THE HOME FRONT

September 1940
ONE SHILLING

Good Housekeeping

The NEW Institute Opens Its Doors

DAPHNE DU MAURIER ★ OSBERT SITWELL ★ HELENA NORMANTON

Good Housekeeping

Christmas Number

1/6

PEARL BUCK · HENRY WILLIAMSON · HOWARD SPRING
LORNA REA · DOROTHY WHIPPLE · LORD DUNSANY
Christmas Play for home acting by A. A. MILNE

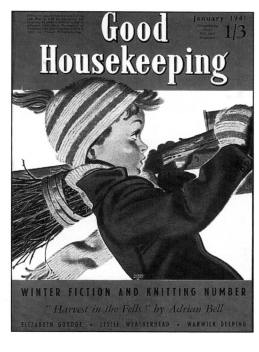

January 1941
1/3

Good Housekeeping

WINTER FICTION AND KNITTING NUMBER

"Harvest in the Fells" by Adrian Bell

ELIZABETH GOUDGE · LESLIE WEATHERHEAD · WARWICK DEEPING

Good Housekeeping
Christmas Number

1/6

Specially written story by Eleanor Farjeon

F. H. GRISEWOOD · WALTER KARIG · MARJORIE HESSELL TILTMAN
CHRISTMAS CATERING BY THE INSTITUTE

Good Housekeeping

1/6

The Next Epoch—A Matriarchy? by Dorothy Thompson

ETHEL MANNIN · ELIA · LADY LISTOWEL · PAUL TABORI
THE INSTITUTE ANSWERS YOUR SPRING-CLEANING QUERIES

Good Housekeeping
April 1942

1/6

Flying Officer X · *Brendan Gill* · *Richard Elwes*
"Lady by Profession" by James Street

Good Housekeeping
Christmas Number

1/6

"There will Always be a Christmas"
by The Lady of No Leisure
Fiction, Features and, of course, The Institute

Good Housekeeping

1/6

"Radio the Unglamorous" by Norman Corwin

FLYING OFFICER X · MARGARET COUSINS · C. PATRICK THOMPSON
The Institute on Cookery for Beginners

Good Housekeeping
April 1943

1/6

"Battlefield Doctor" by C. Patrick Thompson
"THE BRITISH EMPIRE — ACCIDENT OR AGGRESSION?"
The Institute Introduces you to Jugoslav Cookery

THE HOME FRONT

THE BEST OF
GOOD HOUSEKEEPING
1939 · 1945

COMPILED BY

BRIAN BRAITHWAITE

NOËLLE WALSH

GLYN DAVIES

EBURY PRESS
LONDON

Published by Ebury Press,
an imprint of Century Hutchinson Ltd
Brookmount House
Covent Garden
London WC2N 4NW

First impression 1987
Reprinted 1988
Reprinted 1989

ISBN 0 85223 607 7 (hardback)
ISBN 0 85223 751 0 (paperback)

Designer: Glyn Davies
Editor: Suzanne Webber

Printed by BAS Printers Limited, Over Wallop, Hants
Bound by Butler & Tanner Ltd, Frome, Somerset

CONTENTS

Editing Good Housekeeping in Wales

★   ★

ABOUT half of this month's issue of GOOD HOUSEKEEPING has been assembled and passed for press from a perfectly peaceful and remote spot in Wales. We are preparing layouts, reading proofs, sub-editing manuscripts and answering correspondence from trestle tables set up in all the window-recesses of a beautiful old Castle within sight and sound of the sea. There is remarkably little to remind us of the turmoil of the outside world, and we are writing these words before the issue of Peace or War has been decided. But to protect our staff, our business records, and our necessary equipment for bringing out the magazine, this move to the country was decided upon during the last days of August. Vans were loaded with manuscripts, drawings, photographs, stationery, and typewriters; the staff followed, and to-day we are working under singularly peaceful conditions. The reaction from the last few days in London is so great that we seem to be living in another world entirely. By the time these words are published we may be back in London again at our usual offices, but in the meantime the General Post Office officials have undertaken to forward all communications to us down here, from our London address.

EDITOR.

FOREWORD

In my foreword to *Ragtime to Wartime*, the predecessor of this volume, I reminded readers that *Good Housekeeping*, born in 1922 is 65 years old and that I have been one third of its life with it, first as deputy editor and then since 1973 as editor. I said I couldn't remember life before I came to *Good Housekeeping*. But for the benefit of this book, I had to cast my mind back to the war years when I was certainly around, but in no way connected to the magazine.

To anybody who has lived through the war years, the memory of dried egg, spam and clothes rationing is equally as potent as the actual bombing. I was a schoolgirl in London, working for matriculation, and was not evacuated. When I left school at the age of 17, I joined the advertisement department of the *New Statesman*, studied English Literature at the City Literary Institute, doing my homework essays at the Air Raid Post with colleagues playing darts over my swotting head. I was a member of the ARP.

During this time, *Good Housekeeping* was dispensing advice and help on make-do-and-mend and feeding five on £3.10 a week. The wartime strictures that taught us how to exercise good housekeeping, how to make the most out of the least, were lessons that my daughters' generation know nothing about. They of the disposable era who prefer to use paper tissues than wash their hankies!

Some of the pages in this anthology will remind those who lived through the war what it was all about. In adversity, British women perform at their best – it's always been a British trait to do best when up against it.

Good Housekeeping is still here, as we were 65 years ago, to pilot readers through whatever trials and tribulations may be around the corner. We have three generations of readers, some who write to me and who have actually been reading the magazine since the first issue. I started reading it, like so many, when I got married, in 1948 when there was still food rationing and post-war shortages. But we were healthier then as a nation then than we have become in recent more affluent years with an over-indulgence in too much and too rich food.

Health education today is directing us back into more frugal and restrained eating. Unemployment and uncertainties of life are forcing us to be more careful, more economical. We are coming full circle. Our children may smile when someone produces an anthology of *Good Housekeeping* of the Eighties. Or will they, like us, look back with nostalgia at these pages of current behaviour that make human history?

Charlotte Lessing

CHARLOTTE LESSING
EDITOR-IN-CHIEF, *GOOD HOUSEKEEPING*

EDITORIAL
INTRODUCTION

How does a magazine, particularly one aimed at women in the home, cope with a nation at war with the attendant chaos as families were separated, homes destroyed and everyday products limited? That was the situation *Good Housekeeping* found itself in in 1939.

For two decades, it had been dispensing invaluable advice to the new homemakers of the Twenties and Thirties, bereft of domestic staff following the social upheavals of the years after the First World War, and undergoing their own revolution as they found a place for the first time in politics and in the workplace. Now, the Forties had brought a new and unwelcome challenge to women and to the publications that served them.

At *Good Housekeeping*, as in the world it reflected, the war was fought on two fronts: in the front line and on the home front. As well as advising loved ones left behind on subjects from how to write a letter to a front-line fighter (page 71) to how to react when he eventually comes home (page 189), *GH* tackled the role of informing its readers on directing their activities towards helping the war effort at home.

From St Donat's Castle in Wales, to which the staff had decamped in 1939, patriotic slogans – "Beat Hitler's defence by lending your pence", "If you want to win the war, save and salvage more and more" – energy-saving ideas and nutritious recipes were created by the Good Housekeeping Institute to help the beleaguered nation.

The problems of producing a magazine hundreds of miles from the capital and in wartime were exacerbated by paper rationing which resulted in a dramatic reduction in the magazine's size, as you will discover as you read through the book. In fact, *Good Housekeeping*'s continued publication throughout the war years was due, in part, to the Good Housekeeping Institute's collaboration with the Ministry of Food, showing readers how to make delicious and nutritious meals with their rations, and setting up a new cookery school and a wartime meals centre in London's Victoria.

Wartime *GH* reflected the concerns of its readers with families separated by active service and evacuation, and with women adapting to their new role in civil defence, the forces, in factories or on the land. But escapism has always been a natural ingredient of magazines and never more so than when faced with the added anxieties of the Blitz, rationing and loneliness, and *GH* from 1939–1945 provided a staple diet of light fiction and amusing features.

War changed lives overnight: people were encouraged to eat communally in order to save fuel and food, and women who were used to leading fairly private lives suddenly found themselves thrust into a busy working life, compounded by nights spent in air raid shelters surrounded by hundreds of other people. Average weekly food supplies included four ounces of bacon, three ounces of cheese, two ounces of butter and six ounces of cooking fat and margarine. Because of paper rationing, goods were sold unwrapped, shops closed earlier in the winter months to save fuel and comply with the blackout and clothes were rationed so as to conserve cotton, wool, machinery and manpower, all necessary for vital war work. Prices rose both because of scarcity and because of the purchase tax levied on goods which contributed to the war funds. Rationing, of course, meant that fashion wasn't a major ingredient of the magazine during the wartime years – it was more a case of Make Do and Mend.

But despite all the bad news, *GH* tried to look on the bright side. In *Present Day Shopping* (page 42), readers were tartly reminded that "Twenty years ago, there was no war, but there were 1,594,000 men and 444,000 women out of employment. Today, there are less than 90% of that number." Still, a high price to pay for almost full employment!

While food figured largely on the domestic front, its importance in the theatre of war was not ignored by *Good Housekeeping*. While housewives were working out how to make best use of their rations, catering chiefs were coping with a much greater problem. When a British soldier in normal training can burn off 3,600 calories a day, battles can be won or lost by a balanced diet, as *Menu for Battle* (page 164) explains. "Montgomery in Africa gave Hitler's pet general his first surprise taste of what dynamic and scientific rationing can mean. The British commander's success in keeping his troops fully energised and nourished by a balanced battle ration, coupled with new-type supply methods, all planned and meshed with a high-velocity campaign, was a potent factor in the victory which drove the Afrika Korps back whence it came and brought the Eighth Army to fight with undiminished vigour alongside General Eisenhower's invasion forces, 1000 miles west of its El Alamein starting point."

Some of the great writers of the time, among them Daphne du Maurier and C. S. Forester, contributed to *Good Housekeeping* during the wartime years. Daphne du Maurier addressed herself to the strain of separation when, in 1940, she wrote *Letter Writing in Wartime* (page 21). In a brisk, no-nonsense way she advises: "What does he want to be told, this husband, this lover, this son? This is a problem that every individual wife, sweetheart, or mother must solve for herself. No hard rules can be laid down. One thing is certain, though . . . The woman who dares to write 'This agony of separation is too much for me to bear' cannot be forgiven. Whatever she does, and must feel in her heart, of strain and anxiety, no sign of it should appear in any of her letters . . . We must be strong and confident and full of faith, so that some measure of the spirit we would show will find its way to the reader far away, bringing him comfort and hope and a quiet peace even in the midst of very great horror and distress." The subject of separation is one which is returned to again and again, particularly in the fiction (which we have not had the space to reproduce at length here) where more sympathetic tear-letting is encouraged.

The arrival of the Americans in Britain also provided a rich source of material for magazine writers. "As every Briton knows by this time, Americans living here have been politely cautioned that Britons by nature aren't as affable as themselves, are more reserved and not given to wholesome glad handling. To the surprise of Uncle Sam's nieces and nephews, quite the opposite has turned out to be the case!" (*What the Yanks are Saying About Britain*, page 68). And *GH* wasn't afraid to discuss the "overpaid, oversexed and over here" feelings about the Americans. In an article written by One of Them, he gives insights into the various approaches used by GIs to seduce virtuous young British girls. There was the Life-is-too-short-we-may-well-soon-be-dead approach, particularly favoured by airmen; the I'm-so-lonely-you're-the-only-one-who-cares angle and the spider-web technique employed only by those expecting a long war (page 118).

News came through from America, too, about the transatlantic war effort. C. S. Forester in his *News Letter from America* (page 84) writes: "Nothing in the whole war has caught the imagination or excited the admiration of America as much as the dogged British determination under the Nazi air attack. But the American people, living at that time in sheltered comfort . . . reacted extraordinarily . . . They read of the City in flames, of the bombing of Coventry, of the discomforts of air raid shelters, of the difficulties and dangers of daily life whose jobs had to be done no matter what had happened during the night and the first question in the mind of the American citizen was 'How could we help?' "

But perhaps the question uppermost in most women's minds as the war drew to a close was if their men came home again, would they be changed? (*When They Come Back* page 189) "The fighting man will present the worst problem. There is no getting away from the fact that we who have stayed at home, no matter how much we have endured through privation, and bombing, have not changed as much as he. Once a man joins up . . . he at once becomes a cog in the machine, taking orders without blinking, and obeying them instantly, eating, sleeping and bathing in public . . . a mechanised man, trained to do one thing only – kill the enemy."

NOËLLE WALSH

ADVERTISING INTRODUCTION

The most notable fact about the advertising in the war years is that there wasn't a lot of it. Paper was, of course, severely rationed for newspapers and magazines. The paper quota for the magazines was based on a complicated Board of Trade formula which computed pre-war circulation and paper usage. Titles like *Good Housekeeping* managed to produce more pages by reducing the overall format of the magazine, and consequently the type area available to editorial as well as advertising. So the advertiser found himself with far less insertions and considerably reduced space sizes. During the second part of the war *Good Housekeeping* was reduced to Lilliputian proportions.

Considerable priority was given to the bureaucrats with their job of dispensing propaganda and information. Not only was there a comparative abundance of advertisements for the Board of Trade, the Ministry of Food, the Ministry of Agriculture, the Ministry of Fuel and Power and the National Savings Committee, but they were usually granted the luxury of full page spaces, even when the magazine was at its most minuscule and austere.

As a wartime schoolboy, who enjoyed many lessons in the air raid shelter of our Holborn School, and subsequently as a junior editorial assistant on a long-since defunct weekly magazine, a trip through the advertising pages of sixty nine war-time issues of *Good Housekeeping* is pure nostalgia. There were the brand names and products of the war-time generation — many of which have since disappeared — and those old and trusted friends in a sort of advertising battledress, like Bisto, Bovril, Oxo, Heinz, Nescafé, Persil, Elizabeth Arden, Ford, Austin, Pears, W. H. Smith, and Selfridges.

Advertisers had a peculiar problem in those days of rationing and shortages. Their products were not in ample supply on the home front — often they were not available at all. So a recurrent copy theme was an apology that the product had disappeared until the cessation of hostilities or the hope that the reader, with patience and diligence, might discover it somewhere at some-time. Advertisers would also mildly admonish the readers to use the product carefully. "Use less — if you can get it!" was the common cry. Modern day hard-nosed marketeers would shudder at the thought. But the war-time housewife was quite accustomed to the gradual disappearance from the market of rationed and non-rationed goods. We war-time teenagers forgot the sight of a real banana or pineapple and such necessities as razor blades and haircream became sought after items.

Cigarettes on the home front appeared and vanished sporadically. Queues would quickly form when the news spread that the local tobacconist had received supplies. During other times packets of cigarettes found their way into the hands of favoured customers — the vernacular was "under the counter". This music hall joke was matched by the weary shopkeeper's plaintive "Don't you know there's a war on?" This latter remark was particularly comic when delivered to a would-be customer who had spent the night in an air raid shelter or on firewatch. Cigarettes were advertised to maintain brand names and it is interesting to see the Capstan advertisements which advocated, in the interests of salvage, the practice of removing the cigarettes from the packet in the shop, transferring them into a cigarette case (*de rigeur* for the young man about town) and then handing the empty packet back to the tobacconist. A practice not to be recommended these days!

So the shortages of products, coupled with the difficulty of buying space and the often infinitesimal size of the space when obtained, tested the creative resources of the advertiser and his agency. Some advertisements, viewed with hindsight in these days of double page spreads in the magazines and full pages in the broadsheet newspapers, were miracles of compression. Type faces got smaller, illustrations were often eschewed and the selling message had to be precise and particular. However, when the luxury of full pages were able to be used by some of the regular advertisers of the big household names, considerable ingenuity was seen in the presentation of shortages of the product to the public. Photography seemed to be seldom employed and the artist was used on page after page. Cartoon drawings were frequently seen and the advertisement pages of *Good Housekeeping* were no strangers to the work of the likes of David Langdon, Fougasse, the wonderful Bert Thomas, with the strong lines of his Oxo drawings, and the brother and sister team who called themselves Anton.

The big advertising guns, as already mentioned, were the ministries with their considerable task of imparting information to the public. The Food Ministry concentrated on straight recipes, using seasonal fruit and recipes and plaintively suggesting substitutes for real food. Christmas 1941 saw them admitting that "there won't be turkey on many tables this year" and by Christmas 1944 the turkey substitute was a mouthwatering recipe for braised stuffed veal bird. They also ran continuous campaigns extolling the virtues of dried eggs, two words which can still induce a slight gastronomic shudder in a whole generation. The National Savings Committee introduced half way through the war an unpleasant character named The Squander Bug, a nasty hairy creature with big ears and sharp teeth who induced the public to spend their money instead of putting it quite properly into savings certificates. The Ministry of Agriculture consistently pursued their slogan to Dig for Victory, the Ministry for Information helped to recruit WAAFS, Wrens and ATS, the Board of Trade nagged away at the more mundane domestic level and the Ministry of Fuel and Power thundered on about what they could do with all the fuel preserved by rigorous economy on the home front. "Five pounds of coal saved in one day by 1,500,000 homes will provide enough fuel to build a destroyer".

Another recurrent theme was Life will be Wonderful after the War. Pears were particularly prescient with a forecast of high-rise flats, shopping centres and long-haul holidays. Ford took a philanthropic approach with a series of Until Then . . . advertisements. Many other advertisers dreamed of the future, usually with a vested interest. Linguaphone foresaw the need for languages to administer conquered nations and Rufflette curtain tape longed for the end of the "funereal blackout".

A lot of advertising was overtly patriotic, even jingoistic, which was understandable given the circumstances. There was a generic campaign for potatoes that rued the passing of the Vienna Schnitzel and substituted Viennese fish cakes — all potatoes, dried egg and anchovy essence. There were offers to renovate your corsets for 10/6, go mad with your coupons and splurge out on a Harrods suit for $13\frac{1}{2}$ guineas, or a Moygashel dress for 53/–. McDougall taught you how to make a cake without eggs and using saccharine.

Women's liberation was not particularly uppermost in the war-time advertising, perhaps because it manifested itself so overtly in the women's war work and the Services. But ladies in uniform appeared increasingly in the advertising, not only from the Forces but in such innovations as the bus conductress — then dubbed the Clippie, a rather pretty nomenclature that seems to have disappeared alongside the gentleman with the Old Bill moustache and the big driving gloves named Cabbie.

The war-time advertisements in *Good Housekeeping* all drew together a picture of a nation at war, a population of determination and motivation with a common purpose. They present a fascinating review of a society uprooted from its old comfortable ways into a new lifestyle where morale and energy on The Home Front became as vital to survival as any other battlefield.

BRIAN BRAITHWAITE

Making PEACE

WE now realise that "the war to end war," as we optimistically called the outbreak of hostilities in 1914, did not end in 1918: it was temporarily suspended. It might have ended then had we been less weary in well-doing and more assiduous in making a peace with some prospect of permanent duration, but we were exhausted. Like Francisco, the relieved sentry in *Hamlet,* we could say of the Armistice:

> *For this relief much thanks: 'tis bitter cold,*
> *And I am sick at heart.*

Men in that mood are in no state to make a peace that is likely to be of any value. We talked then, very fatuously, of hanging the Kaiser, but the ex-Emperor has been living in comfortable seclusion in Holland ever since the war ended. No hardship or economic anxiety for him. He had five sons when the war began: he had them still when it ended. Not one of them sustained so much as a scratch in the war. One wonders what the Exile of Doorn, now nearly eighty-one, thinks as he sits in his Dutch villa, brooding over his lost empire. Is he glad he is not Hitler? Does he chuckle to himself when he remembers Mr. Lloyd George's election slogan, "Hang the Kaiser!"? Or is he preparing a bed-sitting-room at Doorn for the Führer when his turn comes to run away? Does he feel any shame when he thinks of the millions of Germans whom he left to stew in their own juice while he fled over the Dutch frontier? Has he any cynical thoughts when he reflects that one of his officers, Niemöller, was in a submarine in 1914, but is in a concentration camp in 1940?

We were not in a mood to make a peace that would endure when the war came to its temporary close in 1918. The Peace Conference included too many vengeful minds for it to make a peace worth making. The one man who might have had a profound influence on the Treaty, President Wilson, was so bemused with pedagogic vanity that he did more harm than good. He proposed a League of Nations, which his own countrymen never joined. He was the President of the United States, the representative of all Americans, but he came to Versailles as the head of a political party: he led a delegation of Democrats when his plain duty and interest was to lead an *American* delegation, a delegation of Democrats and Republicans and Labour men, a delegation of *Americans,* not party politicians. He would have done better not to have come himself, but to have sent representatives, but, since he chose to come, he should have come as the head of his nation, not as the head of a political party. A prime and fatal error was committed by the one man who might truly have said he had no axe to grind and no vengeance to execute. But the vanity of the schoolmaster was too much for him. The schoolmarm mind destroyed a great dream.

Our own efforts to make a peace were no less futile. We were more resolved to render Germany impotent than to make peace, and some of our legislators, almost innocent of all knowledge of European geography, sat down to draw maps on a new scale and to shift frontiers. We broke the Austrian Empire into a series of nations, when we should have done better to rearrange it as a federation of self-governing communities, and we left the beautiful city of Vienna in the air: a capital without a country. If London and the Home Counties were to be detached from the rest of Great Britain, with Wales and Scotland as separate nations and the Midlands and the West Country and the North shoved into any group to which they could be attached, we should have some notion of what was done to Vienna at Versailles. Bits were broken off one country and glued on to another. The resuscitated nations, such as Poland, were made up of fragments that did not naturally cohere. Esthonia, Lithuania, Latvia and Finland were detached from Russia, and told to get busy with their independence. A large chunk of Turkey was added to Greece. The Balkans were messed about! . . .

The maps had been redrawn and the frontiers relaid, but there was no peace. The little nations that had been detached from larger nations had little means of support and no means of defence. Some of them, such as Czecho - Slovakia, contained, as was subsequently proved, elements of disruption. The fatuous disintegration of the Austro-Hungarian Empire

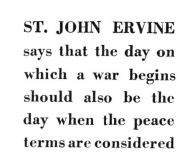

ST. JOHN ERVINE says that the day on which a war begins should also be the day when the peace terms are considered

★

Illustration by Eric Fraser

was in itself sufficient to cause a weakness in the middle of Europe that must eventually bring about war. Statesmen and politicians, it seemed, had learnt nothing from the history of Alsace-Lorraine. Bismarck, by detaching that territory from France in 1870, made the war of 1914 inevitable. The Treaty of Versailles, by its disruption of Austria and the impossible punishment of Germany, a punishment which included the blockade, made the war of 1939 inevitable. The blockade was responsible for the creation of an undernourished and rickety population of young men and women, all of them neurotic and despondent, who were ready prey for a violent demagogue with promises of rehabilitation that no other person but himself could fulfil. Brooding boys and girls, suffering severely from malnutrition, grew into headstrong and impatient men and women, who would not listen to reason, but held up their hands for the loud-mouthed man who offered them the earth in return for their blind obedience. Between 1918 and 1940, a period of twenty-one years, about a dozen wars have been fought in the world, and about half of them have been fought in Europe. Mr. F. L. Lucas, in his *Journal under the Terror*, asserts that England's longest interval of peace between 1682 and 1815 was nineteen *(Continued on page 14)*

JACK'S IN THE NAVY
saving our ships at sea

JILL'S IN THE POST OFFICE
saving her money to help him

Jill's the girl!

She'll never let it be said that the boys who are risking their lives for us were let down because people at home could not make sacrifices.

She thinks before she spends now.

Something saved here by giving up a luxury, something else saved there by doing without a treat. Every penny of it is invested in National Savings. In next to no time she's got a useful investment that grows greater as time goes on. Wise Jill! Some day these Savings may help to start a home— meanwhile they're helping to win the War!

HOW TO LEND TO HELP WIN THE WAR

NATIONAL SAVINGS CERTIFICATES
Free of Income Tax

Price 15s. Value after 5 years 17s. 6d. After 10 years 20s. 6d. which equals interest at £3 3s. 5d. per cent. Maximum holding 500 Certificates including earlier Issues.

3% DEFENCE BONDS

£5 and multiples of £5. Income Tax NOT deducted at source. Maximum holding £1,000.

POST OFFICE SAVINGS BANK & TRUSTEE SAVINGS BANKS

Any sum from 1/- upwards with annual limit of £500. Interest 2½% per annum.

Lend to Defend the Right to be Free

ISSUED BY THE NATIONAL SAVINGS COMMITTEE

Making Peace
(Continued from page 13)

years. "Counting only major conflicts," he says, "we have been at war for about 84 years in the last 286." In the lifetime of every person over the age of twenty-five, there have been two world wars. A Frenchman of seventy can say that he has lived through three major wars with Germany. An Englishman of forty has seen his country engaged in three great wars, apart from minor affrays.

We may conclude from this that war is as much a part of human life as eating and drinking and sleeping, and that all efforts to abolish it are and will be vain. We may think, as Mr. H. G. Wells suggests in his latest book, *The Fate of Homo Sapiens,* that human life is doomed to become extinct unless permanent peace is established. But whatever our view is, we cannot escape from the knowledge that this incessant bickering, these rapidly recurring orgies of destruction must weaken, if they do not ruin, our civilisation. The

That is why the day on which a war begins should also be the day on which the terms of peace are considered. The end of the 1914-18 war brought into the world a horrible epidemic of nationality. Even the Jews, who had had the good luck to lose their nationality, began to clamour for a nation, with the result of a minor, but very bitter and destructive war in Palestine. So little concern had this outbreak of nationality with ordinary human welfare, that great masses of people were treated as if they were cattle, and were moved from their native places to places many miles away. A vast Turkish population was taken out of Greece and settled in Turkish territory in Europe and Asia, while an equally large Greek population was taken out of Anatolia and dumped on waste land in Greece. One saw these Anatolian Greeks almost festering on barren soil about Salonica and the Piræus, living a shanty life that was little better than that of cattle on badly-managed farms elsewhere. The Bolshevists shifted crowds of peasants from one part of Russia to another part, either in Europe or in Asia, and only a few months ago, the Germans were cattle-trucking people from the Italian Tyrol and the Baltic States to Germany. Migration, such as the exchange of Turks and Greeks, might solve some of the racial problems which provoke wars. If the Sudeten Germans could have been put out of Czecho-Slovakia into Germany, if the Germans in Danzig and East Prussia could be removed from those areas to West Prussia and their places there taken by Poles removed from German regions, so that Poland, when she is restored to nationhood again, shall have wide access to the Baltic, a cause of war now and in the future might be removed. But mass movements of men are difficult and dangerous as well as humiliating, and we shall interfere with men's liberty to live where they wish to live at our peril.

The ideal existence is one in which a man has the right to move about the earth as freely as he moves about his own home. I want for myself and for other people the right to go wherever I like in this world, without let or hindrance or fear of robbery or persecution or death. I demand a world in which there are no passports, no customs barriers, no scowling inspectors, no resentful "natives" who spit when a stranger passes by, no people so ignorant that they distrust and hate a man merely because he looks different from them. Can we make such a world? If, out of the ruins of Europe, we can form a federation of States no less secure than the United States of America, we may pardon those who brought the ruin about.

Feeding FIVE

SUNDAY

DINNER

Braised Topside of Beef
Peas   Potatoes
Chocolate and Walnut Whip

SUPPER

Vegetable Soup
Cold Meat (if desired)
Salad
Cheese   Coffee

Braised beef is economical, nourishing and good, served hot or cold. Bone stock, made the previous day, is used for the braise and for foundation of vegetable soup served at supper.

MONDAY

DINNER

Cold Meat   Salad
Potatoes Baked in Jackets
Baked Coconut and Raisin
Pudding
Apricot Jam   Sauce
Coffee

SUPPER

Stewed Kidneys on Toast
Cheese
Coffee

For dinner, mince the " left-over " beef, adding diced cooked vegetables, blended with mayonnaise, and serve on a bed of lettuce with sliced tomato.   Make enough mayonnaise for the week's requirements.

TUESDAY

DINNER

Liver and Bacon
Cauliflower and Sauce
Creamed Potatoes
Rhubarb Fool
Sponge Cake

SUPPER

Curried Eggs
Rice   Peas
Pineapple Sponge
Cheese
Coffee

Supper was to be just curried eggs, cheese and coffee, but two unexpected last-minute guests made a sweet necessary.   Whites of eggs used in the pineapple sponge were left over from mayonnaise.

FOURTEEN shillings per person, per head, on food for a family of five doesn't allow a lot of margin, especially in wartime, when prices are on the " up and up," but by using your head and planning in advance as much as possible, you can produce four nourishing, well-balanced and quite interesting meals for every day of the seven.

To give you a lead we have compiled a full week's menus, together with detailed shopping list, for a typical family consisting of husband, wife, maid and two children aged 10 and 12.

As you see, even jam and marmalade figure on the shopping list, so if you have got home-made preserves, are lucky enough to get fresh greens from the garden, or live in a locality where shops are cheap, you will probably do even better. One thing, though, you must plan ahead, so that all " left-overs " are used up and so that you can buy—and cook —as economically as possible.

SATU

DINNER

Sausage Toad-in-the-hole
Spinach
Apricot Charlotte

Remember to soak the dried apricots

Rationing, though an extra trial to the housekeeper, helps save the pennies! Even with liver and sausages twice a week you will have to choose the cheaper joints of meat to get the quantity you need, while the vitamised margarine that takes the place of butter in sandwiches and on toast, as well as for cooking, will help the budget, too.

The sugar ration can be eked out by using dates and raisins for sweetening puddings, and by making cakes such as Ginger Bread, Date Fingers, Chocolate Cracknels, etc., that use little or no sugar.

Our four daily meals consist of:

Breakfast (cereal, bacon, an egg or fish dish, toast and marmalade, fruit); a substantial midday dinner; family tea with bread and butter and preserves, savoury sandwiches or cake; and supper. The children have hot milk drinks and sandwiches for supper, so no details are given in the daily menus.

WEDNESDAY

DINNER

Steak and Kidney Pie
Scotch Kale
Baked Potatoes
Banana and Pineapple Trifle

SUPPER

Cheese Pudding
Watercress
Coffee

Add the chopped pineapple, left over from Tuesday, to the banana trifle (just layers of sponge cake, egg custard and sliced bananas). A stiffly whisked white of egg, left over from the egg custard, makes a little whipped cream for the top go a long way.

THURSDAY

DINNER

Roast Stuffed Breast of Mutton
Spring Greens
Roast Potatoes
Casserole of Prunes and Raisins
Milk pudding

SUPPER

Baked Stuffed Tomatoes
Cheese
Coffee

Cook the complete dinner in the oven and omit sugar from the fruit casserole, as the raisins will make it sufficiently sweet. Left-over minced mutton is the main ingredient of the stuffed tomatoes for supper.

FRIDAY

DINNER

Mutton Broth
Scalloped Fish
Creamed Potatoes
Date and Apple Layer Pudding

SUPPER

Vegetable Mayonnaise
Cheese
Coffee

Thursday's mutton bones make a good stock for to-day's broth. Use any white fish for the scallops, and make more nourishing by using a cheese instead of an ordinary white sauce. Cook sufficient vegetables at dinner-time for the evening's vegetable salad.

RDAY

SUPPER

Savoury Rice
Cheese Cress
Coffee

overnight for the Apricot Charlotte

(Continued on page 19)

HOLIDAYS OF THE FUTURE

■ This seems a strange time to be thinking about holidays. The last summer holiday we had is now a faded, snapshotted memory, while the next is still an unplanned dream . . . . . hardly worth talking about yet.

Why not ? We take a very optimistic view of the future. Already we are beginning to relish the new opportunities for travel after the war. The possibilities are staggering. Just think for a moment where all this experience in long distance flying, now being so grimly acquired, is going to lead us. To the United States and Canada, for certain. To South America, Hawaii, Tahiti, Bermuda, Mexico.

Aeroplanes now fly the Atlantic in a few short and uneventful hours : civilian and military air pilots cross and recross from Canada and America without mishap.

Soon experienced airmen will be taking us over for our first holiday in the New World. South Africa, Egypt, the Holy Land seem distant places now and impossible for a short vacation, but in the future—well, we'll soon be there ! For week-ends, we shall hop across to Switzerland or to the South of France as casually as to Brighton or Blackpool.

In the future we shall take our 'summer' holidays at any time of the year for the sunshine that we seek for the perfect holiday will always be found somewhere within quick and easy reach of our homes. Luxurious air-liners will ferry us across from autumn to spring, and out of winter into summer. Who knows but that the February of the future will not become the August of today ?

If we have any qualms about the safety of this mode of travel there is one familiar phrase that should reassure us : " All our aircraft returned safely." World-wide travel by air is one of the absolute certainties of the future.

Pears

RENOWNED AS THE LEADING TOILET SOAP SINCE 1789

TP 240/34   *No. 2 of a series of advertisements issued by A. & F. Pears, Ltd., Isleworth, Middlesex.*

Feeding Five on £3 · 10 a Week

(Continued from page 17)

WEEKLY SHOPPING LIST

Grocer

	s.	d.
1 pkt. corn flakes		5
1 pkt. puffed rice		6½
3¾ lb. sugar	1	3
2 lb. marmalade	1	2½
2 lb. jam	1	0
1 jar N.Z. honey		9
1 tin golden syrup		7
1 pkt. dates		7
Anchovy paste		3½
Salmon paste		3½
½ lb. plain chocolate		8
1 oz. walnuts		1½
1 tin pineapple		5½
1 large and 1 small tin peas	1	5
¾ lb. tea	2	0
¾ lb. coffee	1	9
2 lb. cheese	1	8
Cream cheese		3
¾ lb. "Paris" sausages	1	0
½ lb. biscuits		6
½ lb. dried apricots		7
1 lb. prunes		7
½ lb. raisins		4
4 lb. flour		8½
1 lb. rice		3
1 lb. oatmeal		3
2½ lb. bacon	3	9
1¼ lb. butter	2	0
2½ lb. vitamised margarine	1	8
½ lb. lard		3
1 tin evaporated milk		3
1 doz. new-laid eggs	2	0
12 cooking eggs	1	6
1 tin food beverage for children	1	1
	£1 11	11½

Greengrocer

	s.	d.
18 oranges	1	6
2 lemons		2
6 bananas		6
3 grapefruit		7½
1 lb. cooking apples		3
2 lb. eating apples		10
14 lb. potatoes	1	4
1 lb. onions		2
Parsley		1
3 lb. kale		6
3 lb. spring greens		9
4 lb. spinach	1	0
1 cauliflower		4
3 lb. carrots		6
2 lb. turnips		4
3 lb. tomatoes	1	6
3 bundles rhubarb		6
2 lettuces		6
2 beetroot		3
Cress		3
	11	10½

Baker

	s.	d.
22 lb. bread (including some wholemeal)	3	10¾

Butcher

	s.	d.
3 lb. topside	3	6
Bones		2
½ lb. suet		6
¾ lb. liver	1	3
1½ lb. pie steak	1	3
¾ lb. ox kidney	1	1
2½ lb. breast of mutton	1	10½
	9	7½

Fishmonger

	s.	d.
¾ lb. white fish		10
Smoked fillet		8
5 herrings		9
	2	3

Store Cupboard

	s.	d.
Small quantities oil, vinegar, Marmite, seasonings, flavourings, etc., etc.	2	0

Dairy

	s.	d.
26 pts. milk	7	7
½ gill cream		4½
	7	11½

	£	s.	d.
Grocer	1	11	11½
Greengrocer		11	10½
Baker		3	10¾
Butcher		9	7½
Fishmonger		2	3
Dairy		7	11½
Store cupboard		2	0
	£3	9	6¾

Economical Braised Beef

- 2½–3 lb. topside
- 2 good-sized carrots
- 1 turnip or parsnip
- 2 sticks of celery or 2 potatoes and a few celery seeds
- 1 onion
- Small bunch sweet herbs
- 2 oz. dripping
- Cornflour
- Seasoning
- Stock

Prepare the vegetables and cut them in large pieces. Melt the dripping and fry the vegetables in it very slowly for about 10 minutes. Tie the meat firmly in shape if necessary. Add the herbs and sufficient boiling stock almost to cover the vegetables. Bring to the boil. Place the meat on top of the vegetables, and add the bunch of herbs. Cover with a tightly fitting lid and cook slowly for 2–2½ hours, according to the thickness of the joint. Baste the meat occasionally with the liquid. Lift the meat out on to a baking-tin and bake in a hot oven for about 20 minutes, until well browned. Strain off the liquid from the braise, pour back into a saucepan and add a little cornflour blended with cold water. Boil well, season and add a small quantity of meat glaze or gravy browning to colour. Put the meat on a hot dish, pour a little of the gravy round, and garnish with some of the braised vegetables cut into neat pieces. Hand the remainder of the gravy separately.

N.B.—The meat may be stuffed with a veal stuffing if desired. It should be sliced across several times (not quite through) and the stuffing spread on each "slice"; the joint is then tied securely with string.

BE SURE and SAVE

M^cDOUGALL's has a special virtue in wartime. It gives you absolute confidence in the success of your recipes, and successful cooking saves money for you in these hard times! For if there's one thing that runs away with money, it's those costly failures; but there's no risk of such calamities with McDougall's.

Why do we repeat, month after month, that McDougall's is *sure* to make your recipes turn out well? It is because, in our experimental kitchens, skilled cooks perform actual cooking tests on every single batch of McDougall's Self-Raising Flour before it leaves the mills. These cooks regularly bake cakes, scones, puddings, etc., so as to make absolutely sure that *your* cakes, scones and puddings will be perfect every time. That's why we say, you can *rely* on McDougall's.

Recipe for
FAMILY CAKE
(Eggless)

1 *lb.* McDougall's Self-Raising Flour
¼ teaspoonful salt
4 oz. margarine · 4 oz. sugar
3 saccharin tablets (1 dessertspoonful hot water)
14 oz. currants, sultanas, peel
½ pint milk · ¼ pint water

Sieve the flour and salt into a basin, then rub in the margarine, add the fruit and sugar and mix well. Dissolve the saccharin in the hot water, add this and the milk and water to the dry ingredients. Beat very thoroughly and put the mixture into an 8-inch tin which has been greased and dusted with flour. Bake for 1½ hours in a moderately hot oven.

Regulo 4. Other cookers 380° F. Middle shelf.

Letter Writing in Wartime

WHAT sort of letters did we write, in the old, forgotten days before the war ? Those of us who even then had a husband, or a lover, or a son living away from home, and possibly abroad, would sit down comfortably on mail day and scribble pages of light-hearted gossip without that dumb anguish at the back of the mind that perhaps the letter would never find its reader. We talked of the children, of the Browns who were coming over on Sunday, of a possible cold in the head, of a rumoured engagement between old friends, " Fancy old Pat getting off at last," and lastly of approaching plans for the future summer or winter holiday, when reunion was a definite and settled possibility. The envelope was sealed, the Air Mail stamp pressed on the right-hand corner, and then, with one letter to the Bank and another to a London store, the little collection would be left on a salver in the hall for the parlour-maid to take away.

And to-day ? The desk stands as it has always stood, beside the fireplace with the window on the right. Paper, pen, and ink are there before us. But the photograph on the top of the desk stares at us with a new depth, a new intensity—so much so that we cannot bear to look at it too closely, and instead reach for our pen in a rather breathless hurry, only to find we have no words to say.

It is possible that the children have said something funny, that the Browns are still coming over on Sunday, and that a cold in the head does not make for clear thinking—but are these things enough, now ? What does he want to be told, this husband, this lover, this son ? This is a problem that every individual wife, sweetheart, or mother must solve for herself. No hard rules can be laid down. One thing is certain, though. Any murmur of " self-pity " will not be helpful to the writer. The woman who dares to write, " This agony of separation is too much for me to bear," cannot be forgiven. Whatever she does, and must feel in her heart, of strain and anxiety, no sign of it should appear in any of her letters. Men are not always the sturdy, stalwart creatures we imagine, and a yearning letter from home may bring the nervy, highly-strung type to breaking-point. We are not the only ones to wonder, at odd and fearful moments, if the separation is to be final. And so there must be no weakness in these letters of ours, no poor and pitiful hinting at despair. We must be strong, and confident, and full of faith, so that some measure of the spirit we would show will find its way to that reader far away, bringing him comfort, and hope, and a quiet peace even in the midst of very great horror and distress. He will want home news, of course, and local news, too. Here we

by
Daphne du Maurier

can be helpful. No rumours, no grim hearsay gossip from the friend-of-a-friend, but news that will give courage and a renewed determination to endure. The retreat from Dunkirk, wrongly described, would make a fighting-man in another part of the battle feel that the Allied cause was lost, and that nothing was in store for him and his companions but annihilation or grim surrender. Told properly, by someone with understanding and a faith in miracles, the story would read as one of the greatest epics in English history, and fill any man who had not actually experienced it himself with wonder, and pride, and fresh faith in God and his fellow-men.

We must not forget, in our letters, that there is comedy in war as well as tragedy, and that there is a certain sense of fun, essentially English in its quality, that can turn the dullest and drabbest incident — and even serious incidents, too—into a thing of laughter. There is much armchair criticism, on the home front, that can be observed and retold in a letter, with the proverbial tongue in the cheek ; and how many of us, during the last twelvemonth, must have come back from our First Aid lectures, A.R.P. practice, and weekly working parties, in a state bordering on hysteria, only to find an empty house and no companion to chuckle with us from the opposite chair at the tale we have to tell. All these things we can put into our letters—Mrs. Jones who reached for her smelling-bottle when arteries were mentioned—the collapse of the stretcher under a fourteen-stone V.A.D. who had offered herself as victim to our blundering hands—the fanatical gas instructor who whipped a small bottle containing Lewisite under our quailing noses only to be knocked out herself—the lecturer who came to talk on National Savings, and being absent-minded and having mislaid her notes, read a treatise on *Preparing for Baby* to a gathering of spinsters. It is these things that we want to remember in wartime, the idiotic and the heroic, the ridiculous and the sublime, so that we can make a hotch-potch of them in our letters when we write, and the man who reads them will breathe, for one moment, something of our unchanging, foolish world. The grumbles are best forgotten, the rumours of ill-omen, the bitter scraps of criticism, the complacency and selfishness combined. These, alas, have always existed and will continue to exist, but they have never made history ! The man to whom we write and who may yet give his life for his country, does not shed his blood for the little things. When he fights for England he does not think of the blunders, the omissions, the jealousies that governments have shown, and will always show, to the end of time—he sees instead the quiet, intangible things.

Brains can save on the Budget

Three little jackets for dressing-up your "date" frocks

Décolleté evening frocks are dead, except for the grandest parties, but you can still wear those you have. Add-a-jacket is the rule and, incidentally, is there anything better for dressing-up a dull black dress than a sparkling new "top"?

The Chinese Shawl-Jacket after Stiebel

Bring out that embroidered shawl that has lain in the cupboard for the last five years or so, buy a good Butterick paper pattern and carve up your shawl into a little fitted jacket. Victor Stiebel showed his shawl-jacket worn with a pencil-slim evening skirt

The "Glitter-Swing" Jacket after Hartnell

Choose a pastel shade that suits you —and make a wrist-length loose jacket, with long straight sleeves and fairly square shoulders. Work a lavish embroidery design in coloured diamanté or sequins on each shoulder and the top of the sleeves

The Blouse-Jacket after Molyneux

Newest silhouette is the ultra-narrow skirt and bloused full top by Molyneux. Make your jacket soft and full, both back and front, and gather into a corselette waist-band that fits snugly over your skirt top. The sleeves may be either long or short

Trim up your hat and step-up your style

"Small, saucy and smothered" (in flowers or ribbons) sums up the best new hats! They are gay and frivolous, and a glorious relief to this season's simple, practical coats and suits. The sailor leads the way as the most popular silhouette, but basic shapes have not changed much from last season. Luckily the news lies in the trimming, and veritable transformations can be worked with a yard or two of ribbon, some realistic fruit and flowers and a few stitches, as ➤

Taffeta Rosettes

Cut out a dozen circles of taffeta 3–4 in. in diameter, fray the edges to make a soft fringe and shape into the "flower" with a piece of florist's wire, or cotton. Poise two of these rosettes on your plain little sailor— one on each side of the crown or wherever they suit you best. Two contrasting shades look most effective

A Petersham "Fan" Brim

Measure the circumference of the inside of your hat brim and buy a piece of Petersham ribbon three times as long and slightly wider than the width of the brim. Quilt up the ribbon and stitch the pleats in at one side only. Fasten this "fan" round your brim so that the unpleated edge comes just over the brim edge

The Gingham Accent

For your suit make a slip collar, cuffs and pocket flaps of gay, striped cotton gingham, of self-colour rayon, linen, or the new washable chintz. Two sets will enable you to look crisp and fresh. A slip cover for your handbag will add to the effect (make it to button on), and you can use the same material as a hat trimming

A New Fastening

Silver filigree, shiny polished brass or the "sailor" buttons beloved by children, are one idea. Stitch them on your reefer to replace the existing ones. To give an edge-to-edge coat a more up-to-the-minute look, invest in three pairs of military braided frogs with clasps, fastening them one, two and three down the bodice.

A Little "Guimpe"

Schiaparelli is currently featuring the "guimpe" or pinafore dress. Take out the sleeves and lower the neckline of the plain dark dress you are bored with, and make a mock front. Try striped taffeta leg-of-mutton sleeves with lingerie collar and cuffs for when you feel romantic; polka-dotted silk or cotton for mornings

An idea apiece for suit, coat and dress

Never mind if you can't make any big new purchases. People notice the whole effect, not whether the coat you are wearing is this season's or last's. With the small touches suggested above you can give the illusion of a fresh outfit

A Lingerie "Pie-Frill"

Measure the circumference of your hat crown and buy a piece of embroidery edging, four times as long. Cut in half, join lengthwise and run a gathering thread up the centre join, to make a frilly double-sided edging. Put round your hat crown, and finish off with narrow velvet or satin ribbon round the centre join

"Pirate Kerchief" Ribbons

Take off your snood and replace it by two very broad bands of taffeta, or soft satin ribbon. Gauge each band at the edge where you attach it to the hat, then drape over the back hair so that it is almost covered, and tie a big bow low at the nape of the neck. In order to anchor your hat on well, mount a hat elastic inside the ribbons

A "Flower-Piled Platter"

Unearth the season before last's tiny "doll's" hat of the plate or flat variety, or a small, shallow pill-box, and then go and buy yourself a good mixed bunch of realistic flowers and fruit, with one or two tiny feather winglets, and some stiff taffeta ribbon. Arrange all on your hat— and voilà, a model of the most elegant!

"Carry on, Dad!"

Helen Simpson pays tribute to the thousands of men not in the fighting forces who are so staunchly "doing their bit"

THE other day, for a fleeting instant between two buses, I caught a glimpse of a poster. What it advertised I do not remember, but it showed a group of young men in uniform waving, as they departed, to an elderly civilian figure. The caption ran: "Carry on, Dad!"

Dad *is* doing so. The normal life of this country, so far as it continues to exist at all, does so because Dad and his womenfolk have accepted the burden of it. They know perfectly well that for them there can be no limelight—or should we in war-time say searchlight?—no uniform beyond perhaps an armlet, no medals, and finally no thanks. They are content that it shall be so.

Consider one such elderly patriot who has been constantly under my eye. He was in charge of the works staff at a great London hospital, and when war broke out last year was due to retire. He had all the right things to retire on; a bit of money put by, a little house out of town, grandchildren for interest and occupation, a euphonium for the interpretation of artistic impulses. He was all set for a happy fifteen years or so before, as he put it, he need "fold up."

But the war took away the younger men from his staff. They were craftsmen, needed in munitions. Mr. Patriot was asked if he could possibly postpone his retirement. He replied with some scorn that there was a war on, and asked what they took him for? With that question unanswered left ringing in the ears of the Secretary, Mr. Patriot departed to do two or three men's jobs, including the blacking-out of a huge modern hospital constructed almost entirely of glass, besides learning first-aid and helping to carry stretchers when such things were needed. He gets home to that nice little house perhaps once in ten days. He cannot practise the euphonium at all, and this is his sole regret. He will get no commendation, and expects none. It is all in the day's war-work.

Now take a look at Patriot Number Two. He is a doctor, aged about forty-two, who when the war began was making a name for himself as a specialist. That *(Continued on opposite page)*

September all his patients dispersed, his specialist practice dropped to nothing. There were two obvious things to be done; join the Emergency Medical Service as a whole-time public servant, or go into one of the fighting services as medical officer. Either meant that his income dropped to about a third of what it had been, but his rent, rates, income tax still had to be paid. The rent and rates were unchanged, the tax considerably higher than before the war; and these commitments, from which he could not escape, together represented a larger annual outlay than any pay which he might receive from the Government.

"Well," said he cheerfully, "a bankrupt is no use to the Chancellor of the Exchequer." He put ambition aside, and all the special skill which he spent years (and money) acquiring. He went off to a town which had been depleted of doctors, and there took up the general practice of a younger man who had gone into the Air Force. He works eighteen hours or so a day. He is forgetting what a night's rest means, for they get frequent bombers over this particular town, and he is on call in case of emergency. Besides, bombers and their attendant noise tend to bring babies unexpectedly into the world. His wife and the two children live on in the London house, since rent has to be paid for it. They see him rarely. But the Chancellor will get his tax; and the Local Authority the money it needs to keep up A.R.P.; and the landlord will get his rent, which in turn will enable him to pay *his* taxes. And so the wheels go round, to the tune of "Mustn't Grumble."

I am not holding up these two men as anything out of the way, but rather as types. There are thousands of them. They would be surprised if anyone congratulated them on their war effort, which appears to them as simple, necessary, and the only possible course of action. They do not think in terms of glory. They take the world as they find it; and if they find it difficult, shifting, an awkward weight to shoulder—well, the young have even heavier burdens to bear. "Mustn't Grumble."

It is this quality in the English Dad that is probably going to win the war for us. Gallantry the very young have; but gallantry, like patriotism, is not enough. You need doggedness as well as dash to make up a proud nation. If the doggedness fails behind the lines, no amount of dash in khaki or blue will save that nation from disaster. We have an example, a most unhappy one, in the recent cracking of France. It was not the fighters there who failed, but the men behind them; the men who feared for their money and their comforts, who could not conceive a worse fate than to lack money and comfort, and so have lost everything.

If there are such men in England to-day, they hide their heads; the Mr. Patriots are so overwhelmingly numerous that these other deplorable voices cannot be heard. It is not that our older men are fire-eaters. They do not spend their energies exhorting the young to battle while they sit safe; there is less of that sort of thing now than there was in 1914. But there does seem to be among them a quiet, sober realisation of what life under Nazi rule would mean. It would take away that dream of green leisure which most Englishmen cherish. It would kill the easy give-and-take, the small cheerful activities to which both the retired man and the man making his way look forward. Nazism has no use for Dad. Dad knows this, and with such powers as are left him is prepared to fight for England, and what England stands for.

If I wore a hat nowadays I would take it off to him.

In defence of Britain!

This Island Fortress faces the greatest menace in its history. Every man and woman is in the line of battle. Not a particle of our resources must be wasted. Not a working moment can be spared from war production.

Buy nothing for your personal pleasure or comfort, use no transport, call on no labour —unless urgent necessity compels. To be free with your money today is not a merit. It is contemptible. To watch every penny shows your will to win.

This money is needed to defend the fort. So redouble your savings. Lend every pound, every shilling, every penny to the Nation **now.**

Go to a Post Office or your Bank and put your money into Savings Certificates, Defence Bonds, or National War Bonds; or deposit your savings in the Post Office or Trustee Savings Banks.

Join a Savings Group. Make others join with you. **Save regularly week by week.**

There is no time to lose. The need is **urgent.**

Issued by the National Savings Committee, London

"**Mary was a better mother to my child!**"

" When bombing began, I took my little girl to my cousin Mary. Discussing food, Mary said, ' I suppose Pam has cod liver oil ? ' I said no. ' Well,' said Mary, ' I never knew a child that wasn't better for SevenSeaS, particularly now butter's short. Let me try.' I didn't mind her trying, but I didn't expect any result.

It was nearly three months before I saw Pam again. I hardly recognised her ! The way she'd filled out made me ashamed that I hadn't had the sense to give her SevenSeaS before ! "

A well-fed child can be undernourished

A normal, healthy child who has plenty of food can still be undernourished. Children need vitamin-fats, and many foods which seem satisfying contain very little.

Lack of vitamin-fats causes malformation of bones and teeth, lowers disease-resistance. While they are growing, children must have plenty of the growth-vitamins — A and D — that are concentrated in SevenSeaS. You dare not gamble with your children's health; so much of their future happiness depends on the nourishment you give them now. Always supplement rationed foods with SevenSeaS. A small measure *every day* is a wonderful health insurance.

Freshness gives a pleasant taste

All the nutriment-value concentrated in the liver of fresh-caught cod goes into SevenSeaS. Because delay might cause some loss in richness, SevenSeaS is made

immediately the fish are taken from the sea. That explains its purity, its pleasant taste. Men take risks to bring home this clear, golden oil — sure proof of SevenSeaS' importance to the nation's health.

Chemists sell SevenSeaS in three forms. Concentrated liquid, 1/6d (this lasts about a month). Standard liquid, from 1/3d, Concentrated oil in Capsules, from 1/6d

SEVEN SEAS
COD LIVER OIL

makes up for the present shortage of milk, butter, cheese, eggs and fats — foods essential to health. SevenSeaS is concentrated nutri-ment — richest and most dependable natural source of vitamins A and D.

FACTS
and fiction

ONE of the headaches of the editorial staff of a monthly magazine is having to work a good two months ahead. Even during peace, this time-lag between production and appearance of the paper can cause some nasty jolts. In a blazing May, for instance, one plans a holiday issue for July, distinguished by authoritative advice on the way to tan without burning, hints on keeping cool at work and play, ways of tempting the appetite jaded by hot weather, and so on. On press day, the whole thing reads well, and the harassed editor heaves a sigh of relief. On publication date, two months later, and throughout the ensuing month when the magazine is on sale, a cold, wet spell weeps the countryside. A jaundiced look greets any mention of our warm-weather delights, and pages that should have made such pleasurable and profitable reading are skipped hastily with a feeling approaching nausea.

Well, when that's what may, and too frequently does, happen in peace time, you can imagine how much more perilous the task is *now* of forecasting what will be timely and welcome two months ahead. We have to back our judgment and hope that the swift march of events will not be such as completely to overthrow it.

As we write, it seems that the Battle of Britain is about to follow that of France. Detailed happenings cannot be anticipated, but we do know that the days ahead will prove the sternest trial that the great majority of us have ever had to face, and we'll each one of us need all the inspiration (and courage) possible. That being so, we're proud to open this issue with Mrs. Cecil Chesterton's beautiful and moving article, "Sanctuary." Suffering, poverty and hopelessness are no strangers to Mrs. Chesterton—she spends her life in trying to alleviate them and in helping the "down and out" among her fellow-women—so that her words have a sincerity and conviction that go straight to the heart, and that will surely brace and strengthen all those of us who have not yet been tested.

Our leading story, "One Hour of Glory," is also by a woman, and again by a very vital and courageous one. Mary Roberts Rinehart is best known as a prolific and "human" novelist, but she's also fulfilled the varied rôles of nurse, wife, mother, hostess, war correspondent and traveller with marked success. At fifteen, in a family crisis, she determined to earn some money by writing, and succeeded in selling three short stories to a local newspaper for a dollar apiece. She

" You can imagine how perilous the task is of forecasting what will be welcome two months ahead "

wanted to study medicine, but the cost was prohibitive, so she began to train as a nurse. At nineteen came marriage, but not an easy life, for the young couple, with three growing sons, found it difficult to make ends meet. Again Mrs. Rinehart turned to her pen to help out, and since she possesses to a supreme degree the novelist's essential gift, that of story-telling, it is little wonder that she quickly succeeded. "One Hour of Glory" is an American story in an American setting, but there is something about the grand old man who is the hero that's universal in its appeal. Let us know if you don't agree that this latest Mary Roberts Rinehart story is enthralling and inspiriting reading.

Now that we are all racked with anxiety about the morrow, yesterday, when we knew peace, seems a serene and lovely time. A middle-aged man breakfasting in the shade of a lilac arbour; a middle-aged woman, his landlady, waiting on him and telling him the history of those lilacs—it seems a slight enough foundation for a story, yet so beautifully is it told, that the anxious present drops away and one can feel the soft, scented air, experience the serenity of that quiet, country scene. L. A. G. Strong, author of "The Lilacs," must, incidentally, be one of the comparatively small band who combine publishing (he is a director of Methuen's) with the writing of novels, belles-lettres and verse. He has also spent twelve years schoolmastering, is a member of the Irish Academy of Letters, and counts music, walking in the country, swimming and talking dialect as his recreations. An interesting, well-rounded personality.

Laurence Housman needs no introduction to GOOD HOUSEKEEPING readers, and it is with particular pleasure that we present, in this issue, a new "Victoria Regina" playlet. In our view, the most vivid pictures of the great Queen are those that Laurence Housman conjures up, and his latest one of the Widow of Windsor admonishing "Bertie" and receiving "Dizzie" at Balmoral, appeals as a little gem and a marvellous "escape." Turn to it if you feel depressed!

You remember that we promised you the return of a tried friend before very long? We are more than happy to announce that next month Mrs. Helena Normanton will once again lend lustre to the pages of GOOD HOUSEKEEPING. The title she has chosen, "Fidelity to the Future," hints at the challenging, and invigorating, article that we may expect.

Also next month, a famous woman writer of the younger generation, Daphne du Maurier, on a subject of great concern to so many of us to-day—that of "Letter Writing in Wartime." Miss du Maurier writes out of her own experience, for, as the wife of a high-up Army officer, she knows well the pangs of separation and the bitter-sweet pleasure of "talking on paper."

Next month's further offerings must remain a surprise until publication date, but we can promise you a good, well-rounded bag, even though the number of plums in it must perforce be sadly less than in pre-war time. Don't forget to let us know any special preference, or bright ideas, you have; we can't promise to follow them, but they will receive careful and sympathetic consideration.

Results of the Literary Competition next month.

★ ★ ★ ★ ★ ★ ★ ★ ★ ★ ★ ★ ★ ★

Why this issue is the smallest GOOD HOUSEKEEPING ever published

YES, it *is* a thin magazine this month, and it grieves us terribly that it must be so, but the matter is not in our hands. As most of you know, the Ministry of Supply has been rationing paper with ever-increasing strictness, and magazines and newspapers alike have, in the national interests, to reduce their size to an extent that in normal times would be unthinkable.

Since it has always been a special source of joy and pride to us that GOOD HOUSEKEEPING has been famous as a big, "meaty" paper, as well as one of the highest integrity and reputation, we have done, and are doing, everything in our power to retain the maximum number of features and stories. Our revenue depends upon advertisements, but to-day we are turning away a substantial part of that revenue in order not to sacrifice editorial pages. As for the quality of both features and fiction, we mean to let nothing stand in the way of our ideal—that of making every issue of GOOD HOUSEKEEPING yet better than the last.

From the number of letters we get by every post thanking us for the stimulation, help and entertainment the magazine brings, and saying that "whatever luxury goes, it will not be my monthly GOOD HOUSEKEEPING," we know that our readers will remain faithful in this time of crisis.

It is impossible to forecast the future, of course, but we hope to increase the size in forthcoming issues.

Just one last word. We told you before, but we'd like to repeat, that our plan is, so far as possible, to reduce the *length*, rather than the *number* of individual features. As writers of experience know, it takes a riper, more delicate skill to tell a tale or expound an article in the fewest possible words; than to discourse at length. May we not hope, therefore, that this present tribulation will cause the emergence of a newer, and finer, magazine technique, of which GOOD HOUSEKEEPING will be the first and foremost exponent?

THE TOWN OF THE FUTURE

■ There can be no doubt that our future towns will be as different from those we knew before the war as a radiogram is different from our first crystal set. And just as our admiration for the elegance and the greater efficiency of the modern does not in any way impair our affection for the old-fashioned, so we need have no regrets when we come to live in the town of the future.

Towns and cities damaged by the war are already considering their rebuilding plans. Residential districts, we are told, will be designed on the garden city principle of villas or semi-detached houses each with its own garden; or ten-storey blocks of flats surrounded by communal lawns, flower walks and rose arbours. It is gratifying to note that experts are planning for a 'green and pleasant land' with plenty of

space, light and fresh air. In the past, towns and cities have straggled and sprawled, capturing parts of the countryside with the same inevitable disappointment as the caging of a wild bird. The town of the future will be erect and compact, with the trees, the grass and the flowers of the country-side brought to its front doors. Schools and playgrounds for the children will be included as an integral part of the communal plan. These will be so positioned that children will not have to cross main roads on their way to school. The Shopping Centre, in view of its supreme importance to housewives, will

receive very special attention. Architects, remembering the British climate, will develop the arcade principle for greater all-the-year-round convenience, specially appreciated on wet shopping days.

Ancient buildings will be restored and records and relics of a glorious past preserved. The town of the future will retain its cherished character, its unique individuality and its historical associations, yet it will sparkle and shine in its new pride.

New buildings, new services, new homes, rising up from the ruins of the old, will make for happier family life in Britain after the war. The better environment will invite us to make the most of our longer leisure and will encourage us to seek new interests within the pleasant, comfortable and healthy precincts of our new homes.

Pears

MOODS IN

millinery
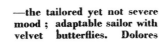

—the smart but conservative mood ; delicately pin-tucked and manipulated felt. Condor

—the gay, sophisticated mood ; piquant pork-pie, with feather mount. Dolores

—the tailored yet not severe mood ; adaptable sailor with velvet butterflies. Dolores

—the New Yorker mood ; challenging, off-face, young and different. Dolores model

. . . Choose for the
tilt of a brim;
the curl of a crown ;
a trimming
that's different ;
a silhouette new—
but most of all
by the test,
" does it suit me ? "

—the wide-eyed, bridal mood ; adaptation of Schiaparelli's " topknot," with soft feather trimming. Condor

29

recovered from the general initial dismay, entered into a period of great and uninterrupted prosperity, though little or nothing can be said for the quality of most of the work that was performed. In all wars for culture, culture is the first casualty, and it is the last to recover from its wounds. The theatre, which is the entertainment of a crowd rather than the entertainment of an individual, feels this effect of war quicker and more extensively than any other form of art.

A novelist can do very well if five thousand people buy his book, but a dramatist has had a disastrous failure if no more than that number of people pay to see his play. Five thousand people will not fill a theatre of average size for a week. The Globe Theatre, where my play, *Robert's Wife*, was performed seats a thousand people. One does not need to be a mathematician to realise that if only five thousand people had paid to see that play acted, the theatre would have been fully occupied only on five nights. If a novelist *sells* a hundred thousand copies of a book—for the number *borrowed* has little relevance to this argument—he is hailed with delight as a "best-seller." It is a sale which very few novelists, even those who are popular and widely-read, ever achieve. There are eminent novelists who have never had a sale of half that number in their lives. It would astonish my readers to learn how many renowned authors never sell more than ten thousand copies of a single book, how many authors whose names are familiar on two continents, account themselves fortunate if they have a sale of twenty to thirty thousand. One of my plays, *The First Mrs. Fraser,* was performed at the Haymarket Theatre 636 times. For the first 5½ months of the run, the variation in the nightly returns was slight, and was caused only by the variation in the number of persons occupying

THE differences between the present European War and that of 1914–1919, which was not, as so many people imagine, the first, are numerous and surprising. The fact that twice as many people were killed by motor-cars in the first five months of the "black-out" in Britain as were killed in the War in the same period is a major difference. The fact that almost the total brunt of the casualties in the present War has been borne by the Navy is another. The British lost more men in the Retreat from Mons than were lost by *all* the Allies in the first six months of the present War. It is not, however, with the major differences that I am now concerned, but with some minor differences, and chiefly with one. The Government has made almost no use of the services of authors in the present War. Those services were freely used in the last. Poets were numerous and prolific in 1914–1919: they have been few and almost sterile since September, 1939. The poets of 1914–1919 faithfully expressed the mood in which we went to war and the mood in which we came out of it. We began in the spirit of Rupert Brooke: we ended in the spirit of Siegfried Sassoon. But our contemporary poets, many of whom are not poets and never have been poets, but are merely political propagandists, express nothing but their own impotence.

My concern here, however, is with the effect of the War on the theatre. That effect was instantaneous and almost fatal. In what we call the first European War—though there have been many such wars since the time of Julius Cæsar to that of Napoleon Bonaparte—the theatre, after it had

THE Theatre IN WARTIME

St. JOHN ERVINE predicts a complete reorganisation of the theatre as a result of present conditions, which are so different from those of the last war

"standing room only." Every seat at every performance was sold during that period, and for a year thereafter the larger part of the seats were sold. The Haymarket seats 900 people. It will easily be calculated, therefore, that 100,000 people occupied seats in little more than three months—reckoning eight performances to the week. And the play ran for eighteen months! These figures show the wide disparity between success and failure for the novelist and the dramatist. If Mr. Priestley, the dramatist, were as successful as Mr. Priestley, the novelist, at least a quarter of a million people would see every play he has performed. If the number of people who bought *The Good Companions* had paid to see *Eden End* at the Duchess, *Eden End* would have played to packed houses for about three years; for the Duchess seats only 494 people.

At the outbreak of the war in 1914, every theatre-manager in the West End of London thought he saw ruin staring him in the face. He had on his hands an expensive building which was expensive to maintain, and so far as he could see, productions were not likely to be profitable. In a short time, however, his feeling of foreboding was changed to one of elation. There was an immense boom in the theatre. Millions of people who had never, or very rarely, been in a theatre in their lives before, wanted to go there as often as they could, and they wanted expensive seats. Rents rushed up to preposterous figures. I knew a lady who had inherited a longish lease of a West End theatre at a weekly rental of £90. Her despair at the prospect of having to find this sum every week was quickly changed, soon after the war began, *(Continued on page 33)*

There are a few plays performing to " big business " in the West End, but none of them is a serious play

"ER — ONE MORE WORD OF ADVICE.
DON'T WASTE YOUR VEGETABLE WATER.
MAKE ʃOUP THE OXO WAY!"

" Cakes and Puddings for Wartime," price 7½d. post free, shows how to manage with less sugar and fats.

The Theatre in Wartime

(Continued from page 31)

to delight on finding that people almost fought with each other for the privilege of paying her £400 a week for her property. She sub-let it at a clear profit of more than £300 weekly. There were theatres, then, which were rented at £600 a week, and it is sometimes asserted that the rent of the Palace in those days reached £700. To-day, theatres are almost like a penny.

Misfortune fell upon the English theatre the moment war was declared in September, 1939. The mere anticipation of the War sent receipts slithering to zero. On Thursday, August 31, 1939, the receipts at the evening performance of a play in a large town were £125 11s. 4d. At the matinée performance on the following day, they were £11 4s. 4d., and in the evening they were £76 0s. 9d. On Saturday night, they fell to £44 10s. 5d. On Monday, September 4, the day after war began, they ceased altogether. Every theatre in the country was closed by order of the Government which, in this matter no less than in others, panicked very badly. Just why a cinema in Budleigh Salterton should be forbidden to open because the Germans might bomb London, was not obvious to anybody but the badly frightened and extraordinarily obtuse gentlemen in Whitehall and Parliament Square. We have learnt to feel contempt for our bureaucracy, which, secured in its own salaries and guaranteed in pensions, showed no scruples whatsoever about throwing thousands of unsecured people out of work. I do not know how many people, including authors, actors, actresses, managers, producers, dramatic critics, stage hands, electricians, programme-sellers, bar attendants, dressers and cleaners, are directly employed in the theatre, nor can I estimate how many people, such as printers, carriers, scene-painters and designers, costumiers, wig-makers and railwaymen, are indirectly employed in it; but it is obvious that the number must run into a great many thousands. If we add to the "legitimate" theatre, the music-hall, the concert room, and the cinema, the number becomes spectacular.

The loss of income by dramatists, apart altogether from regular theatrical performances, has been immense; for, almost without exception, the entire amateur production of plays stopped. It, too, was forbidden at first. Some attempts to substitute play-readings for play-performances were made, but many of these were proposed to be made at the author's expense. Having been deprived by the Government of his means of livelihood, he was enraged by requests from amiable ladies and gentlemen who were eager to amuse themselves, that he should allow them to read or semi-perform his work without the payment of any fee whatsoever! Now that performances are allowed, he is often asked to reduce his fees or to forgo them on the ground that the performance is for some worthy object! A dramatist lately informed me that a month's income from plays had been £2 14s. 2d. instead of the £150 of normal times. The effect of a letter, requesting the right to perform a play free of charge or at a reduced fee, on top of such receipts as those may be horrifically imagined.

We shall not forget our bureaucrats in a hurry. Their reputation for ability suffered a frightful sea-change in 1939. Their behaviour to the people of the theatre, however, could not be permitted to continue, and even bureaucrats become in time pervious to facts. One of the facts to which they had to become pervious was that the total suppression of the livelihood of great numbers of men and women cannot be tolerated, and that it has

consequences for the community almost as grave as those it has for the persons primarily concerned. How, for instance, were theatre-owners to pay their rates and taxes when they were forbidden to give any performances? I do not know how the problem of rates in London will be solved, but it is obviously going to cause great financial confusion to the L.C.C. during the next few months. The rateable value of a West End theatre is high. How many theatres, music-halls, concert rooms and cinemas there are in Greater London, including the West End, I have no means of estimating, but it is a fairly large number, and my readers may easily surmise how serious the rating question, in this one respect, will shortly be.

At the end of a month or two, the prohibition of play-performances was relaxed, and managers were allowed, under restrictions, such as the "staggering" of hours at which performances were to begin and end, to resume their business. But business was not as usual. The "black-out" alone was sufficient to see to that, but it was not the only factor in the situation. Evacuation included not only children and their mothers, but large numbers of adults of every class and age. The theatre audience in vulnerable areas was reduced by evacuation and the "black-out." There was none of the dazzling prosperity in the theatre that there had been in the previous European War. Playhouses could have been hired almost for the price of keeping them aired and clean. The public taste, of course, was for the lightest and most trivial entertainment. That aspect of the last war was, and is, an aspect of this one. There are a few plays performing to "big business" in the West End, but none of them is a serious or moderately serious play. I think I am right in saying that, outside these plays, the receipts at the majority of theatres in the West End, especially at plays of some quality, have seldom exceeded £30 a night, and have often been much less than that sum. The West End, broadly speaking, is a wash-out.

The managers, therefore, turned their eyes towards the provinces, where "black-out" problems, bad though they are, are not so bad as they are in London because places of residence are nearer the centre of the city than they are in the metropolis. A man can, in the last resort, walk home from the theatre in a provincial town, but it is no joke to walk home in London, where home may be anything from four to ten miles away from the West End. All traffic problems are reduced or scarcely existent in the provinces, in comparison with London. That fact is of immense importance to the theatre manager. Our stars, therefore, went on tour, enduring enormous discomfort, because of the disorganised railway service, in doing so. The disorganisation, indeed, was such that in many places Monday night performances had to be abandoned because the companies could not possibly get to their destination in time for them. These provincial tours had two useful effects: they enabled provincial playgoers to see better productions than they were ordinarily accustomed to see, and they helped to keep the theatrical profession alive. Receipts were nothing like what they would have been in peace time, but they were far better than were obtainable in London. Oddly enough, the big cities, such as Liverpool and Manchester and, for obvious reasons, Edinburgh, were less remunerative than smaller places; and we had the strange spectacle of stars acting in towns that had not seen anything but third-rate productions for the best part of half a century. The best theatre towns in Great Britain to-day are Bristol and Oxford. No one could have said that a year ago.

But this touring of stars had one very unfortunate effect: it nearly killed the repertory companies, which had suffered from bureaucratic ordinances no less than the West End had, and were now obliged to suffer the competition of London stars. How far the repertory companies will be able to survive in large cities the competition of the West End, I cannot say. One company, that in Manchester, died in January, but Liverpool is gamely holding on. There is, of course, ample life left in the repertory companies which operate in places unaffected by the competition of the London stars, but even for them the times are harder than they are for the majority of workers. The fact that drama is essential to the life of people is proved by the remarkable number of play-reading societies that have been started since September.

But when all is said that can be said in the way of optimism, the situation is a sad one. What will be the outcome of it, I cannot imagine, nor can any other person, but I hope that we shall see a completely reorganised theatre. I have spent many years in advocating reduced prices and better accommodation. I dislike the thought that the theatre is the entertainment of a small group of people who can afford to pay large sums for admission, and I long for the time when the theatre will once again be the resort of the general community and not merely the resort of a negligible part of it. I like ceremonial as well as anybody, and I like a well-dressed audience, but I hope the evening-dress convention of the West End will drop into desuetude. An evening-dress audience is rare in New York, and is seen there almost exclusively on first nights. At one time people were not admitted to the stalls of a West End theatre unless they were in evening clothes. Mr. Bernard Shaw was, indeed, denied admission to a theatre because he was not arrayed in a suit of solemn black and a starched shirt. Things have changed since then, and I hope they will change still further. An evening-dress drama is a trivial drama. The stars must continue in their provincial courses. Rivalry between them and the repertory theatres will do them both good. Too many repertory theatres, taking advantage of the absence of rivals, have fobbed off their customers with very indifferent performances. We may find London actors more ready to live in the provinces than they have hitherto been willing to do.

It is in the prices of admission that I expect to see the greatest reform. The Income Tax will compel a reduction in them. A tax of 7s. 6d. in the pound, which is fairly certain to rise to a higher figure, will make it impossible for many people to pay 12s. 6d. for a stall in a theatre. At this moment, many people are giving half their incomes in tax to the Government. They will be giving more than half of it before long. I foresee a theatre in which the dearest seat will be 8s. 6d. The price may even be less. Star salaries will drop, but in compensation for that there will probably be more continuous employment. A hundred pounds a week is not, in the theatre, £5,200 a year: it is sometimes no more than an average weekly salary of £10. The dearer the theatre is, the worse it is. Make your seats very expensive, and you make life for the serious dramatist hard. What we want is a theatre of the whole community, instead of one for a clique, and we want a great variety of dramatists, not a close corporation. Never were there such fortunes made in any theatre as were made in the West End in 1914–1919, but who can remember with any pride the plays that were produced then? Out of the present distress, a great theatre may emerge: a better theatre than we have ever had before.

By LORNA LEWIS

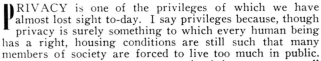

PRIVACY is one of the privileges of which we have almost lost sight to-day. I say privileges because, though privacy is surely something to which every human being has a right, housing conditions are still such that many members of society are forced to live too much in public.

At the present moment, as a result of the war, we are all leading more public lives than can be good for the average individual, and thousands of men and women hitherto nominally unoccupied are engaged on war work direct or on essential civilian work. The chances are that this new work is conducted in groups: that it is reached in crowded trains or buses: and that the midday meal is eaten in a canteen or restaurant. The evening meal is probably taken, for convenience, just as publicly.

Eating communally is indeed encouraged by the Ministry of Food, and is likely to become more and more an essential of daily existence as time goes on.

Then, because of shelter night-life, night war-work, and for many other reasons, town-dwellers have given up their private lives. In the country districts homes are partly occupied by evacuees or troops; and these, however welcome, do not add to the comparative isolation and calm of everyday routine.

Naturally war-workers, town-dwellers short of sleep owing to air-raids, the harassed housewife whose home can no longer be called her own, all need opportunities of escape from this state of unquiet emergency. They want a rest from *enforced* human contacts. But how and where are they to find it?

Hotels and guest-houses are filled with elderly evacuees who have conscientiously left their treasured homes in the danger zones; private houses, cottages and " rooms " each have their quota of soldiers and school-children. The best the tired war-workers can hope for—and I say this in all gratitude—is to stay with friends who are still lucky enough to have a spare room. This can be delightful; but unless the friends are people of imagination and understanding, it may call for adaptability and other qualities which lay too great a strain on overtired guests.

I am thinking of my friends Jack and Althea, a youngish couple who had been married about five years when the war broke out. In peace-time they had a comfortable little home and a hard-earned income on which, by clever management, they lived and entertained modestly but happily. They regretted having no children, but were the best of companions to each other; life seemed good to them.

Then the war came. Jack, a member of the R.A.F.V.R., found himself at once immersed in noisy mess life. Althea joined a big A.R.P. post. Dormitories and public living-rooms were an exhausting contrast to the solitude of her own house and the pleasant prospect of Jack's return in the evenings. She was thankful to get home in her off-duty times, thankful to have a place to which Jack could come on his short leaves. They agreed that, though living

in herds had some advantages if you looked at it the right way (and, really, it wasn't any use looking at it any other way), they were neither of them absolutely cut out for communal life.

One night, when Althea was at her post, a big bomb wiped out her house. As it also wiped out much of the neighbourhood she had some difficulty in getting a furnished bed-sitting-room as a temporary home. It was small, but Jack was now stationed a long way away and leaves were infrequent; she could just manage in it alone. When Jack wrote gaily to say he had seven days' leave, and couldn't they stay somewhere in the country where they would be away from noise, and routine, and crowds of people, Althea replied unsuspectingly that she would fix it right away, it would indeed be simply lovely to be by themselves and just do what they liked.

ALONE *Sometimes!*

After a great deal of wasted time, wear and tear, and expense over letters, telegrams and telephone calls, Althea had to say that, as every place was full up, she had arranged for them to go and stay with their friends, the Smiths.

The Smiths were almost too kind in their wish to make Jack and Althea's leave successful; but it must be remembered that they too had their point of view. They lived in a comparatively isolated village; Jack was a bomber-pilot, with a recent D.F.C. to his credit, Althea was living and working under air-raid conditions. Both of them were therefore " interesting." So strange local people were invited in continuously, who asked innumerable questions, then vanished and were replaced by other strangers. Bridge parties filled up the evenings, prolonged till poor

Jack and Althea could hardly conceal their yawns or see their cards. By day either host or hostess, or both, sat and chatted with their visitors over the only fire, while any expeditions were conducted in foursomes. Jack, if he looked restless, was taken to work in his host's carpentry shed. Althea found herself all too often involved in her hostess's cutting-out for the local Red Cross: a type of work with which she was by now quite painfully familiar.

My young friends did not wish to be exclusive, but they did want a chance of discussing in private such problems as Jack's peace-time business, insurance claims on their bombed-out home, Althea's invalid but obstinate mother's plans, and so on. Mostly they wanted sometimes just to enjoy each other's society, and to be able to pretend that they were back again in happy, hopeful pre-war existence.

At the end of a week's ceaseless entertainment Jack and Althea felt irritable and impatient, almost rebellious. Worse still, being kind-hearted and courteous, they were tortured by remorse over their changed attitude towards their well-meaning host and hostess. They went back to their posts of duty disappointed, rather sad, and still tired: they had been given much on their holiday and were eager to admit it. But the one thing they would have most liked, privacy, they did not get.

So many people have said to me: " I feel selfish being here in the peace and safety of the country. If only I could do something of real use to those who are living and working in danger areas ! "

One of the best things these generous-minded people can do is to open their doors to hardworking friends and even strangers. The Jacks and the Altheas need hospitality badly—if only they can be left alone sometimes !

Rest for the mind, a chance to feel a private person, not just one of the herd, is as necessary as rest and food for the body. It is, after all, for the freedom of the individual, this right to be one's own self, that we are fighting to-day.

*Illustrations by
Gilbert Wilkinson*

A Job for Women:

AFTER three months' "blitz," with Hitler still vainly endeavouring to break the spirit of London by battering its walls, it is appropriate and cheering to look forward to the new City that we shall build out of such ruin as may be made of the old.

I have been talking to numbers of women; women from the suburbs, from central London, from the East End, who all have this in common, that they have lost their homes. Undismayed, they are already looking forward to the new homes they will receive after the war.

When this task is undertaken, I hope those responsible will consult the people for whom they are rebuilding. They have such definite ideas on the subject, and are determined to see them fulfilled.

Mrs. Mellor, wife of an £800-a-year Civil Servant, has had her Kensington house gutted by incendiary bombs. It was a late-Victorian building, ugly and solid, and the Mellors had only lived there two years.

"What annoys me most," said Mrs. Mellor cheerfully, "is all the money we spent on improvements the summer before the war. We'd had a new bathroom in, and new grates, and we'd shut up a terrible basement, and turned a pantry into a first-class kitchen. And now all our planning has literally gone up in smoke!"

I asked her the question that I have repeated many times during the course of my explorations: If you could choose, would you like your house rebuilt as it was before? Mrs. Mellor thought not.

"I liked it at first because it was big. But even with the improvements—and there were plenty more needed—it was very cumbersome to run with only one maid. No, I'd like something smaller. I wouldn't mind a flat, if the building wasn't *too* like a warren—and I should like something less ugly. My husband didn't mind, but I always wanted to shut my eyes when I climbed up the steps to the front door!"

Even more emphatic was the reply of twenty-four-year-old Mrs. Dennis, whose bombed house

How would *you* like to see the new post-war London looking? Do you agree with the people interviewed by Miss Fraser, or have you quite different ideas? Let us know your views

Planning a New London

by Cicely Fraser

was on one of those vast new estates which have sprung up all over Greater London.

"No, I don't want my house rebuilt as it was, because it was just jerry-built. We came here to be near Harry's work, and because it was cheap, but the moment we settled in things started going wrong. Just before it was hit I noticed a great crack along the edge of the ceiling, and I said to my mother, ' If Hitler doesn't knock this place down, it'll fall down of its own accord!'"

"Cheap materials," said Harry. "They look all right to begin with, but they don't last. And they spoil the country, too. I remember this part when it was all fields, and now it's nothing but a jumble of bungalows, all bits and pieces."

Mrs. Dennis's neighbour, however, did not agree.

"I moved out here from Brondesbury," she said, " and I've enjoyed every minute of living in a house that was clean and sunny, instead of dirt and smuts from morning till night, and a chipped bath. That matters to me more than the look of things, or even a few fields."

Her house had been damaged by the bomb that wrecked " The Spinney," but she proudly refuted the charge of jerry-building by pointing out how well it had stood up to the blast.

I spent a night in an East End shelter, among numerous women who had been driven from their homes, and found them very willing to discuss the question of new ones, and decided about what they wanted. They had been happy in their destroyed homes, but it was in spite of, and not because of, the sordid little houses where they had lived. What they want is something new, really new. Many of them had been to the Ideal Home Exhibitions, and though such gadgets as patent dishwashers or even vacuum cleaners seemed beyond their scope, these shows had made a great impression. All the women wanted bathrooms, indoor sanitation, running water, electric light and a decent cooker in the kitchen. They were uninterested in the subject of design, but they approved the idea of big windows and light-coloured walls—though brightly painted doors were vetoed as " fanciful." Some of them, who had never known anything but a paved back-yard, said wistfully that, " a bit of grass, or a garden would be nice, too."

Then they began on the great house-versus-flat argument, and this raged for at least half-an-hour. In the beginning everyone was in

(Continued on page 39)

READY at all times
to cook for all comers

The Aga Heat Storage Cooker was first designed to make peacetime more peaceable. Now it is proving a sure, if silent, aid to victory in wartime. Saving of fuel and labour are a national as well as a private necessity. Efficient service, night and day, in emergency or out of it, can also be counted among the Aga characteristics that will help us to win. The Aga Cooker is guaranteed not to exceed a stated annual fuel consumption and it needs attention only once every twelve hours.

YOU KNOW WHERE YOU ARE WITH AN

AGA
Registered Trade Mark

WITHOUT

reliance upon vulnerable services

•

constant re-fuelling

•

variation in efficiency — night or day

•

big fuel bills

•

dirt, dust or fumes

★ *AGA Model C, suitable for average households. Larger domestic models and models for schools and restaurants are available.*

AGA HEAT LTD. (Proprietors: Allied Ironfounders Limited), COALBROOKDALE . SHROPSHIRE

A Job for Women

(Continued from page 37)

favour of small houses. Regardless of the fact that they had lived in streets too cramped for privacy, regardless also of the way they had now adjusted themselves amicably to completely communal life, they declared obstinately that you could Keep Yourself To Yourself better in a house. But when I pointed out that really large-scale rebuilding of London, with plenty of allowance for space, would certainly mean building upwards in large blocks of flats, most of them changed their minds. They agreed that they would prefer a modern-built flat in their old district rather than a house in a distant suburb.

Though the air-raids have done much, everywhere, to break down old barriers of reserve, I don't think the " my home is my castle " idea, cherished by the English, has been driven away. In a north-west suburb a number of the residents have arranged communal meals, and the men come back from business to an evening supper in a schoolroom, which their wives have joined together to cook. The scheme works very well, but everyone accepts it as a war measure only.

That, I think, is where we differ so strongly from the Nazis. We are gregarious enough, especially in times of hardship, but we shall never acquire the mentality which makes people unhappy except in large hordes.

In fact the only communal suggestion which was not turned down flatly was that of communal laundries. This, a little suspiciously, was allowed as a future possibility. Communal kitchens, however, roused unanimous dissent. The men had an idea that cooking would deteriorate. The women wanted their own kitchens, thank you, without anyone else messing around them.

From the people who want the houses, I went to the men who will help to provide them. I talked with Mr. S. J. B. Stanton, a Fellow of the Royal Institute of British Architects, who (like most British architects since Wren) has dreamed for years of a reconstructed London.

" Residential London is an architect's nightmare at present," he said, " with everything jumbled and unplanned. From our point of view the sudden growth of industrial wealth last century was a very bad thing. Victorian builders were mostly terrible fellows! For the rich they built great, ugly, inconvenient barracks. For the poor their one aim was to jam as many dwellings as possible into the land space, mean, twelve-feet-fronted houses that became slums almost at once. The first thing we ought to do after the war is to make a clean sweep of miles and miles of these places, whether they have been bombed or not."

He pointed out that it is only recently that really new ideas on architecture have penetrated to this country. We have started using new building materials—notably concrete and steel—and we have at last begun to realise that beauty of structure is an end in itself.

" During the last twenty-five years, except for public buildings, and individual jobs where a good architect is given his chance, our best opportunities have been on slum-clearance schemes."

The L.C.C., for example, have for years considered the æsthetic side of rebuilding, as well as the utilitarian. They have a first-class chief architect, with a brilliant staff under him, who have been dotting London with new housing estates which are not only up-to-date, but also pleasing to the eye—more so, in many cases, than blocks of " luxury flats." One of the finest examples is Dover Court, Putney, a charming estate whose little houses, creeper-covered, with bright doors, are grouped round greens. In many cases big trees occupy the centre of the green, and the houses have their gardens, bright with flowers and rich with vegetables, so that the effect is of a model village rather than part of London.

In other towns, too, this sort of thing has gone on. Liverpool, which contains some of the country's worst slumland, has built new estates, designed by the City Architect, Mr. Keay, which are fine examples of what modern architecture can do.

When Mr. Stanton said that something on a really gigantic scale was needed before London could reach the standard that its position deserved, I asked him how long he thought such a scheme would take, and how it should be designed.

" It would take about fifty years to complete on the scale I should like," he answered. " But in that time we could see a new city, more splendidly planned than at any time since they rejected Wren's ideas for reconstruction after the Great Fire."

Wren's schemes were thwarted by lack of vision and vested interests, to the great loss of us all.

" I am not a politician," said Mr. Stanton, " and I can't argue the rights and wrongs of land problems. But speaking as an architect, I should like to see much more control than we have at present. We've had too much spoiling of this country by greed and by uncontrolled jerry-building. No one should be allowed to hinder great schemes for the sake of personal profit."

One of the first things to be avoided in the new London is overcrowding. Narrow streets of narrow houses must be replaced by broad streets, with plenty of open spaces where the children may have light and air. This will mean flats for inner London. If you are pulling down two hundred close-packed houses, and using the same land for erecting only fifty new buildings, you must make provision for the remaining families by building towards the sky instead of along the ground. But in greater London, and in badly-damaged suburbs, it should be possible to make estates of individual houses, preferably on the Dover Court lines. Another important necessity is broad trunk roads.

There are three main types of design suggested for big-scale reconstruction: the square, the circular and the star-shaped. Hitherto most planned estates (as distinct from those which just straggle) have been square, but circular designs are also very effective. O-shaped blocks of flats with circular balconies running round a courtyard look unusual and decorative. Streets leading off a main road, and terminating in circular culs-de-sac, have a pleasantly " self-contained " appearance.

Most modern architects, however, favour the star-shape for any extensive reconstruction scheme. In the centre of your star you have the communal buildings, shops, cinemas, town hall, and perhaps a church with a fine spire as a landmark. Main traffic roads radiate outwards from this centre, and between the main roads run the residential streets, either straight or curved. Not only does the star-shape avoid muddle, and traffic confusion, but it also fosters a sense of community.

What of the houses or flats themselves? It goes without saying that they must have civilised amenities, the baths, electricity, and labour-saving kitchens that the women want. They should have plenty of window space, with windows towards the sun to give the maximum amount of light. And if people can bear the idea of doing without coal fires, and having electric radiators or central heating instead, it would go a long way towards keeping the city air fresher. If the building is carried out on a large enough scale, and under planned control, good materials can be used.

After hearing the ideas of the architects and the future house-owners, I inspected another side of the question, the national side. I spoke to an economist, at present working for the Government. I am not allowed to give his name, but he is well known to the public. He is one of the men who is determined that the muddle following 1918, which led to slumps and unemployment, shall not be repeated after this war. I asked him if a big building scheme, such as the architects wanted, would be impossible from the point of view of the country's finances.

" On the contrary," he said, " it would be a very good thing for our national economy. After the war we must see to it that the demobilised men have work, which will absorb them quickly into civilian life. We must also see that the people already engaged on production are not thrown out of work when armament industry ceases. There are various schemes that can be started to prevent this, but reconstruction is one of the most important. Not only will people need houses, but just think of the different types of labour involved in the building industry. Everything from bricklaying at the beginning to road- and drain-construction when the houses are built. I should like to see large-scale rebuilding schemes, not only in London, but all over the country."

Unlike Mr. Stanton, this man is a politician, and he spoke strongly on the subject of control.

" I want to see the Ministry of Reconstruction maintain wartime · powers after peace," he said. " We must have as much control and co-operation following the war as we have during it. We've simply got to pull together and sink private interests. If there is neither muddle, waste, nor profiteering, big schemes such as you suggest will be a benefit to the nation. But no selfish or greedy people should be allowed to stand in the way, by putting up prices of land and material, and the scheme should be carried out as a whole. Otherwise you will have town and county councils starting piecemeal schemes that will make your friends the architects despair, or adopting inferior plans because they can't afford to do the thing properly. The Government should give grants, and supervise plans, and then we shall have a complete and worth-while reconstruction."

He ended up by saying:

" Rebuilding of London homes is of special interest to all women. It is *their* job to see that things are carried out as they want them. Victory in this war is a justification for democracy—and democracy has got to justify itself in peace as well. So when the Ministry of Reconstruction gets to work, you see it does its job well! "

Let's talk about XMAS FOOD

There won't be turkey on many tables this year; but the Christmas atmosphere will be there and the children's eyes will sparkle at simple treats, served gaily. From what we know of you, you'll make your Christmas catering a grand success in spite of difficulties, and we're out to help you all we can. Here are a few suggestions of general interest from letters we have sent to correspondents. A Happy Christmas to you!

I'd like a recipe for Christmas pudding without eggs.

Mix together 1 cupful of flour, 1 cupful of breadcrumbs, 1 cupful of sugar, half a cupful of suet, 1 cupful of mixed dried fruit, and, if you like, 1 teaspoonful of mixed sweet spice. Then add 1 cupful of grated potato, 1 cupful of grated raw carrot and finally 1 level teaspoonful of bicarbonate of soda dissolved in 2 tablespoonfuls of hot milk. Mix all together (no further moisture is necessary), turn into a well-greased pudding basin. Boil or steam for 4 hours.

SOME HINTS FOR CHILDREN'S PARTY FOOD, PLEASE?

Chocolate squares are popular. Melt 3 oz. margarine with two tablespoonfuls of syrup in a saucepan, mix in ½ lb. rolled oats and a pinch of salt. Blend well, and put in a greased, shallow baking tin, flattening the mixture smoothly. Bake for half an hour to 40 minutes in a moderate oven. Take out, and whilst still hot, grate over it a tablet of chocolate. The chocolate will melt with the heat, and can be spread evenly with a knife. Cut into squares and lift out.

Amusing little figures, cut from short-crust or biscuit dough, go down well. Roll the dough about ¼-inch thick. "People" can be made by cutting small rounds for heads, larger for bodies, strips for arms and legs; pinch the various pieces of dough firmly together. Prick out eyes, noses, mouths, with currants. If you can draw a little or have a friend who can, make thin cardboard "patterns" of animals, lay them on the dough and cut round with a small sharp knife.

Chocolate coating for your Christmas cake. Mix together 3 tablespoonfuls of sugar with 2 tablespoonfuls of cocoa and 2 tablespoonfuls of milk. Stir, in a stout saucepan, over low heat until the mixture is thick and bubbly like toffee; then, while hot, pour it over your cake.

A Christmassy sparkle is easy to give to sprigs of holly or evergreen for use on puddings and cakes. Dip your greenery in a strong solution of Epsom salts. When dry it will be beautifully frosted.

I'll miss my gay bowl of fruit on the Christmas table. Not if you have a bowl of salad in its place. Vegetables have such jolly colours — the cheerful glow of carrot, the rich crimson of beetroot, the emerald of parsley. And for health's sake you should have a winter salad with, or for, one meal a day. Here is a suggestion; it looks as delightful as it tastes.

Salad slices. Cut a thick round of wheatmeal bread for each person and spread with margarine. Arrange a slice of tomato in the centre of each slice and, if liked, put a sardine on top. Surround with circles of chopped celery, grated raw carrot, finely chopped parsley or spinach and grated raw beetroot on the edge. Sprinkle with a little grated cheese.

Issued by The Ministry of Food.   (S25)

A PERMANENT WAVE

is a necessity for women who are doing war work unless their hair is naturally curly. There is no other way to keep the hair always neat and pretty.

The demand for Eugene waves has, naturally, greatly increased this year. We are doing our utmost to cope with it, and while there is some restriction of supplies there is no shortage among Eugene specialists.

Our research laboratory staff, from the start of the war, have been preparing for difficulties of supply that were likely to arise. They are working now on problems that may arise in 1942.

As a result of their skill and foresight Eugene quality is exactly the same as it has always been.

A Eugene wave, carried out by a skilled hairdresser, at a price which enables him to give full time and materials to it, will last comfortably up to eight or nine months. It is the easiest wave to set at home. And it won't hurt the hair in a lifetime.

Pay a good price. A permanent wave using the genuine Eugene materials and Eugene technique cannot be done cheaply.

Keep the hair in good condition by brushing it vigorously with good brushes every day.

Hair that is Eugene waved, regularly brushed and washed with a mild soap is hair at its healthiest and most beautiful. No further time or money need be spent on it.

Permanently Yours

EUGÈNE

Ask housewives which part of their task is most affected

Here is a survey of the whole position

GROW MORE VEGETABLES

Present-Day

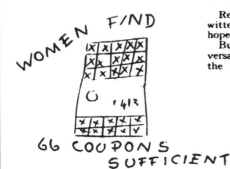

BUDGET YOUR POINTS SHOPPING

WOMEN FIND

66 COUPONS SUFFICIENT

EARLY in January of this year three youths boarded a bus at Kennington and sat near me. It was Saturday midday, and they were obviously looking forward to the week-end's leisure, for they were in the high spirits which spring from freedom after toil.

Their conversation was incessant and disjointed: in a short space of time it covered their work, new jobs and enlisting in the Air Force, while at frequent intervals they left their topic high and dry to comment upon young women to be seen on the pavements and in the roadway, as the bus journeyed on.

All three belonged to the working class, and had no inflated opinions of either their own importance or abilities. They seriously discussed their chances of passing some form of qualifying test for the Air Force. There was considerable concern about eyesight (which, nevertheless, was sufficiently good to detect every pretty girl at no small distance!). One of them was considerably worried, and his tone of voice showed the utter dejection he would feel in the event of failure to pass the test. Immediately the others attempted to revive his spirits by enumerating their friends who had already passed successfully.

"Look at Oldy, he got through," said one.

"Yes," said the doubtful one, "but he has education."

"Oldy didn't have education," said the other. "He went to the same school as me."

Real rough youngsters these, keen-witted, enthusiastic, full of life, fun and hope—ready for adventure.

But it was the next part of their conversation which was of greatest interest to the unwitting listener.

The youth who had doubts about being able to pass the test for the Air Force had two new jobs in the offing.

"Settled which job you're going to take?" asked one of the others.

"No," replied the doubtful one. "You see, if I take the engineering job I'll be able to put away three pounds a week and still have four pounds in my pocket, but I shall be letting Harry down if I don't take the laundry job."

This is not a made-up story: it is one of those true incidents which daily cross our train of thought and influence our opinions and actions. It is strange that such conversations by other people should weave a different strand into our thoughts and produce patterns we had never planned.

We have read much of late of a few cases where boys who have been receiving large wages have fallen into trouble. But the new start given to our thoughts by this conversation makes one wonder about the tens of thousands of young people, well guided in their own home life, who are benefiting from the exceptionally high wage conditions of to-day.

A working lad with self-imposed ideas of saving £3 a week, but with every intention of enjoying life, perhaps not even taking the higher wage because he would be "letting Harry down," and above all, with the lack of selfishness shown by his being more anxious to pass the test for the Air Force than to continue in civilian work, even in the exceptionally favourable conditions offered to him, certainly has in him the right material for the making of a fine citizen. Yet his case will be neglected by the press for the story of the very few who fall into crime.

THE WHEATMEAL LOAF

RUBBE

by the War, and most would reply " Shopping."

by a Market Research Expert

Shopping

But what has this to do with present-day shopping conditions? Just this: it was the new " strand " which wove itself into the pattern that was being worked out for you, and which set me hastily to review the various assembled facts in a new light.

There is no need to tell anyone that shopping conditions have changed considerably since the War commenced. One could fill pages with the disadvantages that now confront the housewife. But the " strand " that high-spirited youth has woven into the pattern induces us to search for the advantages we have gained, instead of concentrating on the depressing side of things. It urges us to accept conditions, see the best in them, and do our best to aid the war effort.

Many people are still unaware that the greatest profession or business is that of housekeeping. There are more people daily employed in it than in any other form of work. In war-time housekeeping becomes even more important than in peace-time: if those who keep house went on strike, the war would be lost in a week.

Most housewives feel that perhaps the most difficult task during the war is shopping. This was true during the first world war, also: in fact, during the present war, shopping conditions are very much better than our mothers experienced then.

At least one of the advantages which has been gained for present-day shoppers is that there are fewer long queues in which to wait for hours, only to find, when your turn arrives, that the goods for which you have waited so long and so patiently are sold. And in the last war this meant no meat, bread and vegetables,

and perhaps failure to provide a meal after wasting an entire morning. Such queues as we now have are mainly for the little " extras," not for essentials.

The allowances of rationed foods are not lavish, but they are sufficient, and in many cases are actually above the average purchased before the war, though they perhaps seem less because other goods are in short supply.

We get four ounces of bacon. Many of us before the war bought much more, but the greatest number of people bought less or none at all, for the *average* purchase in peace-time was in the neighbourhood of four ounces per person per week.

In peace-time some could afford and therefore obtained all they required, others could not buy for want of money. To-day there are few people who cannot afford to purchase their share. And this amazing position has been made possible by rationing, even though we cannot procure the vast supplies we formerly received from Denmark.

There is at present a cheese ration of three ounces for everyone, with higher allowances for certain classes of workers. The supply of cheese appears short because of the shorter average meat allowance, but were a greater quantity of meat available, the average weekly cheese consumption would fall below three ounces per person.

The average weekly butter and margarine consumption per head before the war was not in excess of ten ounces. We did exceedingly well over the Christmas period, and now that butter has been reduced to two ounces, and cooking fats

SWITCH OFF LIGHT WHEN LEAVING THE ROOM

and margarine (which forms the greatest proportion) to six ounces, we are even now not much below the pre-war average, a good position, particularly when we again remember that our large supplier, Denmark, is out of bounds.

There is no shortage of bread, flour, soups, beef extracts, custard powders, cocoa, coffee, pickles, sauces, etc., or of that very important commodity, salt, or for a matter of that, scores of other products which go a long way to making up our food budget.

Of course, some articles of food, particularly fruit from overseas, have disappeared from the shops. We cannot expect to engage in a war of the present immensity, raging right across the globe, without experiencing a great strain upon our shipping.

DON'T WASTE WATER

It is a strange factor in the human make-up that our difficulties are so easily magnified, whilst our many advantages and privileges are ignored. To emphasise these we should make a comparison: the standard should be, not our knowledge of home conditions in the years immediately proceeding the war, but the condition of the rest of Europe. Upon this standard —the only true one—we are the best-fed nation on this war-ridden continent.

So as far as shopping for food is concerned, then, let us conclude that conditions have not changed to anything like the extent we might have expected, and that in fact they are surprisingly good in an abnormal period.

And what of shopping for clothing and similar goods?

Consider the principal changes which have been made:

A clothes rationing scheme has been introduced.

Prices have increased.

We must take our own wrapping paper or carry the goods away unwrapped, unless they are delivered to our home by the tradesman from whom we purchase.

Shops close earlier in the winter months.

THIS IS THE KITCHEN FRONT

GIVE UP UNWANTED BOOKS

Travelling is probably not so comfortable if we are shopping a long distance from home, especially at rush hours.

The rationing scheme which was introduced many months ago was hailed by all and sundry for its soundness and for the measure of protection it afforded the public.

After many months of operation few amendments have been found necessary, and it cannot be denied that most people are happy with it, for they have found that it makes ample provision for their requirements.

As a result of the scheme there has been the necessary conservation of cotton, wool, machinery and man-power, which are all necessary for vital war work. The men and women in the Services must be and are well clothed, and even from the civilians' points of view there is still a wide choice of most of the goods they require.

It is unnecessary to remind anyone that prices have gone up! Many people may consider that this is due to advanced prices at the factory or additional profits to the retailer. They forget that almost every time they buy a recently-made article they are contributing by way of purchase tax to the nation's purse.

If comparison is to be made with pre-war prices, the amount paid in purchase tax must first be deducted, for, like increased income tax, the purchase tax is one of the penalties of war. Although it is applied to certain classes of goods, it has nothing whatever to do with the real value of those goods.

A Notice by the Commissioners of Customs and Excise shows that included among the goods chargeable with purchase tax are:

(i) Garments or footwear made wholly or partly of fur skin (including any skin with fur attached) or silk (except silk used for the stitching of seams or buttonholes): 33⅓ per cent., *and* (ii) Garments or footwear except goods specified in (i) and (iii): 16⅔ per cent., *while* (iii) Garments

KEEP SALVAGE

SAVE TILL IT HURTS

DON'T TRAVEL IN THE RUSH HOUR

or footwear of a kind suitable for young children's wear, except as specified in section (i) above; protective boots designed for miners or quarrymen or moulders; clogs, are exempt.

The note goes on to indicate that garments mean all articles of clothing except headgear, gloves and minor articles of apparel which fall within another class. It covers protective garments such as leather, rubber and other aprons, overalls and boiler suits, and garments such as bathing suits and running shorts. It includes socks and stockings, corsets and other articles.

Hats, caps, cap covers, bonnets, and even wigs and all other headgear, whether trimmed or untrimmed, are subject to a 33⅓ per cent. tax.

Gloves, neckties, scarves, head shawls, handkerchiefs, hair nets, veils, braces, belts, sashes, garters, suspenders, boot and shoe laces, corset laces, hairpins, curling pins, cooking sleeves, and a host of other articles are subject to a 33⅓ per cent. tax.

This tax also affects many other articles in daily use in the home, so if you are inclined to think that prices are high, remember it is partially due to taxation, and not necessarily to traders taking advantage of war-time conditions.

A recent Order has been made prohibiting retailers from wrapping up most of your purchases. This has been done to conserve paper. Paper is an essential war material, and although it is manufactured in large quantities in this country, the pulp from which it is made has to be brought from overseas, at the cost of using shipping capacity which could be better used for very much more essential supplies.

Fortunately paper can be repulped and used again and again, which is one of the main reasons for the present great campaign to collect waste. We must be on the safe side by amply providing everything required for war purposes.

Every time you take your own wrapping paper or carry your purchases unwrapped you are aiding the war effort. It

is an essential service you are performing, something to be proud of, and there is no reason why you should curtail your purchases or consider that present-day shopping conditions are worse because of this imposed necessity.

It is the same for everyone, and to the quietly humorous temperament of the British Public, which has enabled us to survive the heaviest of raids, this new condition appears as a great joke which has been forced upon us.

The fact that shops close earlier is probably a greater hardship to those people who are already giving great service to the country by working in factories and workshops throughout the day, than it is to the average housewife, who can adjust her domestic arrangements accordingly.

War is a dark business in more ways than one. Few of us have not, before September 1939, enjoyed searching brilliantly lighted windows in the hope of discovering a very special present for a close friend, or a bargain for ourselves. We remember, and at times rightfully long for, the shimmering lights, with night as bright as day in every main thoroughfare; the warm atmosphere of well-stocked shops; the service which is at its best when competition is strongest and when the public, not the tradesmen, bestow the favours.

But we have now to regard lights at night as a joy for the future. The price we might have to pay now for well-lighted streets might be tragically heavy.

As for travelling, it must be arranged so that the carriages, trams and buses are free for the workers who must be transported from congested areas to their homes in the minimum time: congested areas must be cleared before night falls.

Even in peace-time transport companies spent thousands of pounds in advertising to induce people to shop early and so leave transport free for the rush hours. If this was necessary then, we can hardly complain if in war-time we do not comply with the request and get caught in the rush, with consequent discomfort.

WE MUST SAVE FUEL

YOUR SEPARATE

GROW MORE VEGETABLES

Those of us who live in areas which have been heavily bombed need only cast our memories back one year, and there will be a unanimous agreement that present-day shopping conditions, whether for food, clothing or any other goods, are many times better than we ever expected that they could be again before the war ended.

And if this is not sufficient for the more pessimistically minded, then let them draw a comparison between the way the average person is clothed and fed to-day and the conditions which prevailed before the war.

There are now no such dreadful and disgraceful terms as "distressed areas." Twenty years ago there was no war, but there were 1,594,000 men and 444,000 women out of employment. To-day there are less than 9 per cent. of that number, and a goodly proportion of these have been certified as unsuitable for ordinary industrial employment.

At least 91 out of every 100 of that large body of people have found improvement in present-day shopping conditions, for there was little shopping on the pay of the unemployed, and a very large proportion of these were the wage-earners or would-be wage-earners upon whom others depended.

And for those who still consider prices high, let us remind them of the position after the last war.

Each month the Board of Trade issues a figure called the "cost of living index." This index shows the fluctuating cost of living, based upon a figure of 100 for July 1914, which was the last month in the peace period before the first great war.

The figures show that what cost £100 in living expenses (namely, food, rent, clothing, fuel, light, etc.) in July 1914 was costing at the end of 1941 the sum of £201. But in December 1918, that is, just after the last war, it was costing £220, and by December 1920 the index had risen to the enormous figure of £269.

The cost of living to-day is therefore only three-quarters of what it cost us in 1920.

How apt we are to forget!

In the case of food only, what cost £100 in July 1914, cost you £165 in December 1941, but in December 1920 you were paying the enormous sum of £282. In other words, you are now paying 12s., after two years of troublesome war, for what actually cost you £1 in the peace year of 1920.

Matters would certainly have been very different had the Government not controlled prices with a firm hand and introduced the rationing of goods as the need arose.

More and more prices are being controlled as the Government finds it necessary to protect your interests.

Such controls may from time to time bring about a greater shortage of the goods than was the case before the control was applied, but bit by bit the goods find their way into the open market again, for it means the manufacturers must accept the control at prices which are calculated to give a fair profit, or go out of business.

Your part in the scheme is patiently to await the return of the goods to the market, and it should be the easier to do so knowing that prices are now—even in these abnormal days—so far below the prices you paid in the years 1918–1920.

With shipping becoming more and more involved in actual war operations, as is bound to be the case with our heavier engagements in the East and the increasing need to supply Russia with more and more war materials, we shall be met with ever-growing restrictions, which will affect shopping conditions of the future. These restrictions are for our own protection, even when they seem irksome.

For instance, a new measure is forecast in a joint statement issued by the Ministry of War Transport, the Ministry of Food and the Board of Trade. Retailers are going to be asked to co-operate

"SAILOR'S BLOOD — DO WITHOUT YOUR CAR"

with the Government in preparing and putting into operation new plans for the "rationalisation" of deliveries to their customers.

Enquiries which have been made by Government Departments have forced them to the conclusion that millions of gallons of petrol could be saved by operating such a scheme. Housewives will be asked to take their shopping home with them, and they will be urged to assist retailers by falling in with the new arrangements made. It is possible that groceries will be delivered on only one day a week, and perishable goods on two or three days a week.

In the name of "Service" there has, in the past, been an enormous expenditure of man-power, machinery and petrol in the distributive services.

For instance, a manufacturer may have sent goods forty miles to a wholesaler, who in turn has brought the goods back to a retailer within one mile from the factory at which the goods were made. Eighty miles of man-power, machinery and petrol all used to effect a one-mile delivery!

This may have been sound practice in peace-time, when expenditure meant employment, and to have saved would have placed even more people out of work. But to-day neither man-power, machinery nor petrol are plentiful, and something must be done to conserve these vital factors.

It was in the months before the war that a very clever student of marketing and a writer of technical articles, Mrs. Chappell, who was at that time engaged upon a wide study of the Grocery Distributive Machinery, wrote:

"One of the points of our study has been the source of supply, and no doubt has been left in our minds that the grocery trade has much to do in order to organise itself in matters of distribution, if, in the event of a major crisis, it is to avoid official action of a detrimental nature.

"In such an event, the conservation of transport, the elimination of unnecessary waste of man-power and petrol will become essential. It will not be possible for a wholesaler to cover the same locality as six other wholesalers. There will be one journey instead of seven, with the consequent compulsion to transfer customers at least for the duration of any crisis.

"We are of opinion that the trade should examine how far mutual arrangements for temporary transfer can be made —organise itself and submit its plans to the Defence Department, rather than have a plan forced upon it at a moment's notice."

Here was sound advice, given almost three years before the Government awoke to the position—the small voice of a clever woman in a wilderness of officialdom. If that advice had been taken in the early days of the war, it would have conserved hundreds of millions of gallons of petrol.

We should not complain at the things which are being done for our protection; rather should we, as Mrs. Chappell did, ask that things should be done which will hasten the end of this ghastly war. Thus, when you are faced with this new delivery arrangement, which will have a distinct bearing upon the shopping conditions of the future, you may care to remember, with pride of sex, that a woman foresaw the need for action which three Government Departments three years later are finding necessary. It may help to ease any little irritations any such new conditions may bring before you have adjusted yourself to them.

So the "strand" which was woven in by the high-spirited youth on the bus-top at Kennington has created an entirely new pattern from the one we had in mind. Instead of finding that shopping conditions are bad, we conclude that, considering all circumstances, present-day shopping conditions are astonishingly good in a very abnormal period, and that great credit is due to those responsible for bringing about the present position, which is far better than we anticipated twelve months ago.—W. H.

TAKE YOUR GAS MASK WITH YOU

SNEEZES — USE YOUR HANDKERCHIEF

MUST YOU TRAVEL TO-DAY?

Patriots must know . . . .

War — world war — has imperiously reminded us that all food comes from the soil and the sea — and that the labour of harvesting is man's primal task.

To Government and Governed alike has come the realisation of the vital importance of the canning industries in overleaping the seasons, and bringing food at its sun-ripe maturity to the humblest kitchen table on any day of the year.

The 57 Varieties have long inspired liking and trust throughout the community — therefore they were sorely missed when the grocers' shelves gave evidence of temporarily diminished supplies.

But patriots must know that all the time Heinz have been doing a big job of National feeding (supplying the Services, the national food reserves, etc). More — they must realise that Heinz have steadfastly refused to lower that standard of quality which gave the 57 its great good name.

It may be difficult to secure them, because the demand is large and retail output restricted, but Heinz 57 Varieties remain unchanged in purity, flavour and excellence.

57

H. J. HEINZ CO. LTD.

LONDON FACTORY

* Make your Salvage pile really worth while—to-day and every day.

YOUR *Paper Salvage*

Results of the December Competition

WE are delighted to find you so keenly alive to the essential points of the paper salvage campaign. By far the greatest number of entries gave ideas for: (1) Establishing a regular and easy routine for collecting paper by installing bags or boxes into which every scrap of paper, cardboard, etc., may be placed; (2) Economising in the use of paper in the three most important directions—in shopping, in firelighting, and in correspondence. These ideas recur most frequently:

● **Carry foodstuffs or sandwiches in cloths, fabric bags or pieces of waterproof material.**

● **Carry home such foods as meat and fish in dishes, jars or tins.**

● **Re-use envelopes or dispense with them altogether, and use scraps of paper or the back of the letter received for letters and notes.**

● **Instead of using paper for lighting fires, use fir cones, twigs, specially prepared firewood, dried bracken, leaves, garden rubbish.**

● **Don't line shelves or drawers with paper, but replace it by a coat of paint, American cloth or "Cellophane," or leave them bare.**

And now for the prizewinners: The following ten people receive National Savings Certificates:

Mrs. I. Mallabourn, 17 Clareville Rd., Darlington, Co. Durham. (*Make firelighter by shaving one end of thick piece of wood to make a sort of " brush."*)

Mr. James A. R. Dryden, 5 Comely Bank Rd., Edinburgh, 4. (*Save envelopes by folding letters into neat oblong and sealing edges with stamp paper.*)

Mrs. H. H. Butler, 9 Homefield Rd., Bromley, Kent. (*Make reversible hessian bag, with recipient's name and address on linen label stitched to one side, and sender's on similar label on inside, so that laundry may be sent to and fro to members of the Forces, etc.*)

Miss Lilian N. Grayling, 26 Lower Hanham Rd., Hanham, Bristol. (*Cut out each day from newspapers and magazines any items to be kept and let rest go to salvage, so giving even flow.*)

Miss Mary Taylor, 8 Cairnside, E. Herrington, Sunderland. (*Have week's inter-family competition, with different type of salvage—e.g. books, papers, souvenirs, cardboard—to be saved each day, and points awarded for biggest total. Biggest total of daily points wins prize.*)

Mrs. M. A. Berry, Thrums, Cranleigh Rd., Ewhurst, Guildford, Surrey.

Mrs. Alice E. Millard, 19 Phrosso Rd., Worthing, Sussex.

Mrs. Noel F. Terry, 14 Craigcrook Rd., Edinburgh, 4.

M. L. Hawke, 1 Beach Villa, Perranporth, Cornwall.

Mrs. Woolford, 43 Vicarage Rd., Chelmsford, Essex.

(Space unfortunately will not permit us to quote the entries of the last five prizewinners, who all sent in groups of ideas.)

now put all these hints into practice!

By

P. L. Garbutt, A.I.C.

Director of the Institute

WHEN planning your budget this year, the accent must obviously be on saving, for, as our footnotes remind us month by month, we must " Save, not spend, to hasten the end." " How much can I save ? " must therefore be at the back of your mind all the time. An extra Certificate perhaps each week, or maybe only an additional Stamp or two—it will all help. The large-scale investor must also try to set aside regularly some definite sum.

Standardised schemes of budgeting never fitted more than a few cases in pre-war days, still less do they do so now. Even with the same income and the same circumstances, no two householders will agree completely as to what constitutes reasonable expenditure. Everyone must, therefore, work out an individual plan, and if this should include any small extravagances, they must be counter-balanced by strict economy in other directions.

This year, financial conditions are not in quite the same state of flux and uncertainty as in the previous two years, for now most people have made the changeover from peacetime to wartime work, from a peace-time to a wartime home, so the present time is a good opportunity to sort things out and get going on a sound footing.

If you are drawing up a draft budget—and this is a very wise thing to do—first of all look through last year's totals, if you kept a record ; next write down your more or less fixed expenses, such as rent and rates ; make the necessary allocations for housekeeping, insurances, etc., and then make provision for savings.. If you have not already used Good Housekeeping *Diary and Account Book*, we suggest that you do so this year, as it will be found a great help in checking up your expenditure.

If, like other people, you wish to increase your savings this year, you will want to know which items it will be best to attack. It is not possible, as a rule, to reduce outlay on such items as income tax, rent, rates or mortgage expenses, nor is it wise to make cuts in insurances or educational expenses. It may indeed even be wise to increase insurances, and perhaps commit oneself to additional educational expenses, such as by taking out an Educational Endowment. In this connection one of the leading assurance companies is prepared to make quotations for benefits for any term required. The yearly payment will vary according to the estimated expenses of a child at Public School or University, but, as an example, an annual premium of approximately £18 for 15 years will assure a sum of £300 payable in three yearly instalments of £100, in the case of a parent aged 30 next birthday. If child is aged 2–3 years and a University education is aimed at, or perhaps some form of technical training, a scheme of this kind will obviously ease things considerably at a time when educational expenses are heaviest.

HOUSEKEEPING and personal expenses generally seem to be the most fruitful items to attack for possibilities of saving.

" What ought I to allow for house-keeping ? " is probably one of the first questions which crosses your mind. The answer depends on what you include under the term. With most people it is expected to cover expenditure on food, cleaning mat-erials, wages of any domestic help, laundrywork and possibly fuel.

As it is always easier to work from something concrete, especially in matters concerned with figures, we will consider an imaginary middle-class, fairly comfortably-off house-hold, consisting of two adults and three children, living in a two-sitting-room, four-bedroom house. We give both last year's expenditure on the various items and the figure aimed at this year.

FOOD

**Last year's average
per week   £4 7s. 4d.**

Food is obviously the most important item of the budget, and admittedly most foods cost more now. Still, as there are few luxury foods, as many foods are rationed, and as nothing must be wasted, costs per head should not be appreciably more, and an allowance of 14s.–16s. per head weekly should be adequate, and even allow of an occasional meal out, at a British Restaurant or else-where. Last year's expenditure, ap-proximately 17s. 6d. per head weekly, was on the high side. Resolved, there-fore, to cut expenditure to 15s. per head weekly.

Resolved for this year, £3 15s. 0d.

Budgeting for Victory

GENERAL MAID

Last year's average weekly wages   **£1 10s. 0d.**

This may not sound very heavy, but with the children now all of school age, it might be practicable to manage either with part-time daily maid or occasional charwoman.
Latter plan resolved on.

Resolved for this year **15s. 0d.**

LAUNDRYWORK

Last year's average weekly cost   **10s. 0d.**

Laundry charges have risen, but if " smalls " are washed at home, it should only be necessary to allow for sheets, table-cloths, large bath towels and possibly men's shirts. Resolved to cut expenditure on laundrywork.

Resolved for this year **7s. 0d.**

CLEANING MATERIALS

Last year's average weekly expenditure   **3s. 6d.**

This figure indicates rather extravagant use of cleaning materials. Resolved, therefore, to cut expenditure.

Resolved for this year **2s. 6d.**

FUEL—COAL, GAS, ELECTRICITY

Last year's average weekly cost   **15s. 0d.**

Strict fuel economy is demanded by the Government, and still smaller consumption must be aimed at by every household. Cut of at least 2s. 6d. decided.

Resolved for this year **12s. 6d.**

HOLIDAYS AND AMUSEMENTS

Last year's average weekly expenditure   **15s. 0d.**

These expenses must be still further cut. Suggest a reduction of at least 5s. per week.

Resolved for this year **10s. 0d.**

RENEWALS

Last year's average weekly cost   **5s. 0d.**

This amount will probably be automatically cut in most households on account of the increasing shortage of supplies.

Resolved for this year **2s. 6d.**

CHEMIST'S BILL

Last year's weekly average   **6s. 0d.**

It is surprising how much we spend quite unthinkingly at the chemist's, but this also will probably be automatically reduced by the shortage of toilet requisites and other non-essential supplies.

Resolved for this year **4s. 0d.**

CAR, CLEANING, GARAGE, TAX, etc.

Last year's average weekly expenditure   **17s. 6d.**

Petrol-rationing means that a car can be little used, and thus running costs are automatically reduced. On the other hand, taxation and insurance are heavy. It is impossible to estimate running costs and repairs accurately, but it was resolved to decrease costs by laying up car for first three months of the year.

Resolved for this year **15s. 0d.**

LOCAL BUS FARES, etc.

Last year's average weekly allowance   **5s. 0d.**

This only allows of occasional bus fares, but it might be possible with care to cut them a little.

Resolved for this year **4s. 6d.**

TELEPHONE

Last year's average weekly expenditure   **5s. 0d.**

It is not always possible to cut this expense, but there are people who still make very careless use of the telephone. Take the hint!

Resolved for this year **4s. 0d.**

CLOTHES AND SMALL PERSONAL EXPENSES

Last year's average weekly allowance   **£2 0s. 0d.**

Clothes rationing effectively reduced expenditure on this item after May last. It should be possible to plan an effective cut here this year.

Resolved for this year, £1 10s. 0d.

IN many households it will, of course, be necessary to make separate provision for husband's, or, in these days, possibly for one's own business expenses, such as season ticket, lunches, etc.

BY pruning expenditure in this way our imaginary family planned to save something like £3 per week. You may not be able to increase your savings quite so spectacularly, perhaps because you have already made very heavy cuts or because your income is very much less. Whatever your individual circumstances, though, do remember it is the small cuts here and there that add up and make something worth-while, although even with the best will in the world, of course, one must be prepared for the fact that some unexpected contingency may lead to unexpected expenses.

HAVING decided to save to the utmost, you must next consider the most practical way of keeping to your resolution, and also decide what you are going to do with your savings. Many ingenious ways of saving have been thought out and publicised, and we must all adopt the most appropriate or attractive method. Many people find one of the group schemes a great boon, for combined effort is always an advantage, and the very fact that one's friends, neighbours and fellow-workers are all taking part in this great savings drive is a real incentive. There is the National Savings Certificate Cycle Scheme. This is very popular with the small investor, who subscribes a certain sum per week towards the purchase of Saving Certificates. Other schemes for the purchase of Defence Bonds by instalments are also in operation, and full details can be obtained from the National Savings Movement. There is, however, no doubt that a firm resolution on the part of every-one in the family, including children, to save some definite sum every week or month, is much more satisfactory for most people than casual saving, which is very apt to become less and less as time goes on.

New ways of Serving CORNED BEEF

★ *All supplies of Corned Beef including **FRAY BENTOS** are now distributed by the Ministry of Food.*

CORNED BEEF PIE

3 rations of corned beef (6d. worth).
1 cup finely shredded raw vegetables
1 Oxo Cube.   (carrot, potato, leek, swede, etc.)
1 teaspoonful chopped parsley.
Small piece fat.
Short crust pastry (6 ozs. flour, 3 ozs. fat).
1 dessertspoon flour.

Melt the fat in a small pan and lightly fry the vegetable. Stir in the flour and cook a few minutes. Add 1 cup of cold water and the crumbled OXO cube. Stir until thickened. Draw off the heat, add cubed meat, parsley and seasoning to taste. Line a small plate with pastry and spread it with the meat mixture. Cover with pastry, seal the edges and decorate with pastry leaves. Bake in a moderate oven 30 minutes.
4 servings.

CORNED BEEF CAKES

8 ozs. corned beef.   *1 teaspoon chopped parsley.*
1 small cupful browned crumbs.   *8 ozs. mashed potato.*
1 dessertspoon flour.   *1 Oxo Cube.*
Small piece fat.

Dissolve the OXO in a cupful of hot water and let it cool. Flake the meat, mix it with the parsley, potato and half the crumbs. Melt the fat, blend the flour with it, cook a few minutes and then stir in the OXO stock. Cook until it thickens stirring all the time. Bind the meat mixture with this sauce and seasoning if necessary. Form into flat cakes, roll in crumbs and press them on. Heat in a well-greased frying pan or baking tin.
About 8 small Cakes.

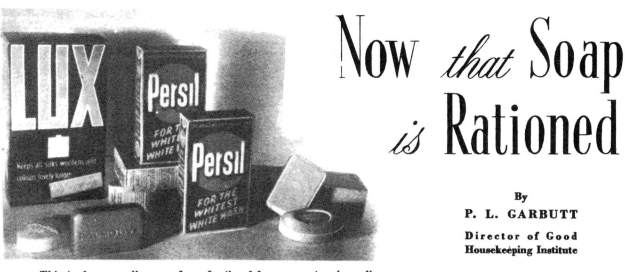

Now *that* Soap *is* Rationed

By
P. L. GARBUTT
Director of Good
Housekeeping Institute

This is the soap allowance for a family of four, apportioned equally between soap flakes, laundry soap, No. 1 soap powder, and toilet soap

Small wonder that there are always laundry problems in the Institute mail, now that soap is rationed and laundries often will not accept new customers. It is not easy to make the soap last out, especially where there are children, but you can help yourself quite a lot by taking a little trouble.

Here are some of the questions we have been asked recently, and among them may be your problem, too. If not, write and let us know your difficulty.

Query I : Soap Rationing

The first question comes from the mother of a family who is anxious to know how she can best soften water and so save her soap ration. This question is published because it is a difficulty shared to some extent by all readers just now.

Our Advice

(1) Install a mains softener if, like our questioner, you live in a hard-water district, are able to secure a model, and can meet the cost. (We ascertained, by the way, that models were available at the time of writing.)

(2) Alternatively, collect and use rain-water for washing and household cleaning purposes, if possible.

(3) If, for one reason or another, the above suggestions are impracticable, use soda to soften the water, but be *very* careful not to use too much, especially when washing delicate articles. Actually, *very little* indeed is required, far less than most people imagine.

The simplest and safest way of using washing soda is to dissolve 1 oz. in a pint of water and bottle this solution, adding about 1 tablespoonful to every gallon of hot water for every 5 degrees of hardness, i.e., for water of 20 degrees of hardness, add 4 tablespoonfuls per gallon. (Your water company will tell

you the degree of hardness of your water supply.) Place requisite quantity of soda solution in a bowl before running in the hot water, and leave for a moment or two, if possible, so that it has a chance of reacting with the hardness before you add the soap. This may sound a little complicated, but is actually very simple once you have ascertained the hardness of your water and measured up the bowl or bath you generally use. Adding the required amount of soda *before* the soap will, indeed, soon become a habit, and a very worthwhile one, which may save you a really big proportion of your soap ration, possibly as much as a quarter.

Query II : Washing Woollens

" After using lukewarm water for years, I have been told that woollens can be washed successfully with boiling water. I should like to have your opinion."

Our Advice

We explained to our reader that there are several satisfactory ways of washing woollens, and that one involves the use of practically boiling water. This method gives very good results, provided care is taken not to immerse the wool in cold water immediately after the hot. If, however,

articles are left in the washing water until cool enough to handle, and rinsing water of about the same temperature is used, no harm will result. Many people prefer to wash woollens in this way rather than in the more usually accepted one, involving the use of water at about blood heat.

Things to avoid when washing woollens are : (1) rubbing, which very soon causes felting and shrinkage; (2) extremes of temperature; (3) the use of strong alkalies, such as soda, all of which are injurious.

Query III : Substitutes for Laundry Starch

" Can you tell me of any satisfactory substitute for laundry starch, which is now unprocurable in my district? "

Our Advice

We explained that satisfactory substitutes for laundry starch are farinaceous substances, such as flour, rice-water, etc., all of which are valuable foodstuffs and should, therefore, not be used for other than feeding purposes in war-time. For thin muslin articles gum arabic is sometimes used, but this only gives very slight stiffening, and may not be easy to obtain at the present time. In any case, it is unsuitable for heavy articles.

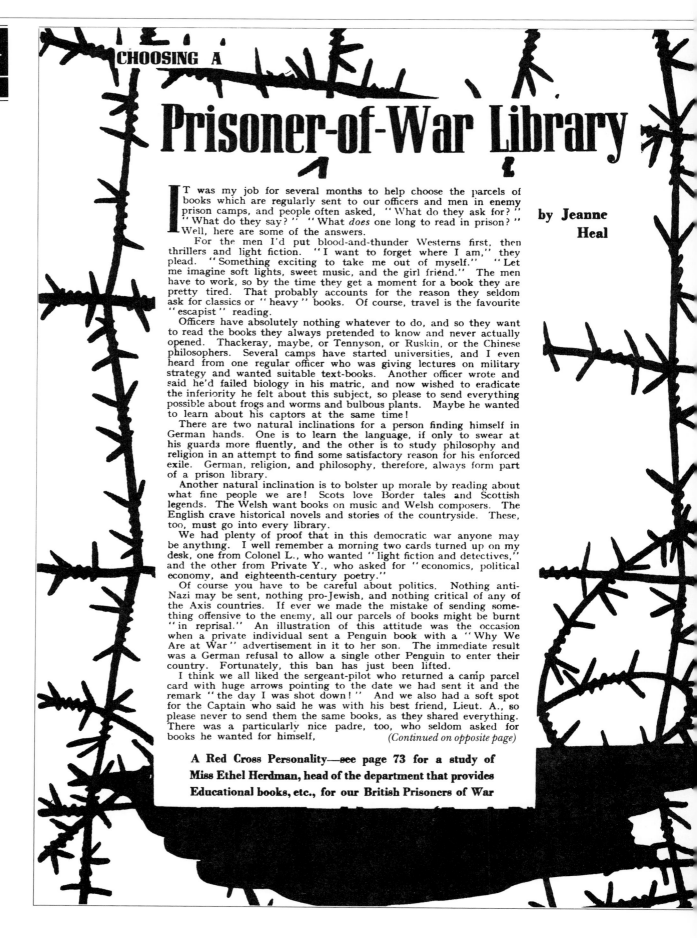

CHOOSING A

Prisoner-of-War Library

by Jeanne
Heal

IT was my job for several months to help choose the parcels of books which are regularly sent to our officers and men in enemy prison camps, and people often asked, "What do they ask for?" "What do they say?" "What *does* one long to read in prison?" Well, here are some of the answers.

For the men I'd put blood-and-thunder Westerns first, then thrillers and light fiction. "I want to forget where I am," they plead. "Something exciting to take me out of myself." "Let me imagine soft lights, sweet music, and the girl friend." The men have to work, so by the time they get a moment for a book they are pretty tired. That probably accounts for the reason they seldom ask for classics or "heavy" books. Of course, travel is the favourite "escapist" reading.

Officers have absolutely nothing whatever to do, and so they want to read the books they always pretended to know and never actually opened. Thackeray, maybe, or Tennyson, or Ruskin, or the Chinese philosophers. Several camps have started universities, and I even heard from one regular officer who was giving lectures on military strategy and wanted suitable text-books. Another officer wrote and said he'd failed biology in his matric, and now wished to eradicate the inferiority he felt about this subject, so please to send everything possible about frogs and worms and bulbous plants. Maybe he wanted to learn about his captors at the same time!

There are two natural inclinations for a person finding himself in German hands. One is to learn the language, if only to swear at his guards more fluently, and the other is to study philosophy and religion in an attempt to find some satisfactory reason for his enforced exile. German, religion, and philosophy, therefore, always form part of a prison library.

Another natural inclination is to bolster up morale by reading about what fine people we are! Scots love Border tales and Scottish legends. The Welsh want books on music and Welsh composers. The English crave historical novels and stories of the countryside. These, too, must go into every library.

We had plenty of proof that in this democratic war anyone may be anything. I well remember a morning two cards turned up on my desk, one from Colonel L., who wanted "light fiction and detectives," and the other from Private Y., who asked for "economics, political economy, and eighteenth-century poetry."

Of course you have to be careful about politics. Nothing anti-Nazi may be sent, nothing pro-Jewish, and nothing critical of any of the Axis countries. If ever we made the mistake of sending something offensive to the enemy, all our parcels of books might be burnt "in reprisal." An illustration of this attitude was the occasion when a private individual sent a Penguin book with a "Why We Are at War" advertisement in it to her son. The immediate result was a German refusal to allow a single other Penguin to enter their country. Fortunately, this ban has just been lifted.

I think we all liked the sergeant-pilot who returned a camp parcel card with huge arrows pointing to the date we had sent it and the remark "the day I was shot down!" And we also had a soft spot for the Captain who said he was with his best friend, Lieut. A., so please never to send them the same books, as they shared everything. There was a particularly nice padre, too, who seldom asked for books he wanted for himself, *(Continued on opposite page)*

A Red Cross Personality—see page 73 for a study of
Miss Ethel Herdman, head of the department that provides
Educational books, etc., for our British Prisoners of War

Choosing a Prisoner-of-War Library

but rather for a bagpipes tutor, a song book, or an Ethel M. Dell novel he knew someone else was longing to have.

We liked hearing about the men from relatives, who visited us and read us parts of their letters. There was a sergeant captured by the Italians in Libya, whose family wondered if it were worth while sending anything since he was bound to end up in his own lines again with his captors in irons!

Incidentally, to readers whose relatives are prisoners, I would like to say that from all the inside information I have received it does seem that British prisoners are among the best-fed people in Germany. This is because the food they receive from the Red Cross is far better than anything their guards ever get, and consequently their guards almost bribe them for something to eat!

I heard from one officer that he had been playing cards at the Camp Kommandant's house, and when he went back to prison had great difficulty in persuading the guards to let him in again!

Who is the most popular author? It's an impossible question, of course. It might be Dickens or Edgar Wallace or Hugh Walpole. Equally, it might be Bernard Shaw or Georgette Heyer.

And the most requested book? *Gone With the Wind* or *Busman's Honeymoon*? *Cold Comfort Farm*, *Whiteoaks*, or *Fanny by Gaslight*? No, perhaps it's an inexpensive little book of patience games—but I should not like to commit myself!

THE HOUSING PROBLEM
by Ralph Wotherspoon

It mustn't be too small,
It mustn't be immense,
(The Newlyweds are planning
Their future residence).
It mustn't be too draughty,
It mustn't be too hot,
Dry points may line the drawing-room,
Dry-rot of course may not.

It mustn't be too old,
It mustn't be too new,
Internally—some cupboards,
Externally—a view ;
Not ghostly in the country,
Nor ghastly in a slum,
No swingeing charge for "fixtures,"
And not a premium.

It mustn't be too this,
It mustn't be too that,
Wanted—a house, a cross between
Nirvana and a flat,
A castle in the ether,
Unique and duty-free—
It is a drop to Surbledon,
And suburbanity.

Do you remember when the headlines said—

"No potatoes for this Sunday's joint"

While thousands of housewives enjoyed another little grumble, the wiser families who had dug for victory enjoyed their Sunday joint with all the potatoes and other vegetables they wanted. Learn from experience. To be sure of the family's vegetables, you must grow them yourselves—women and older children as well as men. If you haven't a garden, ask your Local Council for an allotment. Start to

DIG FOR VICTORY NOW!

POST THIS COUPON NOW (Unsealed envelope, 1d. stamp)

TO MINISTRY OF AGRICULTURE, HOTEL LINDUM, ST. ANNES-ON-SEA, LANCS.
Please send me copies of free pictorial leaflets, "How to Dig" and "How to Crop"

NAME ....

ADDRESS..

B.99

ISSUED BY THE MINISTRY OF AGRICULTURE

Important Note

We recommend these goods for the immediate consideration of customers—such values can never recur, even if the goods can be produced.

The "Derry Post" will be sent on receipt of subscription of sixpence for the next six numbers.

The **Derry Sale**

DAILY 9 to 4

Household Linens

DERRYS COTTON SHEETS. *Snow-White bleach. Plain hemmed. In single bed size, 2 × 3 yds.*	**25/-** *per pair* Two pairs for **49/6**
COTTON SHEETS. *Two-row cord. Very hard wearing. In double bed only, 2½ × 3 yds.*	**35/-** *per pair* Two pairs for **69/6**
HORROCKSES' SHEETS. *Two-row cord. Snow-White. Ready for use. Single bed size, 72 × 104 ins.*	**32/6** *per pair* Two pairs for **64/-**
SUPER QUALITY EGYPTIAN COTTON. *Exceptionally fine two-row cord. Single bed size, 2 × 3 yds.*	**52/6** *per pair* Double bed size, 2½ × 3 yds. **59/6**
LINEN SHEETS. *Irish. Superior quality one-row cord hem or hemstitched. Single bed size, 2 × 3 yds.*	**73/6** *per pair* Two-row cord, double bed size, 2½ × 3½ yds. Per pair **95/-**
COLOURED COTTON SETS. *Fast colours. Pastel shades: Coral, Blue, Lemon, Green. Sets comprise 1 pair sheets and 1 pair pillow cases. Single bed.*	**49/6** *per set*
HORROCKSES' COLOURED FLANNELETTE SHEETS. *Colours: Blue, Green, Rose, Gold and Camel. 70 × 90 ins. State second choice colour.*	**29/6** *per pair* 80 × 100 ins. Per pair **37/6**
PILLOW CASES. *Plain hemmed Egyptian Cotton. Housewife style. Size 20 × 30 ins. Post 4d.*	**3/6** *each* Six for **20/6.** Post 8d.
PILLOW CASES. *Hemstitched Egyptian Cotton. Housewife style. Size 20 × 30 ins. Post 4d.*	**5/6** *each* Six for **32/6**
PILLOW CASES. *Two-row cord Egyptian Cotton. Size 20 × 30 ins. Post 4d.*	**5/6** *each* Six for **32/6**
PILLOW CASES. *Hemstitched or two-row cord Linen. Housewife style. Size 20 × 30 ins. Post 4d.*	**10/11** *each* Six for **65/-**

ALL WOOL CELLULAR BLANKETS. *In pastel shades of Blue, Green, Gold and Rose. Size 60 × 80 ins. 70 × 90 ins. 55/- each. 80 × 100 ins. 65/- each.*	**47/6** *each*
COLOURED FLEECY FLANNELETTE SHEETS. *Made especially for people who suffer from rheumatism. Pastel shades of Pink, Blue, Green, Gold or Cream. Top sheet hemstitched, under sheet plain hemmed. Single bed size, 68 × 100 ins. Double bed size, 80 × 100 ins. Per pair 39/6*	**35/-** *per pair*
CREAM FLEECY FLANNELETTE SHEETS. *Beautifully soft and warm. About 60 × 80 ins. Post 8d. 70 × 90 ins. 21/- 80 × 100 ins. 26/6*	**16/6** *per pair*
WHITE TURKISH BATH SHEETS. *Post 7d. Each*	**17/6**
IRISH LINEN GLASS CLOTHS. *24" × 33". Post 6d.*	**6 for 17/6**
TURKISH TOWELS. *Derrys well-known White. Size 24 × 42 ins. Post 4d. Six for 29/-*	**4/11** *each*
KITCHEN CLOTHS. *Irish. Strong for hard wear. Size 24 × 33 ins.*	**Six for 21/-**

Quilts and Bedspreads

Art Silk Taffeta Quilts and Bedspreads with dainty ruched work in centre filled purified feather down in Gold, Blue, Green or Rose. Double Bed Quilt with plain hemmed Bedspread to match. Size 90 × 100 ins. — **75/-** *per set*

Single Bed Quilt with plain hemmed Bedspread. Size 70 × 90 ins. — **57/6** *per set*

Quality Fabrics
for making up at home

Ceylon Flannel

Twill weave for pyjamas, fast colours, thoroughly shrunk. 29 ins. wide. Limited quantity only. 1¾ coupons. — **1/9½** *Per Yard*

Derrys Union Flannel

For shirts and pyjamas, etc. Stripes and colours. Thoroughly shrunk and fast colours. 29 ins. wide. 2¼ coupons. — **5/3** *Per Yard*

Black Ring Velvet

Beautiful lustre and deep pile. Ideal for frocks, coatees, etc. Black only. 36 ins. wide. 2 coupons. — **8/11** *Per Yard*

Boucle Stockinette

For two-piece, frocks and skirts. Colours include Wine, Green, Saxe, Red, Ice Blue, Lilac, Mist. 48 ins. wide. 4 coupons. — **14/11** *Per Yard*

Dress Crepe

All Wool Dress Crepes. Greens, Greys, Red, Browns, Fuchsia, Rust, Navy, Black, etc. 54 ins. wide. **12/11, 11/9** *and* **10/11** *4½ coupons. Per Yard*

Crepe Manila

Beautiful fabric of lovely texture for lingerie, etc. Pastel shades, including Pink, Azure, Nil, Champagne, Peach, etc. 36 ins. wide. 2 coupons. — **5/11** *Per Yard*

Milanese

The remainder of a stock of this well-known fabric in checks, over-checks and stripes. In widths varying from 46 to 72 ins. **46 ins. 3 coupons. 72 ins. 4 coupons.** — **9/11** *Per Yard*

Tweeds

In various weaves, designs and colours. To suit all tastes. For coats, two-piece, wraps, suits and skirts. 54 ins. wide. From **21/9** *to 4½ coupons.* — **8/11** *Per Yard*

Derry & Toms
Kensington W

Telephone: Western 8181

Telegrams: Derrys, Kensington, London

A Trip Around

"**G**OOD old Lady London Town" has seen many changes and lived through many upheavals. Her widespread grey skirts have given refuge to a weird and wild assortment of exiles; and if her houses and streets are of stone, her heart certainly isn't—for here thousands have found bread and kindness in their plight. In her long life she had offered a haven to Huguenot and Fleming, to Russian revolutionary and Chinese republican. But never before have men and women of a score of nations looked upon her as the last stronghold of freedom in Europe; never before have they brought their heartbreaking misery and their dreams of resurrection with such trust and hope to London, the citadel of a free world. Foreigners there have always been in great numbers among London's teeming millions; but they came here to study and work, not to fight. To-day, with very few exceptions, these aliens are allies—whether they belong to an allied nation or to one of the countries blackmailed or cajoled into co-operation with the "New Order"—and they share in our struggle just as they will share our victory.

The vanguard of the great modern migration was made up of Germans and Austrians who were unable to live under Hitler. With pitiful remnants of their possessions they came. Some were Jews and some Aryans; some had luck in finding a niche at once, and others had to slave at tasks seldom congenial. For some reason a great many of them settled in Hampstead and Golder's Green; and their numbers were so large that some native wit declared Hitler had every right to claim as his "last territorial ambition" the incorporation of these North-Western parts of London in the Third Reich. Another joke current in the early war months related how someone went into the courtyard of a big apartment house in Hampstead, shouting: "*Herr Doktor!*" whereupon all the windows flew open. Others again maintained that after passing Swiss Cottage bus conductors invariably called out the names of the stops in German. In the hectic days after Dunkirk many of these flats emptied, their possessors scattered between Huyton, the Isle of Man and even Australia, but most of them came back and have shouldered the duties which the citizen soldier has acquired in this total war. They have their own daily paper and several periodicals; the Austrians have revived the Viennese cabaret in their St. John's Wood theatre and club-house; other Austrians run a small theatre in Bayswater, while there are several churches where one may hear services in German. A great many of these "enemy aliens" do yeoman work in propaganda, in the factories, laboratories and even government offices.

Next came the Czechs, though their number before the collapse of France was comparatively small. To-day the big building that forms the home of the exiled Czech republic is a veritable hive of activity; they have numerous papers (some of them in English), and the Czech Institute has created a home for Czech music, art and literature. Their co-operation with the Poles was born here in London, and may be counted as the first definite step towards a happier North-Eastern Europe.

When the Czechs relax, they like to do it with music and good food; the latter they find in a recently opened restaurant of their own in Edgware Road. Civilians, soldiers and airmen of the exile army enjoy in this simply furnished place the dumplings and other substantial food which they must have missed during their days in France—even if they have to forgo the *steins* of foaming *Pilsner*.

Most of the Poles are stationed in Scotland, but they, too, have their contingent in London, with its centre, "The Polish Hearth," in South Kensington. Here they gather for social evenings, for concerts, and go to

Europe in London

school again to learn English. The literary activities of the Polish colony are really amazing; not only does it turn out a number of dailies and weeklies expressing various shades of political opinion, but there is also a large, well-directed publishing house, which has already issued many Polish books. M. Stronski, the Polish Minister of Information, has gathered around himself an excellent staff of journalists and broadcasters. The Polish Choir is well known to radio listeners, and the Poles also run several schools.

The new French community in London has two official centres: one in South Kensington, the other in St. James's. The first is the long-established Institut Français, where, under the most capable direction of that fine essayist and lecturer, M. Denis Saurat, lectures, recitals, exhibitions follow each other in a courageous attempt to keep the free spirit of France alive. The Institut is the intellectual home of Free France in England; its activities find permanent form in the daily *France* and the admirable *La France Libre*, edited by André Labarthe, both of which enjoy a large circulation far beyond their own numbers.

General de Gaulle's headquarters are in Carlton House Terrace, next door to the venerably bohemian Savage Club. Waggish "Savages" repeatedly tell the story of how they were accosted in error by young ladies who wanted to join the Foreign Legion. Founded by Mme Mathieu, the French A.T.S. can boast of having the prettiest personnel of all the Allies. A bevy of these girls travels daily from South Kensington to Pall Mall, offering a Free French conversation lesson (complete with idioms) to anyone who cares to listen in!

For the third centre, this time an unofficial one, of Free France in London, you must go farther East, to the "York Minster" and other French pubs in Soho. Here the company usually includes bearded *matelots* exchanging badinage with waiters from the Savoy, and lovely French dressmakers transplanted from the Rue de la Paix to Grosvenor Street. The atmosphere in these pubs is a strange and not unattractive mixture of Britain and France; the talk in many languages and the jokes universal, though broad. Recently the French have been complaining, half-jocularly, that their pubs have become too popular among writers, actors and stockbrokers, delighted to find some new local colour in Soho, whose one-time glory has been dimmed by the war and the black-out.

Soho's Italian population has considerably decreased, though many have passed the Aliens' Tribunals with satisfactory results. Waiters are at a premium in the West End, for hundreds of Italians have joined the Pioneer Corps, or gone into munitions. Some Italian restaurants have closed, but a few still linger on. Incidentally, there are beginnings of a Free Italian movement, which wants to link up with the Italian population of the United States.

London, however, has had another "Latin" invasion in the shape of hundreds of Gibraltar women and children, billeted mainly in Kensington and Shepherd's Bush. Almost all of them speak English, but on their shopping expeditions they discuss quality and price loudly in their native tongue, which sounds like the fastest in the world. Dark-eyed beauties saunter along Kensington High Street, dragging olive-skinned, cherubic-looking offspring at their heels. There are also some Maltese in London, but most of the inhabitants of that dauntless island have preferred to remain at their post in the front line. *(Continued on page 61)*

PETER STAFFORD visits the new

foreign colonies that have

sprung up in the capital

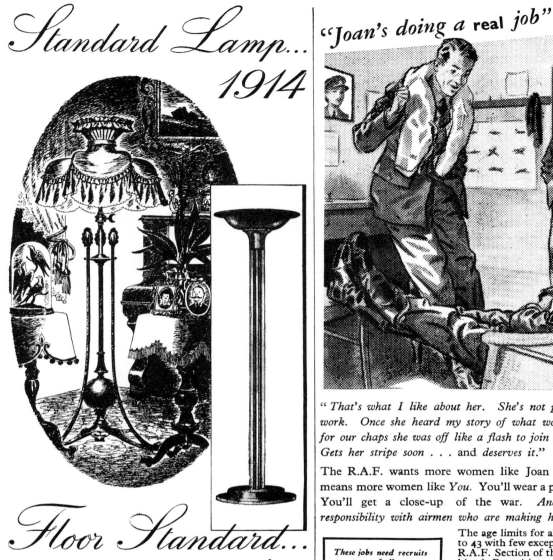

A Trip Around Europe— in London

(Continued from page 59)

Our Scandinavian colonies have remained more or less stable, for both Norwegians and Danes were overrun too suddenly to escape in large numbers. Those who did escape were mainly seamen, who continue sailing the seas with the Allied navies. But the Danish club in Knightsbridge, the "Three Vikings" in Mayfair and the Norwegian Sailors' Club, are great meeting-places for the husky sons of the North, who can settle down there to a nourishing *smörgasbord*. They also overflow into the local cafés of Bloomsbury, explaining to proprietors, by means of gestures and wide smiles, the items they want from the "1/9 Three-course Dinner." Norwegian women and children have also taken part in those dramatic voyages across the North Sea from occupied Norway, but they are usually evacuated to the country on arrival here.

Belgians and Dutch belong to the smaller groups of London's foreign communities. Both of them have their own papers and broadcasting stations (the latter in co-operation with the B.B.C.). The Dutch have peacefully invaded Stratton Street and Park Lane; in the former place their offices occupy a large block of flats, and the receptionist wears the picturesque silver-braided black outfit which is among the most dashing of the Allied uniforms. The Belgians have had a great success with their musical ensemble, the Belgian Quartet, and also with their new tri-lingual monthly paper, *Message*.

You could hardly call the Americans foreigners, and they are certainly not Europeans, but let's just glance at their particular haunts. The Eagle Club in Charing Cross Road is the magnet for American airmen, both those in the R.A.F. and the Ferry Service. The musical slang of London's Tin Pan Alley mixes here on the pavements with the twang of the Middle West or the Southern drawl. And no survey of London's foreign colonies would be complete without mentioning the Savoy, now "taken over" by American correspondents and broadcasters for the duration—at least they behave as if it were! They are a high-spirited, hard-working and (according to Mr. Brendan Bracken) hard-drinking lot, who celebrated Thanksgiving Day by publishing their own *Savoy Standard*, and dining off turkey and pumpkin pie.

Small, but compact, is the Hungarian colony in London. They now rank as "enemy aliens," but almost all of them are staunch and proven friends of this country, who stayed with us during the *Blitz* rather than return home to a Nazified country. Before the war Magyar domestic servants were in great demand in London, and about three thousand remained here when their unfortunate land was swept into the Hitler orbit. They have their Club, which organises lectures and dances. There are also three semi-political movements of Free Hungarians. A couple of Hungarian restaurants form the most popular meeting-places for intellectuals and business men, while for writers the P.E.N. Club has a Hungarian group.

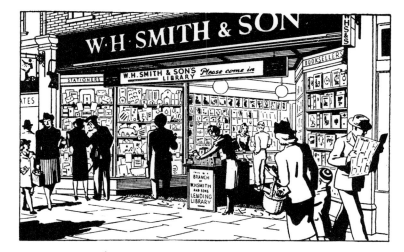

W. H. Smith & Son can still supply a fair choice of writing papers.

But use it carefully—both sides of the paper please, little or no left-hand margin, and smaller writing and closer-spaced lines.

You get more on to a sheet if you use it lengthways instead of upright.

It's not simply a matter of making a little go a long way. Paper makes MUNITIONS so please don't forget to put out for salvage every scrap of old paper and cardboard in the house

PRIZES FOR PIONEER DIET RESEARCHERS

WOULD you like to contribute to a really valuable piece of dietetic research—and at the same time stand a good chance of winning a worth-while prize of National Savings Certificates ? If so, all you have to do is to keep a very simple chart, or diary, of the health of each member of your household over the next six months.

Send us a postcard, saying you are entering for the competition, and we will post you a form explaining clearly the few straightforward details required on your chart.

Each month we will give six Savings Certificate token prizes for the six most informative charts, with a further six prizes of Five Certificate tokens to those whose *series* of six monthly charts have been most helpful.

You'll enter ? Good !

Now here is where the dietetic research comes in. On each of your charts you must state clearly the kind of bread used in your household, for example, white, National Wheatmeal, brown, half white, half wheatmeal, etc., and also give a rough idea of how much is eaten daily. This is particularly important for the whole purpose of the " Health Diaries " you are keeping is to provide material that will clearly prove whether or not the kind of bread eaten materially affects our well-being. Laboratory research indicates very strongly that it does, but only practical research among a reasonably large number of people, over a period of months, can accurately assess results. That is why, in the interests of national health, GOOD HOUSEKEEPING has planned this competition.

If your friends are interested, and we think they will be, as the matter is of real importance to every mother, tell them to write for forms, too. The greater number of people who complete the simple charts, showing days absent from school or work, colds and other illnesses incurred, the more valuable will be the results.

Send your application postcard to " Diet Research," " Good Housekeeping," 28–30 Grosvenor Gardens, London, S.W.1.

No surrender . . .

War gives us a chance to show our mettle. We wanted equal rights with men; they took us at our word. We are proud to work for victory beside them. And work is not our only task. We must triumph over routine; keep the spirit of light-heartedness. Our faces must never reflect personal troubles. We must achieve masculine efficiency without hardness. Above all, we must guard against surrender to personal carelessness. Never must we consider careful grooming a quisling gesture. With leisure and beauty-aids so rare, looking our best is specially creditable. Let us face the future bravely and honour the subtle bond between good looks and good morale.

PUT YOUR BEST FACE FORWARD.. *Yardley*

HER SAUCEPANS WERE A PRESENT

Ten years ago to-day,

And, thanks to Vim smooth cleaning,

As good as new they'll stay !

" As good as new " is good news in these days !
For rationing of metals makes saucepans scarcer,
and dearer too. So, thank you Vim ! It's Vim,
of course, that makes saucepans last so long,
because it cleans *smoothly*. It doesn't scratch.
You can't say that about harsh scourers. They *do*
scratch. But use Vim—and you'll get long service
from everything it cleans. And always ask for
Vim in the new 6d canister—such bigger and
better value !

Use Vim for POTS · PANS
BATHS · TILES · ENAMEL · WASHBOWLS
SINKS · DRAINING BOARDS · COOKERS

Save and lend to hasten the end.

Salve your conscience, and save your salvage.

*Be careful in the blackout and obey the Highway Code – And you'll
stand a chance of dodging death upon the road.*

PLANNED ECONOMY

COUPONS have taught us the importance of careful planning, and the result is the type of all-purpose outfit with interchangeable accessories you see here. (It's important to build your wardrobe round either black or brown accessories—good bags and shoes are expensive, and not easy to find.) Black and white herringbone is a clever choice for a suit, because it can look formal or casual, according to what accessories you wear with it. The one illustrated is a *Harella Utility model*: from Bon Marché, Liverpool.

For the country or travelling, it looks grand with a lipstick-red topcoat (this one is from *Nicoll Clothes,* obtainable at Nicolls of Regent Street), and a mannish felt hat. Don't, however, overdo the red—stick to black gloves and shirt. For extra warmth when you wear the suit without a coat, choose a jersey like this lovely soft angora, buttoning up the front and with a nipped-in waist—so elegant you could wear it with a long black skirt for dinner: *Robert Pringle* jersey of the type stocked by Harrods. The amusing-looking clogs are the newest idea in country shoes—they have thick wooden soles covered with rubber, and tops of sturdy black suède banded with scarlet leather: *Lilley & Skinner*. For town occasions, dress your suit up with a sunflower-yellow shirt with the new American neckline—this one in fine wool is made by *Nicoll Clothes*, obtainable from Nicolls of Regent Street. Drape yourself a becoming turban from a yard of matching jersey. High-heeled, laced black calf are the smartest shoes for any town suit: *Russell & Bromley*.

Fight the Battle of the Atlantic in your planning – save, don't spend!

Fight the Battle of the Atlantic in your cooking – be resourceful, never wasteful!

Fight the Battle of the Atlantic in your shopping – do without and lend!

"The Edinburgh castle is really a swell place."

"Hello, mother, I'm enjoyi

"Hello, sweetheart, I'm ha

WHAT THE YANKS ARE SAYING ABOUT BRITAIN

By

Eugene Warner

**Director Public Relations,
American Red Cross in
Great Britain**

THE Americans are amazed, pop-eyed, unbelieving, delighted and overwhelmed by the rather unexpected warmth of friendliness shown them everywhere by the people of Great Britain. That goes for soldiers, sailors, marines and the pretty Red Cross girl welfare workers, too.

In my job I've had an unusual opportunity to listen while they "sound off" on every subject, from beehives to Britannia, and one of the most frequent topics is "how swell the British are." As every Briton knows by this time, Americans arriving here have been politely cautioned that Britons by nature aren't as affable as themselves, are more reserved, and not given to wholesale glad-handing. To the surprise of Uncle Sam's nieces and nephews, quite the opposite has turned out to be the case!

One of the numerous undertakings of the American Red Cross in Britain is to broadcast messages from the U.S. fighting forces to their mothers, sweethearts and pals back home, via the B.B.C. These messages are in the form of spontaneous, unrehearsed interviews: in them can be heard the unprompted feelings of the Yanks about British hospitality. The British public does not hear these broadcasts. Here's what they say.

(The following are verbatim excerpts from a typical broadcast, this one from Glasgow.)

Seaman 1st Class Claire Warfel, to his mother in Ohio:
"Well, Mum, I'm O.K."
"Having a good time over there?"
"Oh, a very good time. Fine."
"Are the people friendly?"
"Oh, too friendly." (Laughter.)

Gunner's Mate 3rd Class George Frank, to his mother in Wisconsin:
"Hello, Mum, I hope you're all right. I'm feeling fine."
"What's been happening to you over there in Glasgow?"
"Oh, I've been having a swell time over here."
"Have you been having as much fun as the others?"
"Oh, yes . . . but I'm making out better than them." (Laughter.)
"Do you find it hard to understand the Scots people?"
"Well, the men yes; but the women I understand all right." (Laughter.)

Seaman 1st Class William Bernard Oldiges, Cold Springs, Kentucky, to his mother:
"Hello, Mother, I'm enjoying my trip over here very much."
"Have you been to London yet?"
"No, I've not been to London but I've seen Edinburgh."
"What did you see there?"
"The Edinburgh Castle. It's really a swell place."
"Did you see the Royal Jewels?"
"No, they must have locked them up—I guess they must have known I was coming." (Laughter.)

Private William LaRue to his mother in Nebraska:
"Hello, Mother and Dad. We're having a fine time here and I'm in the best of health."
"Would you like to send a message to your girl?"
"Which one?" (Laughter.) "Last night we went to a

*We can't all fight, that's true enough — So find some war work,
do your stuff!*

The woman who will save and lend is the fighter's truest friend.

y trip over here very much"

pretty fair time here – considering I'm married!

jitterbug contest. The champions of last year won."

"You don't mean to say Scotsmen beat out you Americans?"

"That's true. The only difference between Scotch jitterbugs and American jitterbugs is they're shorter—and better."

Corporal Ray Adams to his mother in Nebraska:

"Mother and Dad, I want to tell you that I'm all right and the treatment we're all getting over here is fine, and my health is good."

"Would you mind telling your first impressions of Glasgow?"

"Why the bobbies and the horses. The horses are unusually large horses. And the bobbies have their funny hats on."

"Are the bobbies polite to you?"

"Oh, sure. Very polite. They treat us very nice. So does everyone."

Seaman 2nd Class William Fraser to his mother in Virginia:

"Hello, Mum. Having a great time over here in England."

"How do you like the English people?"

"It's a fine place and the people here are swell."

Sergeant Max Altman to his wife in New York:

"How do you spend your leisure time, Max?"

"Oh, palling around with the boys. Manage to have a pretty nice time."

"Have you seen any sights?"

"Loch Lomond was one of the gorgeous places. The art gallery and various other well-known places."

"Say, where did you get that heather that's pinned in your buttonhole?"

"That was given to me by one of the lovely ladies of the city. It means good luck, she told me."

"You wouldn't mistake it for another kind of vine or vegetable we have back in the United States?"

"Well, I was thinking of using it for mistletoe." (Laughter.)

Sergeant Raymond Manes of Brooklyn, N.Y., to his wife, Marie:

"Hello, sweetheart. I'm having a pretty fair time here—considering I'm married!" (Laughter.)

"Did you hear those bagpipes out in the street to-day?"

"Couldn't miss 'em." (Laughter.) "They're a bit different from the music at home, but it was very appealing."

"After meeting the English girls, d'you find them friendly?"

"Yes . . . but I still love my wife. Sergeant Max Altman— the Scotch call him 'MacAltman'—and I are both married and we're trying to keep out of trouble." (Laughter.)

Sergeant Frank Radevich of Chicago to his wife:

"Hello, Laura and Mum. I sure do miss your cooking. The beer over here isn't comparable to my favourite brew, but it'll do, and there is an excellent substitute for chicken here. They call it fish and chips. I'm making out very well. I'm gaining weight and losing altitude. The people are treating me fine."

"How are the girls treating you?"

"The girls are giving you plenty of competition, Laura. As for their cooking, they haven't demonstrated their ability yet along those lines."

It's the same story everywhere *(Continued on page 70)*

Illustration by Horace Gaffron

Make "lend" not "spend" your motto.

Diphtheria is a dangerous thing – inoculation kills its sting.

What the Yanks are Saying About Britain

(Continued from page 69)

I've been. At the American Red Cross clubs scattered throughout the British Isles I've talked with scores and hundreds of soldiers and sailors about British hospitality, and one hears great and enthusiastic elaborations on that theme of friendliness which dominated the Glasgow broadcasts sketched above.

To a man, the soldiers and sailors under the Stars and Stripes are impressed, happily impressed, with the kindliness and cordiality of the British populace. Many of them have expressed surprise to me that a race which they half expected to be reserved was in actuality so eagerly hospitable, and so sincere about it.

Red Cross nurses have told me how a group of Cockney workmen near St. Paul's in London laid down their picks and shovels and came up out of a hole to shake hands and welcome them to Britain, how pages in hotels smile and tell them they're glad they're here, how people on the streets, in buses, on trams, find no difficulty at all in speaking to the American strangers and telling them, "Glad to see you; it's nice to have you with us."

It's all making a profound impression on the Yanks. It augurs much for the post-war period. It proves again that democracy is more than a term. It indicates that the common people of all the world are just people, and have much in common. Every American mother knows by this time, through letters home and through the nation-wide broadcasts from her son, that the people of England are good friends, fast friends, and with that mighty body of public opinion —millions strong some day—a great and powerful force will be at work at the peace table.

Home to meals
that mother makes

Ah! **BISTO**

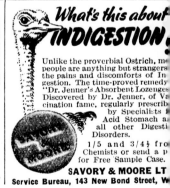
Break Hitler's Defence by Lending Your Pence.

Put it in the bank, it'll help to buy a tank.

A job with the hoe is a stab at the foe.

From the Middle East Mail—

LETTER FROM A HOME-FRONT FIGHTER

Dearest Jack,

You always used to jeer at my " habit of joining things," but this time I think even you would approve—I have become a Salvage Steward.

I'm not pretending that it's a job I should have rushed at in peace-time, but, you know, it certainly has its humours and compensations. I don't feel nearly so lonely now I'm on calling terms with so many people. On the whole, people are very co-operative, especially when " the reason why " is explained to them. Naturally, everyone is inclined to say, " But my little bit won't make any difference," when tackled about failure to salvage something or other. Quote them a few figures, however— provided they're the kind of figures that the average person can grasp—and you soon make them as enthusiastic collectors as yourself.

Paper and cardboard are fairly easy to collect nowadays—such a good job has already been done in educating the public that, so long as they have reasonably good means for disposing of their paper collections, the results are fine. Metal, too, is collected quite easily, and I think rubber will come in all right once people have got used to saving it. Rags present more difficulties : when you mention the subject, housewives are apt to retort indignantly that they're wearing their rags these days, and what with clothes rationing, they'll have to go on wearing them to the end of the war ! However, if you quote a few of the war purposes for which rags, string, rope, etc., are required, they usually calm down and promise to go through their pieces bag, worn-out stockings, string box, and so on, and often, the next time you see them, they produce with pride a well-stuffed paper bag or cloth bundle.

The job that really requires all my powers of salesmanship is persuading housewives to save meat bones. Despite the fact that figures show some hundreds of tons of bones pass out via the butchers each month, women assert that, with the present meat ration, joints are so small they don't have bones. The next gambit is to say that, anyway, the dog needs the bones. When you point out that the Government is quite glad to have the bones even after Fido has had his go, they bring out their real objection—bones are so difficult to keep until they are collected. It's quite true that flies and the neighbourhood dogs are attracted in equal proportions if you don't clean the bones and cover them securely, but if only people would dry the bones in the oven after the gas has been turned off, and if only they'd devote ten minutes to improvising a dog-proof bin — !

Well, enough about my newest war-time job—though I must just add that I get a real thrill out of thinking that maybe the bones, paper, metal, rubber and rags saved by Lime Road, under my auspices, will help to equip you with bullets, Uncle Tom with depth charges, and young Bob with a seat for his 'plane !

I was so glad to hear about your leave, though I wish . . .

Not many souls to-day alive who speed along at seventy-five.

Everyone who lends and saves, Helps Britannia rule the waves.

Dig and hoe and plant and sow – That's the way to beat the foe.

How do you look when he comes home?

WELL, how *do* you look when he comes home?
I'm not thinking of the man who comes back on leave
after a prolonged absence: then, of course, it would be a
very strange woman who did not feel that was an occasion to look her best. I'm thinking of the man who comes
home every evening after a day's work, a man who has been
married to his wife for a number of years.

Even in the days of peace most women reached a phase in
their life when they felt they were entitled to take a holiday
from good grooming, on the score that they had reached an
age when that sort of thing wasn't supposed to matter.
To-day there are so many good excuses to let appearance
slide there is no need to search for one. There's the war, the
shortage of cosmetics, and there's the one about working so
hard there isn't time, anyway.

But, at the risk of being called frivolous or superficial, I'm
sticking to my opinion that a woman's job of keeping herself attractive is as important now as ever it was. This is as
true of older women as younger folk.

Ask any man who comes home tired after a long day's
work, in surroundings which are probably anything but lovely,
and he'll say there's nothing more restful, more stimulating
than seeing his wife looking fresh and charming. It makes
him think, Well, anyway, the day has been worth while. All's
well at home. But if he comes back to a wife who is drooping
and looks weary, it is disappointing and unsatisfying.

I'm not suggesting for one second that it isn't both right
and vitally necessary to be economical, but lean periods are
the times of all times to be as attractive as possible. Moreover, by keeping up the good work in a small way, but with
regularity, we spend less in the long run. The habit of
Letting Yourself Go has a way of leading you to the inevitable
moment when you can't stand yourself as you are for another
second, and by that time repairs and a general overhaul run
into a lot of time as well as money.

War work and war-time conditions keep us frightfully busy.
But remember this: Interesting women are busy anyway,
war or no war, and these are the women who realise that
some of that busy time is wisely spent in keeping themselves
as others like them to look.

So if, after a little self-questioning, you come to the con-
clusion that you are slipping into the habit of thinking
"Nobody's going to see me but the family," pull yourself up.
The beauty problem certainly presents more difficulties than

By Susan Drake

Look Home?

it has ever done before, but none of these is insuperable. Supplies of worth-while creams and powders and other aids to skin charm are still available, and we can still find a happy medium between the liberally and obviously applied glamour of peace-time—which didn't suit many people, anyway—and the shiny-nosed, pale-lipped look which suits nobody at all.

I'm not going into details here about how to apply the various beauty aids which you select, because each face, in my experience, responds to different methods. But there are two ingredients we can all use to good advantage—time and patience!

Getting to the hairdresser is often a difficult job these days, and hairpins are scarce, but you can still get ribbon and some hairpins, and there's always water if setting lotion runs out. It is also interesting and often effective to try out new styles, because if you are wearing the same style as you did ten years ago, the chances are you'd look better with another, because your hair, face and skin have altered meanwhile.

Should you be pestered with straggling ends because you need a new perm, remember what I said about ribbon and tie a length around the crown of your head, roll up those back ends over the ribbon and tuck them underneath. What pins you have can then be concentrated on side or top curls.

Dress, too, has its limitations, bounded by coupons, but utility clothes have great blessings—they do give us good style, sound wearing qualities and a basis for individuality at a price which need not make any budget sag. And we still have our irons for pressing, our own pet methods for dealing with shine and stains, which, if steadily applied, give a crisp, clean look to clothes—and that means you not only feel but are well-dressed.

So you see, when you get down to it, you can make any sort of excuse you like for Letting Things Slide and not caring much how you look for your husband, but none of them holds water, and you won't be wise if you try to make it do so.

No woman can afford to neglect to keep up her husband's morale. Stimulating the spirits of the person with whom you live, and doing so efficiently, but without his noticing it, is what makes anybody a good wife, daughter, or whatever your feminine rôle may be.

The truth is that economy and a right attitude to wartime conditions should be as nearly invisible as possible. This doesn't mean pretence. We are restricted—and quite rightly—from over-spending on clothes, cosmetics or anything else to the point of extravagance, but that doesn't necessitate letting the results stand out like an ugly mark. It's as important, no, more important than ever, to live as serenely as possible and help our menfolk and our families to do likewise.

Stamp them out with your Savings Book.

Food waste in the kitchen means waste of life at sea.

British propaganda shares certain traits with most ⟨of⟩ our activities: "Typically slow and insufficient," say the impatient; "Typically dignified and fair-minded," say the good-natured. This article on th⟨e⟩ British Council may shed a fresh light on the subje⟨ct.⟩

CAST your memory back to 1934, or turn back th⟨e⟩ pages of a contemporary history book. A year ⟨of⟩ incidents even more fateful than they then seemed—Pilsudski's Treaty with Hitler, riots in France, rio⟨ts⟩ in Vienna, and the three major assassinations of Dollfus⟨s,⟩ King Alexander of Jugoslavia and Barthou, the trucule⟨nt⟩ but far-seeing old statesman who had done much in eigh⟨t⟩ months to repair the waning prestige of the Fren⟨ch⟩ Government.

One event you will not find recorded; new eras a⟨re⟩ seldom recognised at their inception. The British Foreig⟨n⟩ Office, in a somewhat hole-and-corner way, gave birt⟨h⟩ to a love-child. That is, in tardy response to urge⟨nt⟩ representations from British diplomatic missions abroa⟨d,⟩ it created a peculiar kind of semi-official organisatio⟨n⟩ which not even its inaugurators recognised for what ⟨it⟩ was—a new page in British diplomatic history.

Those British missions abroad, stately administratio⟨ns,⟩ conducting their country's affairs with the secrecy and solemnity proper to the gentlemanly traditions of their calling, for some time past, and to their dismay, had found the upstart totalitarian governments playing the ancient game of statecraft with new rules and, from one aspect, with lamentable success! Hitler, long before any other politician, realised the implications of popular education and the importance of "the people" and, equally, the power on the people of the press and the radio and the cinema. Harnessed to his service, he could us⟨e⟩ these twentieth-century genii as millions of mouths⟨.⟩ Partly because Britain disdained to give the lie to fals⟨e⟩ allegations, partly because her confused diplomacy an⟨d⟩ divided domestic mind seemed to support such whispers⟨,⟩ it was not too difficult to circulate the legend of he⟨r⟩ decadence, her past greatness but present incapacity⟨.⟩ "Yes," said a Swede regretfully. "I would love t⟨o⟩ spend a holiday in England. But I'm a manufacture⟨r.⟩ I must see what's new in the way of factory machinery⟨.⟩ And so I'm going to Germany." The British engineer t⟨o⟩ whom the words were repeated said wonderingly: "Bu⟨t⟩ we make the best machinery in the world!" Yet th⟨e⟩

SELLING BRITAI⟨N⟩

Summer inoculation means winter immunity – Save your child from diphtheria now!

Safeguard Britain's stocks of food – Kill Master Rat and all his brood.

Better be safe than sorry – children not inoculated die of diphtheria.

By Marjorie Hessell Tiltman

swede, and his orders, had gone to Germany. That little story is just one of the straws in the wind which British trade, British prestige, found blowing against them. How was it manipulated, this gigantic game of "Come and Sit On My Chair!"? You yourself may remember some of the blandishments used by both the Reich and by Italy—the handsome reductions to visitors on the railways, the attractive tourist posters, the marvellously illustrated brochures. Publicity! That's what the totalitarian governments wanted and they were prepared to pay for it. The German publisher distributed his books in foreign countries on terms that would have bankrupted his British colleague. His Government subsidised the difference. It would come out of the twenty millions at which some critics have estimated Germany's annual expenditure on propaganda, direct and indirect, or, in Italy's case, out of the million pounds which even her poverty-stricken government budgeted for the same purpose.

It was in reply to such measures that the British Government took steps. Belated steps typical of those pettifogging 'thirties. In two rooms in a block of offices on the Thames Embankment it installed the British Council for Relations with Other Countries and made it a grudging allowance of £5,000 a year.

Now there were at that time (in spite of Hitler) various Anglophile societies established abroad; and in Paris and Florence there were Institutes where British studies could be methodically pursued—places of pattern equivalent to the Institut Français in Kensington. The Council decided that their plan of campaign might well begin with the gradual extension of such places. The British language was always in demand; its study could there be amplified by classes and lectures, libraries, educational films and cultural exhibitions. And so at strategic and sympathetic points the Institutes were founded, one by one. There were fifty of them by 1940; the exigencies of war have naturally narrowed the ranks since then.

But that is anticipating. In 1937 the late Lord Lloyd was appointed chairman. He was a statesman who combined vision with a genius for organisation, who saw the illimitable possibilities before the Council, and who applied himself tenaciously to their realisation, bludgeoning the Treasury in the process to such effect that its allowance had been raised to £335,000 by the time the war broke out. Humble though such a sum for the task before it might be, it was obtained in the teeth of much opposition. Ignorance and prejudice dictated the hostile cries in the popular press at the idea of the taxpayer's precious money being spent on such projects as sending theatrical tours abroad (the memory of the last-minute escape of the Sadler's Wells Ballet company from Holland may recall this agitation), entertaining foreign visitors, making large presentations of English books abroad, arranging European lecture tours by distinguished speakers.

These are, it is true, very general and somewhat unsensational methods of propaganda, but small as was the original form of the Council, it began with one great aim—it was to be unpolitical. It was to be pro-British, but anti-nobody. The obnoxious but necessary replies to Goebbels are the affair of an entirely different body.

Now the Germans and the Italians have never completely dissociated cultural from political propaganda; this was borne in mind when they carved up the world into spheres of influence. The Italian Government pursued their ambitions to be the great Mediterranean Power as far as Palestine. There is no doubt what sort of schemes were put into the head of the Arab student who accepted their offer of a complete education in Italy and all living expenses for £2 a year, or what creed was taught *(Continued on page 77)*

(Continued on page 77)

TO THE WORLD

Illustrated by Jack Matthews

Do you care for clothes ?

IF YOU CARE FOR CLOTHES you naturally want to *take* care of your clothes. This is a really important war job for every woman to take seriously to-day. Fortunately you are rewarded for the extra trouble, not only by feeling that you are helping to win the war, but also by looking your best all the time. *And* you save money as well as coupons.

MAKE DO AND MEND

Every sailor knows his "rig" may have to last him a long time. So definite times are set aside each week for the sailors to " make and mend," clean and repair their clothes. Follow their example. Every time you avoid buying new clothes by mending, altering or "freshening up " something you already have you are definitely helping to beat Hitler and his gang.

PUT YOUR BEST FOOT FORWARD

There's a lot more wear to be got out of every pair of shoes than some people realise. Here are some simple hints. Never put your shoes near the fire or on a radiator. When leather is exposed directly to heat it soon dries up, curls out of shape and loses its toughness and flexibility. Never go out in new shoes for the first time in wet weather. Wear them indoors for a few days instead. Always rub polish well into leather shoes and brush suede and fabric shoes *before* you put them away—on shoe trees if you have them

A WRINKLE ABOUT WRINKLES

Creases and wrinkles should never be allowed to stay. When you take off your clothes at night shake them and smooth them and hang or fold them up at once. Crumples and wrinkles should be tackled at once, before they become " set," by using a damp cloth and a hot iron.

Count your Coupons

When you are thinking of buying some garment or piece of material, count over your coupons and think of the warm things that you will need in the winter time. The cold weather is only a few weeks ahead. Better hold your coupons. Perhaps you can " make do " for the present with the clothes you have. Once your coupons are gone they're gone.

ISSUED BY THE BOARD OF TRADE

Why be careless on the road? Remorse is such a heavy load.

Save now for a safe tomorrow.

Selling Britain to the World

(Continued from page 75)

in the sixty-two Italian mission schools in Egypt (to the thirty-nine British). Egypt and the Middle East therefore formed one of the four main areas in which the Council decided to concentrate preliminary efforts and action.

The other three were the Balkans, South America and Portugal. Of the strength of the Nazi efforts in all these regions the war has given us only too devastating a proof. By the time the British Council was born, German " merchants . . . technologists . . . advisers . . . tourists . . . " had become another Trojan horse, or, as we say, fifth column. Roumania fell, Bulgaria fell; Portugal, in spite of the doubling of the German community there in six years, still holds out. As for Greece, she suffered a fate so gallant, so glorious and so tragic that it seems impertinent, although it is not irrelevant, to recall here that on the day the British Institute at Athens was opened, its doors were besieged by four thousand people instead of four hundred, and that one of the policemen called to the rescue, having shut them out and himself in, said : " Now I wish to enrol ! "

And South America? It takes an economist or a member of one of Great Britain's trading communities to realise the inestimable importance of this enormous, rich, only partly developed half-continent. Those inhabitants of it who are pro-British are enthusiastically, even emotionally so. Their practical efforts to keep the mere name of Britain alive in the face of the German determination to smother it had been herculean. Now at last and at least they have some support from the British Council. To take one example—over the field of medicine Germany had almost complete control, owing to the colossal sales of German drugs. The Germans used these contacts with less objectivity than is usual in science, and when the medical department of the British Council began to send out summaries of British work and findings to scientific and medical journals, they were printed and reprinted sometimes sixteen times.

I have mentioned the strength of the German propaganda; it has, however, its weaknesses. Like a courting parvenu, it demanded results both prompt and tangible, and often followed its kisses by blows when rewards were not forthcoming. Moreover, in its determination to impress, it was crude, it was blatant, and it was not strictly truthful—and truth will out, usually at inconvenient moments. And so it comes about that honesty is indeed the best policy. If you have read Mr. Harold Butler's brilliant survey, *The Lost Peace,* you may remember that he says: " To be successful, propaganda does not have to be mendacious, for in the long run, truth is more telling than fiction, but it does require to be coherent and persistent."

That is precisely the policy of the British Council. Perhaps in the past the British have found it easier to be truthful than to be coherent and persistent, but it seems as if the Council at least is acquiring those excellent habits. For example, one of the small routine jobs undertaken by its Books and Periodicals department is the supply of literature (such as *The Illustrated London News, The Wireless World, Radio Mechanics*) to seamen's clubs in all the great ports of the world. After six months, a letter is sent to enquire if the selection is a useful one and welcoming alternative suggestions. It has lately sent out Reference Libraries to the Emperor of Ethiopia and to the Emir of Transjordania. About two hundred thousand books a year, chosen with some regard to their permanent value, are sent abroad to libraries, schools and institutions. This, needless to say, is only one branch of the Council's work, which attempts to embrace all the expressions of the British twentieth-century way of life, in science, music, drama, the fine arts, films, education and so forth.

The tale is too long to tell here. But if world peace, as the most enlightened spirits of our time declare, is to rest in future on a truer understanding, the British Council has, as the liaison officer for our nation, a future so limitless as to justify—in spite of the fact that the first £5,000 has jumped to £500,000—the optimistic words spoken to me by one official: " Yes, our expansion has been amazing. And yet, even so, in my belief, we're still only scratching the surface! "

They also serve who save their waste.
The news you tell in secret ear, hark now from every side you hear.

SPENDING & SAVING

By Norah Ramsay

SAVE TIME

. . . By planning the week's meals in advance and dividing out ration
and points. You may have to make changes, but a list does help.

. . . By serving some meals in the kitchen. In the winter the kitchen is
cheerful place and you will appreciate food hot from the stove.

. . . By putting extra potatoes in the pot for Potato Cakes, Potato Pastry
etc.; by cooking vegetables in their skins; by making a double quantity of
white sauce and saving some for next day's use.

. . . By having all your information at hand. Keep your cookery books
on a kitchen shelf and pin beside them lists of homely measures, basic
wartime proportions, "Food Facts" cuttings and so on.

. . . By training yourself to work methodically, to keep things in their
proper place, to wash up in an orderly way and to think ahead.

SPEND TIME

. . . To learn about food values and to collect new ideas in cooking and serving food.
Go to cookery demonstrations, listen to the 8.15 a.m. "Kitchen Front," be alert
to all food news.

. . . To turn out every corner in search of salvage. Tins, bottles, rubber and rags
are all urgently needed. And you will, of course, be specially conscientious about
bones.

. . . To pack a basket of fresh vegetables to take to your friends in Town. Country-
dwellers will appreciate a cake from the pâtisserie or any non-point cooked meat
you may see.

. . . To label your store jars, so that you know what is in them. Paint tins blue
or red or yellow and add gaiety to your kitchen. List your emergency food-store,
date the packets and tins, and replace old by new whenever an opportunity occurs.

SAVE LABOUR

. . . By making full use of your mincing machine. Mince the
vegetables for soups and cut out tedious sieving; mince dried crusts
for raspings; mince crisply fried bacon rinds for flavouring.

. . . By planning your cookery. While the main meal is cooking,
prepare a one-pot dish for supper or lunch. Or serve a "health"
meal of raw vegetables, cheese and milk.

. . . By serving foods in the dish in which they are cooked, when
possible. For example, fish baked on a bed of diced vegetables,
haricot bean casserole, rabbit and mushroom pudding.

. . . By cutting down the putting-away and getting-out. Lay the
table for the next meal as soon as you have washed up, or if this is
not practicable, leave everything ready on a tray.

. . . By covering the kitchen table and shelves with light-coloured
linoleum (the substitute kind will do). It stands up to any amount of
hard wear, and needs only wiping with a damp cloth to keep it clean.

The Ministry of Food

*Many a mickle makes a muckle — whether it's money, work or
salvage.*

Think before you light up — fuel waste helps Hitler.

Is your conscience clear? There's war work waiting.

Officially this article was approved by the Ministry of Food. Unofficially, we feel sure that several other Ministries will also be delighted if you follow its suggestions—and you and your family will certainly benefit

SPEND LABOUR

. . . On learning how to make one or two good drinks for cold winter nights. We suggest Blackberry Cordial, Honey and Ginger Punch, Spiced Apple Tea.

. . . On chopping fresh parsley to add to soups, sauces and salads—but don't chop it *too* fine, or it loses value. Raw parsley is a valuable source of Vitamin C, so the more you eat the better.

. . . On cooking a really good meal when the occasion demands. If you are single-handed, concentrate on an interesting main course, followed by a cold sweet and good coffee.

. . .. On rubbing fat really well into flour when making pastry—on beating sauces to make them smooth—on whisking salad dressings and custards to make them light.

. . . On entertaining from time to time. however simply. Your guests will appreciate bowls of steaming-hot potato soup, sausages and mash, mushrooms and potatoes au gratin, and similar unrationed dishes.

SAVE MONEY

. . . By using coloured tiles, lined with baize, instead of linen mats on the dining-table. The tiles look decorative, last indefinitely and reduce the laundry bills.

. . . By learning to do all the odd jobs yourself. Every woman should know how to mend an electric fuse, fasten the head on a broom, re-washer a dripping tap.

. . . By making do. Sort out worn tea towels and roller towels, machine the thin ones together in pairs. Crochet a shopping bag from an old string hat or some string belts, if you have them. Put strong new handles on that old fish basket and carry it proudly to market.

. . . AND FUEL. By cutting down the amount used for cooking. De-fur the kettle with a weak solution of vinegar, fill the oven to capacity when it is on, cook complete meals in your steamer, SAVE FUEL in every way you know.

SPEND MONEY

. . . On necessities only. Think twice before you get anything new for the kitchen; when you must make replacements buy Utility ware. Utility ware is well-designed, durable and good value for money.

. . . On foods that are plentiful and likely to help out other foods. Prunes and haricot beans are notes for your shopping list. Haricot beans are particularly good value for points, because they help to bring up the amount of protein in our wartime diet.

. . . On the excellent books and leaflets published by the Ministries of Food and Agriculture. For small cost you will get much valuable information.

. . . On letting your daughter take a practical training if she is too young to join up. Cooking, gardening or nursing will stand her in good stead not only in wartime, but all her life.

has approved these Ideas

Do you keep your gas mask a prisoner at home?

Stuff the salvage sacks and starve the dustbin.

Coughs and sneezes spreads diseases – so use your handkerchief.

Fruitful results from vegetables

Eating fruit is a pleasure we don't often get nowadays, and there's no denying we miss it. But, from the point of view of *health*, we can more than make up for the lack of fruit by eating extra vegetables.

The main health value of fruit is in its Vitamin C. Vitamin C clears the skin, prevents fatigue, and helps you to resist infection. And it's by no means confined to oranges, as people are apt to imagine. Some vegetables, indeed, actually contain *more* of this health-giver than oranges do.

To get your requirement of Vitamin C you should eat daily a salad which includes a good portion of at least one of the following:

Watercress (all the year round)

Raw shredded sprouts (December to February)

Raw shredded cabbage (May to August, October to March)

Raw shredded spinach (all the year round)

Shredded swede or turnip (September to March)

The Vitamin C value will be increased if you use parsley or mustard and cress as a garnish.

Increased servings of

Cooked green vegetables

Cooked swedes and turnips

Cooked potatoes

will also help to maintain the Vitamin C value of the diet at a high level.

Vegetables are most "fruitful" of Vitamin C when you serve them raw!

And, by the way, the dark outer leaves of vegetables are richer in vitamins and minerals than the paler insides. So when they're too tough to eat raw, or to cook in the ordinary way, be sure to put them into soups or stews.

Our old friend the carrot, although not so rich in C, is important for its anti-infective Vitamin A.

Have YOU tried DRIED EGGS yet?

Dried Egg from America is now in the shops—soon there'll be enough for one 1/9d. tin on every ration book. They are *extra* to your regular egg ration. Each tin contains one dozen fine fresh eggs, dried, and in powder form. Nothing is taken away but the shells and water. All the rich goodness and fine flavour of fresh egg remain.

You get your Dried Eggs from where you are registered for shell eggs. Mix with water as directed on the tin and use just as you would use freshly beaten egg.

ISSUED BY THE MINISTRY OF FOOD

Before you travel, ask, "Is it necessary?"

When using petrol or imported foods, remember the men who brought them.

THOUSANDS OF WOMEN

AGED 17½–50 WANTED

TO BECOME COOKS

IN THE ATS AND WAAF

As the climax of the war approaches, every fit man is needed in the fighting line. There are thousands of men cooks in the Forces. Women are asked to take over their work, now, in the ATS and WAAF.

Experience is not needed. You'll have three to six weeks' training, then a cookery course to give you experience in cooking for large numbers. Pay for unskilled work starts at 2/- a day and all found, and is increased when you pass your test.

There's not a wife or mother in the country who doesn't feel it a part of her life's work to feed her man right. And there's not a man who wouldn't admit that his health, his good temper and his courage depend on the food he gets. That is why cooking for the Forces is a key job, and every woman who joins the Services now to do it will be doing one of the really important jobs of this war.

In addition to cooking, there are over 100 other types of work open now in the two Services. Recruiting Centres and Employment Exchanges will tell you about them.

Every woman who is not doing vital work is needed now in the Services to release men for the offensive.

The need is urgent and the sooner you can go to a Recruiting Centre or Employment Exchange the better. *They* will find out whether you can be spared from your present work. If you cannot go at once, send in the coupon. But remember, time is short.

If you were born between January 1918 and July 1922, you may now be accepted for the ATS or WAAF, but go to the Employment Exchange in the first instance.

IF you cannot go to a Recruiting Centre or Employment Exchange at once, send in this coupon

---

297 Oxford Street, London, W.1   *LA.1*

Please send me full information about the training and service as a cook in the

☐ *ATS*   ☐ *WAAF*   ☐ *BOTH*   Tick which you want

Mrs. ⎫
Miss ⎰ ....
                Cross out " Mrs." or " Miss "

Address ....

County......................................Date of Birth........................ *In confidence*

"Better be safe than sorry" is the motto for blackout travel.

If it's paper, it's on loan – return it to the nation now.

To win this scrap you must save scrap.

FRONT of RUMOUR

By Lyn Arnold

RUMOUR is a weapon of war. As far as Hitler is concerned, it is by no means a secret weapon: in *Mein Kampf* he has set out his plans for spreading "alarm and despondency," and in the fall of France and the Low Countries campaign we saw these methods at work.

This country has not (at the time of writing) had to bear invasion. Apart from German parachutists dressed up as nuns ("and, my dear, I *actually* SAW the thick black hairs on her hand!") we have had no rumours in the Russians-with-snow-on-their-boots class.

Nevertheless, rumour of a far less sensational but dangerous and insidious type runs rife.

"After all, when one's separated one's salvage, the dustmen just tip it all together again...."

"My husband actually saw it—crates and crates and crates of rotten eggs, when WE haven't had one for a month!"

"My dear—I know for a fact: munition workers just stand and knit beside idle machines...."

All these rumours have a common purpose: they give those who believe them an excellent excuse for doing something they want to do, or for avoiding something they don't want to do.

It's a nuisance to separate salvage; if you believe that dustmen undo your good work anyway, that quietens your conscience when you skip sorting salvage "just this once."

You'd like to get eggs on the side; if you believe that crates of eggs rot, and in fact rationing doesn't work, your better feelings will not forbid a very-small-scale black marketing.

If munition workers are not working anyway, why leave your nice, bright, comfortable home just to help them waste time?

Trivial as these rumours may seem, in greater or less degree they all result in a definite sabotage of the war effort.

How do rumours arise? Some undoubtedly are put out by enemy agents—but they depend utterly on the fools who pass those rumours on. Most are started by credulous malcontents who would strenuously—and sincerely—contest the suggestion that they are not one hundred per cent. patriotic.

Why do people start rumours? First, as we have seen, rumour may give a good excuse for a course of conduct which is either unpopular or forbidden. For instance, if invasion comes, the woman who feels compelled to run away (entirely forgetting that in England there is, in any case, no place to run to!) will be very likely either to start or to pass on stories about hundreds of other people who are not staying put.

Second, to start or to pass on rumour gives a sense of power. Most people live drab and unexciting lives; war brings "glamour" only to certain classes. The soldier gets his stripes; the munition worker made foreman carries no mark of promotion. His only method of impressing his importance on disinterested, perhaps disbelieving friends, may be to start a story which proves he is "in the know." Very many secrets have been given away by workers anxious to show that they are in the confidence of their superiors—and rumour is a snowball; if it starts with a stone of truth, that truth is very soon overlaid with wild exaggerations.

But the most dangerous type of rumour is, of course, the one which has—even to sane, sensible, level-headed people—every appearance of truth. For instance, a newspaper recently reported the complaint of an instrument mechanic employed at an ordnance depot. He and his friends had actually seen soldiers filling new *(Continued on opposite page)*

The Rout of Rumour

:king-cases with broken bricks and ikers, and packing them down efully with straw. As a "distinguished visitor" was due in a days, to say the least of it, this ked peculiar.

Now the newspaper investigated. ch facts were correct—the pack--cases had been filled as de-bed, and the distinguished visit s arranged. But these two facts no bearing one on the other, the first had a simple and completely satisfactory explanation: the es were being filled with bricks weigh exactly the same as if they been packed with war material, so save the use of vital goods a proposed transport exercise.

n this instance, no damage was ie because the instrument-maker had the sense to report the in-ent and call for action, instead of rely passing on the story.

But what amazing damage that iour might have done if it had under way! The workers in the tory would have felt: Why sweat guts out working like this if the iy goes through such idiotic pre-ces at work just to kill time? rkers' wives might have felt: iat's the good of trying to do t-time work if my husband is de a fool of like this? There is iost no end to the repercussions. low then can we prevent our-ves falling victims to these tales? By applying a Test for the Truth Rumour.

et's try it on the munitions-rkers - who - stand - and - knit - idle-machines story.

. *Do I—or does the rumour-nger—*WANT *it to be true?* In s case the answer is yes. However patriotic and high-minded and voted we are, there is in almost of us a streak of selfish, lazy, age female who wants first and emost her own comfort, and uld be glad to hear some story ich made the effort of munitions-k unnecessary.

f the answer is yes, we must bly stringent tests of accuracy.

. *Can I check the truth—or erwise—of the story?* Similar cases have been reported and sub-stantiated; but when you start to run a rumour to its source, you almost always come up against the dead end of "Somebody in Such a Frightfully Hush-Hush Job that I Couldn't Possibly Give You Any More Details"; or you find you have been told either direct lies, or at least gross exaggerations.

3. *Has a more or less isolated case been enlarged into a "My Dear, but* EVERYONE, *I Know for a Fact?"* Here the answer is obviously yes—or Hitler would already be walking down Whitehall!

4. *Has a wrong interpretation been put on facts which are actually true, but capable of explanation?* Again the answer may be yes; the Ministry of Labour report that a week of bad shipping losses may hold up the raw material which workers need. If there's no raw material, there's nothing to do but sit and knit; only when the raw material does arrive, *twice* as many workers will be needed to make up for lost time!

Very, very few rumours pass all these tests without showing a flaw. If we see that a rumour is untrue, what should we do?

First, make the truth as widely known as the original untruth.

Second, *remember* the person who started the scare—for scaremongers are usually congenital scaremongers—and watch her next time.

Third, where there's still a doubt, and the story is exciting or amusing —DON'T pass it on—not even with the safeguard "I can't vouch for this, of course." For the listener may pass it on without the safe-guard—probably conveying, if not actually saying, that a friend of hers (i.e. you!) did vouch for it.

If the story appears to be true? Don't talk—act! Report it to the proper authorities—write to your M.P., your local councillor, to your newspaper, to the right Ministry.

Rumours of slacking or scroung-ing food, etc., make it easy and tempting for others to follow suit; but action to prevent such abuses strengthens the morale of all.

RUBBER ROBBERY

You've seen in your papers that the Axis has taken 90 per cent. of the world's ubber. Have you done anything about it yet? You may not be able to free he rubber plantations of Malaya and the Dutch East Indies of the enemy, ut you can search your home from roof to cellar for Rubber Salvage. What about that rubber girdle, that bathing cap, those old tennis balls, that orn bathroom mat? They're wanted NOW.

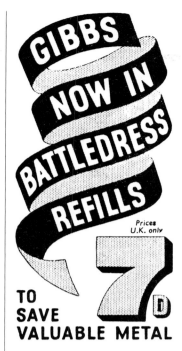

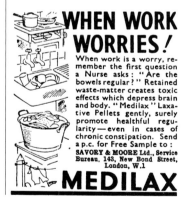

Munitions are no good in the home – turn out that waste paper.

If every home gave a book a week, it would make 240,000 tons of waste paper a year.

San Francisco Examiner

Women Go.....
.....Everywhere

By Marion McEniry
Woman's Editor, The Examiner.

WHAT are the women of England reading? Or do they have time to read?

We've just seen the March British edition of GOOD HOUSEKEEPING—and you'd be surprised.

Surprised, first of all, at its normalness. No stories or articles at all about the horrors of war. The " I Escaped from a Nazi Prison Camp " school of writing is conspicuously absent.

All the love stories are just love stories—except one that has a delicately military slant, and the scene of that is laid in Seattle ! There is one article on the functions of the British Broadcasting Company in wartime and one on the world AFTER the war by the ubiquitous Dorothy Thompson.

Reading this magazine it is easy to see why British women have kept their heads so well ; they insist on keeping their lives as normal as possible.

The fashion pages, beauty page, numerous stories and articles on children, the big book review section (larger than that of some of our peacetime American magazines), the gardening section . . . all tell where women's interests—even under fear of enemy invasion—still deeply and fundamentally lie.

And you wouldn't know the hats on the fashion pages from our own ! Saucy, individual little numbers they are, and tilted as crazily as any Montgomery Street stenographer's.

* * *

LOTS OF HUMOR in this magazine and—smack in the center, illustrated in color—is a whacking good mystery story !

NOT THAT British Good House-keeping ignores the war. On the contrary there are many pages devoted to articles that never would have appeared except for war ; how to get the most out of your coupons ; news of new rationing orders, and the like. But the slant again is that—war or no war—families must be fed, Junior put to bed, a new school dress managed for Mary.

Six pages were devoted to " Healthful Meals Spell Victory."

* * *

INGENIOUSNESS AND lack of grumbling characterize such " hints to housewives " as how to create a hat trim from odd bits of woolen cord and " blousettes " from old blouses. And how to change dresses, worn at sleeves and neck, into smart new V necked jumpers !

* * *

Particularly appealing was one of the few advertisements that inferred a shortage. Under a picture of a pretty girl the copy read : " Although she cannot buy Blank's chocolate candy, she is thankful to get a small share of Blank's fruit drops."

NEWS LETTER

Sent to us by **C. S. Forester,**

Come at Dawn," is

HERE in America one moves in a land of plenty. So far rationing has not yet begun, and, except in the matter of conscription, the war has hardly touched the private lives of American families. There are the gravest shortages just over the horizon and the strictest rationing is being arranged for, but at present, and for a few more weeks to come, it is possible for an American woman to go through a quite normal day without any reminder of the war. Let me add quickly that no American woman does do this: the American public is alive and awake to what war means.

The figures are beginning to come through which tell of the help to England that has been given up to the time of the American entry into the war, before the whole industrial power of this vast country was mobilised for the purposes of production. Some of the figures are quite astonishing. From the enormous food supplies here, about 80 million pounds of meat and fish products have been sent under the Lease Lend agreement—nearly 20 pounds for every man, woman and child in England. A thousand million pounds of grain, 800 million pounds of fruit

TIME

Have a paper-chase next week-end, and see how much you can collect.

Every newspaper you use to light the fire helps Hitler.

Make "potential production" into a reality — turn out your waste paper for munitions.

FROM AMERICA

...hose vivid war story, "Commandos
...ow being filmed

...d vegetables, and 800 million ...unds of milk and egg products. These figures, of course, deal ...ly with goods supplied by the ...overnment of America to the ...itish Government. But the ...merican people is the most ...nerous public in the world, ...ways ready to open its purse-...rings in response to any appeal. ...thing in the whole war has ...ught the imagination, or excited ...e admiration, of America as ...uch as the dogged British deter-...ination under the Nazi air at-...ck. When the war is over, any ...man of England who went ...rough the blitz will be able to ...ld up her head with pride; the ...itish public was steadfast in the ...tack as a matter of course, and ...ose people overseas who knew ...d loved England were not sur-...sed. But the American people, ...ing at that time in sheltered ...nfort, and only knowing Eng-...h people through novels and ...e caricatures on the American ...ge, reacted extraordinarily. ...Warm-hearted and sympathetic, ...eir imagination was touched by ...e news which filled the Ameri-...n newspapers. They read of ...y in flames, of the bombing of ...ventry, of the discomforts of ...e air-raid shelters, of the diffi-...ties and dangers of daily life ...en jobs had to be done no ...tter what had happened during ...e night; and the first question ...the mind of the American ...izen was, "How could we ...p?" Contributions in money ...d kind poured into the agencies ...t addressed themselves to the ...—the Red Cross, British War

Relief, and the others. There were regions which actually sub-scribed sums averaging more than a dollar—five shillings—per head of population, adults and children, rich and poor. The women set themselves to knit; one agency alone, the British War Relief, sent over two million knitted woollen garments, made from 800 thousand pounds of wool supplied by the agency, and they sent as well two million used garments, which they cleaned and repaired on this side before despatch.

No one who saw it could doubt for a moment the sincerity of the sympathy of the workers. Ameri-can women are free from self-con-sciousness; they are accustomed to organising themselves for collective effort; they have a good deal less of that tendency to shrink from expressing their ideals in words which has made England occa-sionally misunderstood. They threw themselves into the work with the express determination to help as far as was in their power the people who were fighting the Battle of Britain, civilians no less (if anything, more) than members of the fighting forces.

After the incendiary attacks on England, when roof watching had to be instituted on a large scale, an appeal went out for warm out-door clothing. It was exactly the kind of vivid appeal to make to the American public—it pre-sented *(Continued on page 87)*

On their July ...s,
forty mill... ...ies
Americ... ...zines
...Old Glory...
...symbol of the U.S.A., bringing
...mind, without words,
...rous history
of the past,
...he stern demands
...resen...

Just one of your envelopes will make a cartridge wad.
Modern magic transforms waste paper into munitions.
That old "A.B.C." will make four gun fuses.

Little cubes of carrot

Leeks and 'taters too

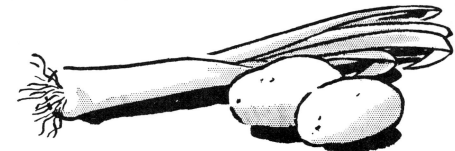

Simmered with some

BOVRIL

Make a beefy stew

VEGETABLE HOTPOT: Peel and slice about a pound of mixed vegetables—carrots, parsnips and a small swede make a good variety, with a leek or an onion if possible. Do the same with 1 lb. potatoes. Melt 2 ozs. dripping in a casserole, add all the vegetables, season well and fry lightly. Make ½ pint of stock by dissolving 1 dessertspoonful Bovril in boiling water. Pour over vegetables and cook about 1½ hours in a moderate oven.

Letters, bills, ledgers, books, everything's grist to the waste-paper mill.

Waiving the rules won't help to rule the waves – play fair.

News Letter from America

(Continued from page 85)

problem whose nature Americans could grasp at once, and the depôts were flooded immediately with outdoor clothing, and the women set themselves to the task of stitching together the quantities of furs which came in into rough-and-ready but satisfactory coats for roof watchers. In the same way, the American housewife could visualise the difficulty of feeding workers whose homes had been destroyed, so that in a single year British War Relief sent over nearly 300 mobile kitchens, to say nothing of the ambulances, which, with the Stars and Stripes and Union Jack painted on their sides, are familiar sights in England.

That brings us to the great, the burning question of the moment—the question of the shortage of shipping. In America there is all the goodwill in the world; compared with England, there is an abundance of the necessities of life. All that hampers the transfer of these necessities to England is the lack of ships to carry them. It is not merely food that must be sent to England; it is weapons of war and the materials with which to make them.

Hardly anyone needs to be reminded of the factors which make for this shipping shortage—apart from the losses caused by U-boats, there are all the other difficulties of infinitely longer voyages and zigzag courses. The fact remains that the shipping shortage is probably the most pressing problem to-day.

It is not merely air-raids which cause general staffs and planning committees to look upon the women and children in England as serving in the front line. Food and comforts must be sent to them; when they are sent they take up space which could otherwise be devoted to munitions of war—to the 'planes which are rolling off the American assembly lines, the ammunition for the guns, or, for that matter, to the troops which America is sending to England. The Governments of the two countries, Mr. Churchill and Mr. Roosevelt in consultation, have to draw a very fine dividing line between what is necessary for the English family and what it is possible to do without. A small reduction in the British ration may mean that every month an extra American division arrives

in Northern Ireland.

It is for this reason that British home production is of so much importance—the man or woman who grows a ton of food, by that very action makes it possible to send another ton of materials of war from America; the housewife who fights against waste in her kitchen is at the same time fighting against the Japanese in the East. The expression "global war" takes on a heightened meaning when viewed in the light of the shipping shortage.

From the same point of view, therefore, one of the most vital contributions that America can make, and is making, to the British people is to step up her shipbuilding programme. Mr. Roosevelt anticipated the approaching shortage long before America's entry into the war, and the increase in production has continued with growing acceleration. The goal that has been set is a production *fifteen times* as great as before the war; so that one has only to stop and think for a moment to realise what this means in the way of demands upon the skilled workers in the shipyards, and of careful planning.

In all the inlets of the sea in America there are shipyards hard at work—at one such place the writer of this article recently saw no fewer than twenty-three ships in process of completion, where only a few months ago there was no activity at all; and the American public realises the importance of the work; the new ships are being christened not by the wives of the magnates of the companies, but by the wives of the men who have helped to build them.

The American nation is, in fact, fast becoming conscious of the sea and of the influence of sea power to an extent far greater than ever before. The first sign of it was noticeable when the news reached the U.S.A. of the battle at Oran. For a week or two previous to that, after France fell and when there was grave doubt about England's power of resistance, America was faced for the first time with the possibility of a hostile nation in command of the Atlantic, and the news of the crippling of the ships which might be used against her sent a genuine wave of relief throughout the country. Since that time damaged British ships have arrived

often enough for repair in American ports, and in the streets of American seaboard towns the British naval uniform is frequently seen.

American mothers have made the men welcome. One of the most charming things that has come to the writer's attention is the arrangement made by an unofficial organisation of American mothers in a town with a navy yard. A British ship came in for repair with an unusual number of boys in her complement. Each mother adopted one boy, adopted him almost literally for the time the ship was in port. The boy was given a latchkey to the house, and was told to regard himself just as if he were a son.

All this has helped to give Americans a clearer picture of the importance of the sea and of the closeness with which England and America are linked. When the settlement comes after the war I do not think that lesson will be forgotten, and a permanent peace can only be ensured by the closest co-operation between the two countries. And, with the weight that American womanhood has in American counsels, the more conscious those women are of the nearness of the two countries, the better.

For the winning of the war, and for making the final settlement a permanent one, the accumulation of stores of food and of the essentials of life in America is of the greatest importance. The starving people of the subject countries of Europe, and the discontented masses of Germany, are already thinking with longing of the abundance which will be poured out freely to them the moment their Nazi masters are disposed of. The thought of it is influencing them every hour that they are hungry, and that is every hour of the day. The riches of America are a tradition among them. And they know that the moment their master admits defeat, those riches will stream across the Atlantic. For England it will only be the restoration of variety and luxury in food, but for Europe it will mean the end of actual starvation. And the terms of the Atlantic Charter are a definite promise of peace and security for everyone.

Your wise housekeepng is a vital part of the war effort.
Save your fuel and foil the Fuhrer.

FARMER'S BOY—1942

MARJORIE HESSELL TILTMAN

**investigates the
Land Girl Situation
in her own
inimitable manner**

THIRTY-SIX thousand young women, drawn from every conceivable calling in civil life, from modelling to domestic service, are now ploughing and sowing and all the other things which before the war hefty young country lads were rather inclined to cold-shoulder, in preference for the more sociable and less rigorous town job.

It is, admittedly, a hard life and a dirty one—this work on the land. "Mud and muck," some farmers have termed it. Yet these girls have chosen it in preference to dashing uniforms to which official-dom allows a discreet touch of lip-stick, or munitions-making with the possibility of high wages. At the beginning of the War they volunteered. Now that conscription is applied to the (comparative!) youngsters, they put their tick against the Land Army in the Second Priority column of the Ministry of Labour form, and hopefully await an interview. Curiously, only one branch of the Land Army—timber and forestry—comes under the heading of "Essential Works"; there are sensible reasons for this, but no room to discuss them here.

To begin, then.

You must imagine a Labour Exchange—one of the temporary offices which have been set up all over the country to deal with the enormous turn-over of wartime labour. Offstage—telephones and typewriters. Left—benches and chairs. Right—a trestle table with two women behind it, one in the uniform of the W.V.S. They can be placed at a glance—the type of Englishwoman whose creed (often unspoken) social service offered wi modesty, with selflessn and with devotion. If were one of the you things lined up opposi the beating of my he would die down before t reassurance of those cal kind faces.

The first applicant of n particular day was a da ling blonde, escorted her mother. Her profession? Commercial arti The reiterations of the chief interviewer about t long jump from a studio to a cowshed do n deflect her wishes. Horticulture is discussed. Y she does like heat and does not believe the chang in temperature between a hothouse and a c garden would affect h health. Next to apply a sturdy young ca worker, who wants join her Land Arm sister in Kent, "She ever so happy there The interviewer omits recall the fact that sa sister ran away from sa job in its early stage and files the applicatio Another waitress, th time as slender a delicate as a you gazelle, who says h mother thinks that wo in the open would " the making of her." Th question is discussed some length and will referred to the docto who has to pass eve applicant as suitable for agricultural work.

Here the sequence is interrupted by anoth brand of applicant—a woman with white hair, well-tailored suit and a rough-haired terrier. (the face of it, she is well-qualified for the post Land Army Hostel Warden, about which she h come to enquire. Her leading question is, ho ever: "And could I keep my dog?"

There follow in succession a nice little girl w has had a nervous breakdown, which she thin farm work might finally clear up; a neat lit mouse with swimming grey eyes, whom some fre of circumstance or mentality has prevented fro

EDITION

Drawings by Rowland Hilder

...rning to read or write, a woman with a ...personal history" who would like to do ...nd work if "they" would undertake the ...re of her baby, an irate father who wants ...s daughter (about twice his size) to work ...here the parental eye can be kept firmly ...on her, and a more than irate mother ...hose daughter, by some technical error, ...ds herself booked for the A.T.S. and ...o stubbornly affirms that Government ... no,' she'll be Land Army or nothing, ...d rather defies the Prime Minister to do ...s worst!

...So the scroll of humanity is unfolded. ... is very interesting, very touching and ...ghtly comic. One is shown tragedies ...d hardship, courage and promise which ...ems likely to be better than performance, ...metimes quiet efficiency, sometimes a ...nt of illusion which the interviewers tact-...lly do their damnedest to shatter. ...Dairy work is dirty work—carting ...anure, swilling out cow-stalls. Could ...u get up early? Are you afraid of cows? ...o you like animals? Picking tomatoes ...s a devastating effect on the hands. . . . ...ave you had any major operation? How ... your general health? . . . How do you ...el once a month. . . .?"

...Every precaution possible is taken to fit ...uare pegs into the same shape holes. ...his is not philanthropy but common ...nse. One dissatisfied or inefficient young ...male can afterwards cause as much time, ...ouble and expense as the ninety-nine ...ore normal sort. In theory, the precau-...ons should be foolproof, both as regards ...e applicants and the places of employ-...ent to which they are later recommended. ...ut in fact, side-issues are likely to sprout ... the most unlikely places. One girl may ...ave cherished a fond picture of herself ...waggering round in her breeches, emerald-...een jersey and felt hat like a perpetual ...incipal boy; she finds herself in dungarees ...ost of the time. Another may develop ...ilblains. One actually registered the ...rth closet as a reason for her resigna-...on; another was offended by the biological ...pect of the farmyard. As for the farmer, ... is a conservative creature at the best, ...d his preliminary approach is one of ...ained sufferance. That is soon replaced ... more positive *(Continued on page 91)*

Learn to regard every type of waste as a crime.

Make salvage your watchword.

You are often at your local branch of Smith's changing your library books, or paying your newspaper account ; buying a writing pad or some envelopes, or choosing books or other gifts for friends in the Forces, but do you know that while you are there you can buy your National Savings Certificates ?

As in the last war, Smith's are honorary official sellers for the National Savings movement, and our manager will be happy to supply, or obtain at short notice, whatever National Savings Certificates you may require for yourself or your family.

Make a habit of regular savings—it's the *regular* contributions that are specially valuable to the country's war effort.

W. H. SMITH & SON. LTD. Head Office: STRAND HOUSE, LONDON. W.C. 2

Waste helps the enemy.
Justify the risks British sailors take – don't waste their cargoes.
Get the paper-saving habit.

THE CENTRE OFFERS—*Soft water to double your soap ration and save your hands. This good-looking softener is easily fixed to any cold tap, and will give you a permanent supply of beautifully soft water. A testing set is supplied with the outfit, and the only other requirement is an occasional handful of salt. From Good Housekeeping Shopping Centre (30, Grosvenor Gdns., S.W.1), price £6 8s. 4d., plus carriage.*

Farmer's Boy—1942 Edition

(Continued from page 89)

motions—sometimes respect, sometimes thankfulness, good-humoured tolerance; sometimes by the blunt criticism that "They giggle."

I've talked to Land Girls working on five different types of agricultural work—on "hospital" or reclamation work under the direction of the War Agricultural Committee, at market-gardening, glasshouse work, dairy work and general farm work such as hedging and ditching. The only serious complaint (because it was an economic one) came from a market-gardener who employed a gang of six girls living at the nearest hostel to lift two tons of carrots. Time they took was four days. The charge at ruling rates for the labour was £10 plus 12s. for fares. The selling price for the National Marketing Board was £7 a ton. Thus the balance of purchase money left to pay for seed, rent of land, sowing, thinning, hoeing, collecting, shooting into bags, weighing and tieing was £3 8s.—a pretty hefty deficit, which not unnaturally left the farmer wondering. This example cannot be taken as the average, for have been given glowing accounts of the prowess of these "gangs" at potato planting, bush-pulling and threshing, but it is worth quoting to illustrate the high place which labour costs can take in a farmer's

budget, even when nicely adjusted.

Accounts generally, and, it seems to me, perfectly naturally, seem to show that young novices do best where there is some sober supervision. On the Duke of Norfolk's estate in West Sussex, seven are employed in the ten acres of kitchen garden, under the direction of an experienced head gardener. Although he talks wistfully of one girl who must have performed prodigies before she entered the Forces, he yet conceded a measured enthusiasm for those still in his charge. "Oh, ay; they're good lassies. They'll try anything, and if they do wrong, they're willing enough to learn right, if you'll show them how." And Mr. B. J. Bunbury, the agent for the estate, was even more unequivocal in his praise. "I had 110 acres of sainfoin—a valuable crop in these days. One of the girls cleared it of thistles and dandelions in one week. That's good."

There's a big firm of glasshouse growers near this estate, which has an extremely businesslike manager in charge of its vast output of tomatoes, mushrooms, salads and wartime quota of chrysanthemums. "I've got fourteen permanent Land Army girls here, and I find them pretty good—not as good as a skilled man who's been on the job

all his life, of course, but actually better at some jobs. They come to me straight from civil life, and I give them a month's training. It's tricky work and I can usually tell pretty well at the end of a week if a girl is going to be any good at it. My chief complaint is that they're not keen on doing overtime, and I have known them call a day's absence lumbago when it's really the boy friend on leave. But I can say this—that I shall always keep on a few women, if they'll stay."

Dairy work is said to be the most unpopular of all branches of agricultural work. It means putting the alarm to 4.30 a.m. winter and summer—that is, 3.30 a.m. by our grandmother's time! However, I talked to a nineteen-year-old ex-student of elocution who works with a friend on a 2,000-acre West Sussex farm, and this was her version. "We came here six months ago, after a month's training at Plumpton. Oh yes, the first two mornings were perfectly frightful, but we go to bed early, and now we both wonder how on earth we ever stuck life indoors and how we're ever going to stick it again! Milking is a fascinating job, and the people here are awfully nice to us."

She was helping to tread down young grass in a silo, while one of the men sprayed it with treacle. She was hot and sticky, but she radiated brightness.

"And after the war?" I enquired.

"Oh, I shall go back to elocution. I've got to try for the gold medal."

Those are a few glimpses of how they work. Space has run out before I've described how they eat and sleep. Some may live with the farmer and his wife; that may work out well or it may not. Others are billeted with countryfolk who do not object to the early hours their lodgers must keep. The luckiest of all find a home in one of the three hundred hostels set up by the Ministry of Agriculture in requisitioned manors, castles or even stables! I went to see twenty-seven girls living in what was formerly a fashionable golf club-house. A few players still strolled about the greens, while lambs bleated round them and a lorry decanted a gang of girls by the entrance. While the water ran for their daily bath, they sat round the fire and talked to me. They all plumped for the joys and jokes of communal life, the warm kindness of the warden and the excellent cooking. I sampled the two last, and I can endorse their enthusiasm.

A Special Page for Children

Superintendent Salvage, with Detector-Inspector Wast take charge for the holidays

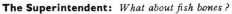

The Superintendent: *Now, Inspector, let's have your report.*

The Inspector: Well, sir, everything's mostly according to plan. I have my men in every house and a Sergeant acting directly under each grown-up Salvage Steward.

The Superintendent: *Good. How's the Bone Hunt progressing?*

The Inspector : Things are moving. My house constables check up on every joint that comes to the house and personally superintend plate clearance after each meal. They are also present at each emptying of the stock-pot and take account of all bones given to the dog. These are all reclaimed and put into the Bone Tin. Every other day, the house constable takes the tinful to the street collector's post and adds it to the bone collection.

The Superintendent: *What about fish bones?*

The Inspector: Ah, we don't make the mistake of putting *them* in, but all other little bones, even rabbit bones, are carefully salvaged.

The Superintendent: *Keep going—if every bone in every house is saved the country will have the bones to produce nitro-glycerine to propel hundreds of thousands of shells.*

The Inspector: The Waste-paper Search is going on relentlessly. The instructions are as follows : Every day, house constables collect the previous day's newspapers and any finished-with magazines, together with letters that have been answered and all wrappings from parcels.

The Superintendent: *String is included?*

The Inspector: Certainly—string is a vital ingredient in paper-making. Once a week old cheques ar receipts are collected from the grown-ups and taken to the bank for repulping. No secrets leak out this way !

The Superintendent: *What about paid bills?*

The Inspector: They're collected once a week from Mothers' shopping baskets, and odd bus tickets are searched for, too, and the kitchen drawer inspected in case too many paper bags have accumulated.

The Superintendent: *Have you tracked down that case of Pig-swill Poisoning yet?*

The Inspector: Yes, sir ! At No. 4 Home Drive one constable was not alert enough in seeing that NO coffee grounds and rhubarb tops went into the bucket with vegetable trimmings and plate scrapings. He knows the seriousness of this slackness, and won't offend again.

The Superintendent: *Well, carry on, Inspector, and don't forget that the Case of the Elusive Rubber must be tackled next. Not an old hot-water bottle, a rubber boot, a worn-out rubber ring, or an old bicycle tyre must escape.*

The Inspector: Very good, sir. The Squad is on the job !

MOTHERS

Make the children responsible for Salvage Collections. They'll enjoy doing a worthwhile job and they'll probably help to keep you up to the mark yourself.

SALVAGE STEWARDS

The youngsters make good helpers—especially if you appeal to their imagination. The above are suggestions for getting them interested. Organise your Street Squad these holidays, and watch the Salvage pile up !

Turn waste into our biggest war weapon.

Every scrap of paper saved, Helps to free all those enslaved.

THE MODEL ILLUSTRATED
IS **WHITSUNTIDE**
CC 41 UTILITY PRICE 53/-

MOYGASHEL FASHIONS

DISTRIBUTORS **MOYGASHEL FASHIONS** *Liberty House* · 222 REGENT ST. LONDON W.I.

Rubber articles past Home Service are needed for War Work.

Salvage is the Housewife's weapon.

Men must work and women must – Dig for Victory!

ood Housekeeping Institute: Principal. Phyllis L. Garbutt, A.I.C.

TO ALL OF YOU . . .

Two years of clothes rationing have come and gone. There are 0,000 fewer workers making civilian clothes than before the war. at is a saving of man-power of which we can all be proud.

To all of you who have so cheerfully made-do, who have mended d managed and got months of extra wear out of your own, your sband's and your children's clothes, I say—thank you.

Thank you for the raw materials you have saved the country ; r the shipping space which you have freed to bring vital nitions of war to these shores and to take them where they are st needed ; for the men and women you have set free for the ghting Forces and for direct war production.

Remember that every coupon unspent means less strain on the untry's resources. To wear clothes that have been patched and rned—perhaps many times—is to show oneself a true patriot. e " right " clothes are those we have worn for years, and the rong ones those we buy, when we don't absolutely need them. Making-do may at times seem a little dreary. Nearly every man, and some men, would like something new to wear. But, en when old clothes aren't exciting, they are a war-winning shion, to follow which will speed the day of victory.

Hugh Dalton.

Waste paper's only waste if YOU waste it.
The factories need your salvage for the Forces.
Have a Salvage Treasure Hunt today.

Egg and rice loaf with mushroom sauce is a delicious dish for dinner

DRIEI

By Nora Ram

DRIED eggs are one of the best foods that wartime rationing has brought us. Always available, always fresh and ready to use, they help the cook in a hundred ways. More than that—they provide every member of the family, from one year old up, with valuable body-building extras for the winter months. Take your full share of dried eggs, learn to use them really well, and you will be doing your household splendid service.

Here are some practical points to remember and some tested recipes for every meal of the day :

When reconstituting dried eggs, first mix the powder to a smooth cream with half the given amount of water, then stir in the remaining liquid. Do not mix the eggs until just before they are needed.

Eggs can be sifted dry into the flour when making batters or " rubbed-in " cake mixtures. For " creamed " cake mixtures, the eggs can be beaten in dry, or reconstituted.

Keep the packet of eggs in a cool dry place, but not in the refrigerator, as they tend to go lumpy.

FOR BREAKFAST : ....

Bacon Omelette

For two people, allow two reconstituted eggs and a small rasher of bacon, or half a rasher. Cut rasher into small pieces and fry in the omelette until crisp. Add a nut of fat to cook the omele if necessary, then pour the seasoned eggs into pan and stir rapidly several times with a fork, u the mixture is just set but not brown. Fold quickly, turn on to a hot dish and serve at once.

Egg and Potato Fritters

1 large raw potato	1 dried egg
1 tablespoonful flour	Dripping or bacon fat (for fry
Salt and pepper	Milk if necessary

Put the flour, egg and seasoning into a basin mix thoroughly. Peel the potato, then shred v a coarse shredder into the flour. Make a hol in the centre of the ingredients and, if necess stir in milk to give a thick batter. Drop spo

The Ministry of Food

A sustaining winter breakfast—savoury egg moulds with sauté potatoes

EGGS

*...mbined Domestic Science
...Diploma, Edinburgh)*

... of the mixture into hot bacon fat or dripping, and ... gently until browned, then turn and fry the other .... Serve immediately. Diced cooked bacon or ... cooked sausage can be added to the fritters, if ...ilable.

Parsley Eggs

...econstitute the desired number of eggs and add ...oning and sufficient chopped parsley to colour ...n. Steam in a greased egg poacher, or bake in ...o patty pans in a moderate oven until set. Turn ...o rounds of toast or mashed potatoes, and pour a ...ll spoonful of tomato sauce, mixed with a little ...uant sauce, over the top of each egg. Serve ...y hot.

Potato Surprises

...lix one cupful of mashed potato very thoroughly

with one egg (mixed dry), and season to taste. Add a cooked sausage cut in dice or any small pieces of cooked meat or fish which you have available. Form into flat cakes on a floured board and fry in a little hot fat until lightly browned on both sides. Serve very hot.

FOR LUNCH:

Egg and Rice Loaf

1 pint vegetable boilings	1 tablespoonful chopped
3 oz. rice	onion
3 dried eggs (reconstituted)	1 tablespoonful tomato
1 tablespoonful chopped	sauce
parsley	Seasonings

Parsley or tomato sauce to serve

Put the rice into a saucepan with the stock, cover and cook gently until the rice is tender and all the stock absorbed. Reconstitute the eggs and add them to the rice with the parsley, onion, tomato sauce and seasonings. Turn into a greased pudding basin or a cake tin and steam or bake in a moderate oven (375° F.) until the mixture is set. This will take about 1 hour. Turn out and serve with parsley or tomato sauce.

...has approved this article

THE LADY OF NO LEISURE ACQUIRES A CHAR

AM just jotting down in House Book, "what w
wrong with the Rock cakes," so that I shall kr
next time, when I receive an excited visit fr
neighbour-over-the-way (with whom have not
changed a *word* since was obliged to send crisp r
last summer about her dog at our dustbin, and she
plied with complaint about my chil-
dren swinging on her railings. Well,
she hasn't any railings now). Over-
the-way says do I know that the
new people at the corner house, who
only moved in four days ago, have
actually found a charwoman? Say
impossible! Not a char in the
neighbourhood. Even Local Busybody to be seen cleaning her own
windows! Over-the-way says she
knows they have a char. Has seen
her arrive in the morning with neat bundle, and hu
away at noon with less neat and larger bundle. O
the-way asks what are we going to do? As older reside
we have first claim on only char in neighbourhood.
that short of kidnapping her, I don't see what we can
Over-the-way says we must unite, without unity noth
can be done. Do not know what plans she has
combined operations, and cannot wait to enquire, as
due at fish-shop at twelve o'clock, word having g
round that consignment of bloaters expected at that ti
Neighbour and I part somewhat coldly. Do not pass
information about bloaters.

Reflections in queue . . . odd that queueing up
anything, whether it's bargains in clothes or food, d
not draw women together, as one might suppose. On
contrary, it brings out the very worst in them . . .
sharp looks of hate, the pointed elbows, shopping bask
used as battering rams, the place-snatching, the "exc
me's" if you step an inch out of line, and the gene
atmosphere of wariness. Reflections disturbed by si
of girl-friend Christine sailing by with basket appare
crammed with bloaters. Abandon place in queue (h
been able to get some nice vegetables, so we'll h
Woolton Pie for lunch. Won't smell out the kitcher
bloaters would—hope they're high), and join Chris
at bus stop.
During journey home pick up following interes
pieces of information.
Christine has had no trouble in getting either s
wool, floor polish or custard powder.
Christine is without a charwoman, too, but ne
lets the house get *her* down. Christine has finis
everything by 10.30 and not another thing to
all day. (Don't they eat, then?)
In Christine's house they never finish up
week's rations before the next are due. On
contrary, they invariably have enough butter, su
and even tea to carry over until at least the mic
of the following week.
Repeat all this to Bored Husband later on,
ask if Christine is a much better manager than
B.H. says, No, just a liar, and I feel very c
forted. Dear B.H. drinking his tea out of a s
bowl without a murmur! Every time I hear ab
the acute shortage of crockery I seem to br
another cup.

Your country expects YOU to make a big Salvage contribution.

Every paper scrap saved is worth a banknote.

Save till it hurts – and go on saving.

Drawings by Emett

Am obliged to leave B.H. in charge of house and
…ld with feverish cold, while I go to work at war-
…e canteen. Depart with usual feelings of appre-
…nsion, as B.H. (kind as he is over soup bowls) is
…ken reed where household help involved. Never
…ows where anything goes, even after twelve years
…one house.

…Meet Local Busybody in bus and discuss this
…ious characteristic of B.H.'s, never knowing
…ere the bread is kept or the margarine goes.
…cal Busybody says they *do* know, of course. Hers
…just the same. Pretends he doesn't know, so that
…won't be asked again.

…Again manage to get on the wrong side of the
…k at the Canteen, who receives me with a majestic
…ou may wash up.'' Should much prefer to be
…ving out tinned plums and custard to tired
…rkers, and say so, whereupon Cook puts me in
…arge of pig buckets, and I spend two hours stand-
… in area outside kitchen window receiving the
…ods and sorting them into buckets.

…Reflect that cooks always a frightening species and have
…ways been queens of the kitchen. This one certainly is,
…h her attendants of '' gentlewomen '' trembling in chintz
…ralls. Have good mind to fold up own chintz overall
…d leave the canteen for good, and if anyone tells me
…in it's total war . . .

…Drop in to office on way out and ask organisers of

Voluntary Canteen Helpers
if I couldn't have something
different to do. Mention
lightly that my friends consider me a born organiser.
Note curious stiffening of
their ranks and make mental
note that born organisers
are not popular. Feel rather like
wolf bursting in upon sheep.

On reaching home find ap-
prehensions fully justified.
B.H. has made several nuisance raids on larder
…d spilt jug of coffee, which has been left, drip-
…g like blood from shelf to floor. Washing-up
…ored, with used plates and cutlery placed on
…r and even decorating mantelpiece and piano.
…ld apparently thriving in pigsty and croaks
…ve her handkerchief that B.H. has been won-
…ful nurse, filled her hot-water bottle and given
… lovely tea of meat roll (taken from emergency
…lf) and fish-paste sandwiches. Can see B.H.
…ening himself behind newspaper.

…Am electrified next morning to receive visit
…m charwoman, who says she can give me a
…ple of hours a day, as she has three young
…ldren and not likely to be called up for war
…rk. She also informs me that she is very
…chy and liable to ''take everything funny,''
…d if I don't believe this I can ask her
…osband.''

…Can hardly believe this good fortune, as had
…g ago given up any hope of either Heaven or
…Registry Office helping *(Continued on page 101)*

IF Bored Husband, friend
Christine and the rest are new to
you, you're due for a delightful
discovery . . . and if they're old
friends, by now you'll be busy de-
vouring news of their latest doings

FUEL COMMUNIQUE

ACTIVE SERVICE on 12,000,000 Fronts

Britain's 12,000,000 households are 12,000,000 battle fronts in this great drive to save fuel. Each one counts. Each one must do its part. An *active* part, for it isn't enough to stop wasting coal or gas or electricity or paraffin; there must be *economies* in the use of fuel in all its forms.

So much depends on Women

Housewives, you have done splendidly so far—you have put your hearts into this great effort to help the war effort. Colder weather makes the struggle harder for you now—*but keep it up*. Put your wits to work as well as your will-power and plan your own special ways of saving.

YOU CAN DO IT—

Save a fire one or two nights a week by sharing with friends and neighbours.

Save coal or coke when using the oven or boiler by banking the fire up with slack. This prevents cold air entering.

Save on your gas fire by not turning it full on; or if you have an electric heater which has two or more bars use only one.

Save in cooking by using the small gas ring instead of the large one.

Save hot water by never using more than 5 inches in the bath; and by doing the day's washing-up all at one time.

KEEP YOUR EYE ON YOUR FUEL TARGET

Issued by the Ministry of Fuel and Power

Mend and lend . . . Waste not, Lose not.

Unremitting war on Waste will hasten the Cease Fire.

Factories are looking to housewives for raw materials – don't let them down.

The Lady of No Leisure Acquires a Char

(Continued from page 99)

ne. But how can I keep this bright
pirit, touchy temperament or not,
ith all the neighbourhood looking
or help, and maid-stealing now prac-
ised so openly? Go round the family
nd beg everyone to be on their
est behaviour, and go about myself
ith bright, fixed smile, which be-
omes rather wearing as day goes
n, and Helper seems to spend most
f her precious two hours finding
ew places for everything. Cannot
ut my hand on anything and
egin to feel I'm working in a
aze, as the brooms and dusters
nd even the scouring powders are
eterminedly whisked into new and
cret hiding-places. If I indulge
so much as a raised eyebrow,
n see Helper darting for her hat.
Observe curtain of neighbour-
ver-the-way's window twitching.
as she seen Helper arrive, and
ill she lay booby trap for her de-
arture? Could B.H. be induced
escort her firmly to and fro be-
een our kitchen and her own?
ecide that eyebrows must at all
sts be kept from rising, an effort
hich results in heavy scowl from
hich children flinch in alarm.
(Query: Is not all this repression
tremely bad for one? Should
ve to be thoroughly *cross* just for
ce. Have one glorious day of
apping at B.H., slapping the
ildren, telling the tradesmen just
hat I think of them, withering
ristine with eyes and tongue,
umbing my nose at Over-the-way,
d telling Helper that I do not
e to see the coffee-filter (my last
k with France) lying in the dust-
n (the filter is obviously French,
this unaccountable gesture of
rs must have some political sig-
ficance), and that I have more
an a sneaking sympathy with
n'oosband."

B.H. comes in from Home Guard
arade with all-too-familiar signs of
epression. (Was the news bad?
-too busy myself to tune in at
ne o'clock—or is it only his feet?)
Endeavour to cheer him up by
ying war can't last for ever, and
at in a few years' time our in-
rance policies will fall due and
e can have a gorgeous holiday.
B.H. says we'll be too old to
joy a holiday then.

In VIENNA then... In ENGLAND now

When Vienna was still a city of song the excellence of its food was known throughout the world. In those care-free days Wiener Schnitzel (veal slices dipped in egg and crumb, fried in butter) was a popular Viennese dish. Potato cookery too was carried to a fine art in Vienna. The other day a team of Viennese cooks made a special potato breakfast dish in London. (Recipe given below.) Try it yourself. It is a simple recipe and it makes good use of our home-grown potatoes — the splendid crop that saves our ships.

VIENNESE FISH CAKES

Cooking time: 15 minutes. *Ingredients:* ½ lb. of boiled, mashed potatoes, ½ teaspoonful dried egg, ½ teaspoonful of anchovy essence, 1 tablespoonful of breadcrumbs, pepper, salt to taste. *Quantity:* For four people. *Method:* Mix all the ingredients together and form into little cakes. Fry in a little fat until golden brown on both sides.

Potatoes
are part of the battle

P 3

Collect all your shopping, and save paper, labour and petrol for Victory.

Make your dustbin serve Britain's arsenal.

Wage unceasing war on Waste.

Don't be an armchair strategist – go on Active Salvage Service.

Good Housekeeping Institute: Principal, Phyllis L. Garbutt, A.I.C.

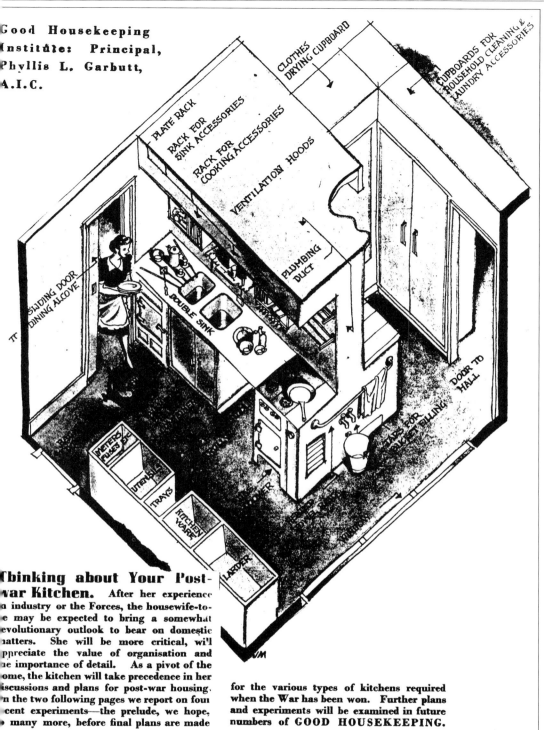

CLOTHES DRYING CUPBOARD

CUPBOARDS FOR HOUSEHOLD CLEANING & LAUNDRY ACCESSORIES

PLATE RACK

RACK FOR SINK ACCESSORIES

RACK FOR COOKING ACCESSORIES

VENTILATION HOODS

PLUMBING DUCT

SLIDING DOOR TO DINING ALCOVE

DOUBLE SINK

DOOR TO HALL

TAP FOR BUCKET FILLING

METERS FUSES

UTENSILS

TRAYS

KITCHEN WARE

LARDER

Thinking about Your Post-war Kitchen.

After her experience in industry or the Forces, the housewife-to-be may be expected to bring a somewhat revolutionary outlook to bear on domestic matters. She will be more critical, will appreciate the value of organisation and the importance of detail. As a pivot of the home, the kitchen will take precedence in her discussions and plans for post-war housing. In the two following pages we report on four recent experiments—the prelude, we hope, to many more, before final plans are made for the various types of kitchens required when the War has been won. Further plans and experiments will be examined in future numbers of GOOD HOUSEKEEPING.

Everything that could float mattered at Dunkirk — Everything save-able matters NOW.

A darn is a badge of loyalty to-day.

Children —

ANTHONY

(Born during my leave)

When my son smiles, in trust content,
  His eyes like starry midnights shine;
Fists fast about my finger bent
  Claim me his own, as he is mine.

As on his mother's breast he lies,
  My arms enfolding both, I see
In each my present paradise,
  In him my immortality.

Grey ships unshackle from the buoy,
  The convoy weighs, and leave is done,
But grief can never quench my joy,
  For I have lived to see my son.

Personal, deadlier, bolder now
  Each blow I strike, so Anthony,
His harvest sure, in peace may plough
  My wilderness of victory.

                                    D. C. BRAY

CHILD ON THE GRASS

When I was a child,
I longed to know where the sky ends.

On the cool grass, silent for hours,
I watched the clouds pass by.
Clouds,
I thought,
Are toy balloons that the wind blows up.
And stars are really tiny cracks
Where light from the Golden City shines through.
There is God's house.
Sometime when I am old,
I shall know where the sky ends;
I shall know God.

I am older now,
But still I wonder where the sky ends.

                              BEATRICE M. C. RISLEY

MOTHERS AND SONS

All women fear the men-children they bear,
Seeing in their bright faces, ghosts of wars
And earliest sighs of hurricanes that tear
Across the world, homes in their windy jaws.
Helpless and quiet and proud, they watch them grow.
See the soft, childish cheeks turn brown and lean,
Feel them draw shamedly from their bosoms, so
The circle of maleness widens to let them in.
Marble, the mother then, and terrible,
Holding the frayed end of her silver cord,
Dupe of an old ruse she knew full well,
Her loving womb betrayed by fire and sword.
Yet for that offshoot of her suffering flesh
She would deny herself, and die afresh.

                              WRENNE JARMAN.

MATERNITY WARD

Cream-panelled walls look down on our ease,
Long, shining windows reflect the green trees;
In bright, liquid ripples, the summer sun pours,
Distilling the brightness of glass-polished floors.
Outside the French windows the gold privet blazes,
Inside blue nigella peeps out of its hazes.
Peace, after striving, in dark waves of pain,
Calm, after suffering, a treasure to gain.

DINE LISTER.

SOLDIER GIRL, SOLDIER BOY

I stood at the top of my stairs to-day,
And watched my ghosts go down.
First came a girl with a snood on her hair,
Gold hair deep-tinted to brown.
She carried a racket, a bag of balls,
Her limbs were sun-kissed and free.
As her white-clad figure danced down the stairs,
She turned and smiled up at me.
The sweet, soft shyness of first love's gleam
Lay deep in her clear grey eyes.
Her fresh young voice called gaily to me,
"I'm playing with *him*," she cried.

(Ah, lovers parted by distance dumb!
Ah, death that lurks between!
Oh, years of struggle alone, alone!
And an End that cannot be seen!)

Thus I stood at the top of my stairs and watched,
And it seemed that the banister rail
Was hid from my sight by a boy's strong frame,
A teasing voice gave hail,
"What, dreaming, old dear? Day-dreaming again?
What price the holes in my sock?"
A muscular arm seemed round my back,
Brown hand in my elbow's crock.
A pair of blue eyes; rough thatch of gold,
Man's mouth, yet a cupid's bow.
An old tweed coat, and flannel "bags,"
Soft shirt and a tie aflow.
A bag of golf sticks, a pocket of balls,
A body pulsating, alive—
"I'm off with the chaps for eighteen holes,
You wait, I'll be back at five!"

(Ah, waiting years and deadly game!
Oh, guns that belch and roar!
Oh, empty stairs that my ghosts go down!
And my heart alone and sore!)

Then over my stairs there seemed to come
In whisper faint yet clear,
A boy's strong voice, "Cheer up, old dear!
I'm fine, and it's grand out here.
You wouldn't have liked me to stay behind!
You're proud of my badge you wear?"
And a girl's voice echoes, "I'm fine. . . . It's
grand . . .
Remember we're glad you're there. . . ."
Slowly I gaze into empty rooms,
Shrines of two lovely lives.
Then slowly descend and go out to where
The scene of my own work lies.
That moment's pause at the top of my stairs,
That chat with my two gay ghosts,
Renews my courage, tells me again
We three can be one at our Posts.

(Oh, Courage, shine bright in youthful hearts!
Oh, Faith, give patience, release!
Come Life, come Death, bring benison!
Love waits at the Gates of Peace!)

So, soldier girl, and soldier boy,
True hearts admit no parting.
And here where all your treasures are,
I wait for your home-coming.

E. WHEATLAND.

WARMED UP FOR WINTER

Here are some simple home recipes that add
warmth and variety to a
wilting wardrobe

Take one or more tired frocks and spice them up with a cheerful sleeveless pullover made from the brightest scraps of woollen in your piece-box. Cut strips, join them by machine in the gayest colour combination you can manage, then cut out your pullover from this length of material. Line with oddment of strong cotton or woollen for firmness and extra warmth.

Take a faithful old tweed suit, press and brush well, and garnish with bonnet, mitts and spats made from brightly-coloured felt or skiver skins. Have a back-flap on the bonnet and fit it well over the ears, to obscure draughts. The fingerless mitts will go over woolly gloves, and the spats should button on the outside. A similar set would delight small daughter. Diagrams and instructions on page 55.

Spend wisely, save generously.

Rubber is a vital war material – give up every scrap you can spare.

Paper Salvage has innumerable uses – increase your quota today.

Take a dated glamour-jacket of long-haired fur and bring to a high standard of usefulness with a few pieces of firmly-woven fabric. Add deep cuffs to the three-quarter or seven-eighth sleeves, drawn into a buttoned band, stitch a scarf-length to the collarless neck and gather the lower edge into a snug waistband, buttoning at front.

Take an elderly fur coat, rip off sleeves and collar and neaten lining at neck and arms. Wear as a loose slip-coat under overcoat or mackintosh, or, fur side out, as an indoor extra for fuelless days. But always remember: that fur is cut on the back with a sharp razor blade—that sewing is done from the back with a close over-and-over stitch—that pieces must be joined so that the hair of the pelt runs always in the same direction.

Take the rest of the fur collar and sleeves to a furrer and have him make it up into a round cape collar, buttoning at the throat, and a tiny barrel muff with inset pocket: wear with your town suit and street frocks, to give them a lift.

" More tanks for Russia ? "
Flo says " Right.
I'll stay and make
a few to-night "

She fairly takes the biscuit!

—*and Weston* MAKES *the biscuit*

The girls on munitions use up a lot of energy. They use up a lot of biscuits too! Biscuits are fine food for energy.

Busy people often rely on biscuits for a light, sustaining meal—easy and quick to eat—needing no getting ready, no clearing away, no washing up.

Look at it however you like—weight for weight, penny for penny, point for point—you cannot get better all-round value than biscuits.

WESTON
Biscuits

MADE BY THE LARGEST BISCUIT MAKERS IN THE EMPIRE

"Rest-therapy"—a successful treatment for INDIGESTION }★

REST IS the finest remedy for strain. And Indigestion is a severely strained condition of the digestion. Give your digestion a course of rest and you provide the right conditions for it to recover its natural powers. So, follow this simple rule. Never eat a full meal when you are tired or worried or feel digestive discomfort. Instead, drink a cup of Benger's. Benger's soothes the stomach and gives your digestion a chance to recuperate and build up its strength. Yet it provides warmth and nourishment which you must have in a form you can fully absorb without the least discomfort or strain on your digestion.

Household Milk Powder and Tinned Evaporated Milk both make delicious Benger's. Try it!

Why Benger's is so good for you

Benger's is rich nourishment in a form which requires very little effort on the part of the digestive organs. It contains active enzymes which partially predigest milk so that you absorb the full value of this valuable food whilst giving your digestion the rest it needs.

Benger's, to-day, is as easy to make as a cup of cocoa. From all chemists and high-class grocers—The Original Plain Benger's, Malt Flavoured or Cocoa and Malt Flavoured.

Benger's Ltd., Holmes Chapel, Cheshire

"Cartage" is obsolete – "Salvage" is its successor
Become a "snapper-up of unconsidered trifles" – for SALVAGE.

MINISTRY NOTICE BOARD

Topical advice from the Ministries of Health, War Transport and Labour, and the Board of Trade

A Career for Intelligent Women

The Ministry of Labour and National Service still lists nursing among the services for which there is an ...t priority need for recruits.

Volunteers and "call-ups" who opt for nursing will be welcome for most branches, but there must be many modern-minded women who can find particular satisfaction and interest in the field of mental nursing. Nowadays this means psychological study, rather than straight jackets and padded cells, and scientific treatments for the mentally sick are profoundly interesting. There is good scope for skilled nursing, also, as mental illness in many cases produces a state of physical collapse and exhaustion. A high proportion of cases are curable, so that the work is hopeful and satisfying.

Women attracted to this form of war service and available for it should apply to the nearest Appointments Office of the Ministry of Labour and National Service, or to the Appointments Office, Ministry of Labour and National Service, 24 Kingsway, W.C.2.

"Clippies" are Wanted

—and it's worth-while work, says the Ministry of War Transport

Transport must be kept going, and every woman who takes on the tough but interesting job of a Bus or Trolley Bus Conductress is doing as important war work as those in the Services or at factory benches. At the moment, with so many calls on labour, there are not enough conductresses to service all the buses, and more volunteers are needed.

If you are liable to the call-up, you can opt for bus-conducting, and, of course, if you're above the conscription age, but are fit and keen to try your hand, you can volunteer. Wages compare favourably with many jobs in industry, and for the woman with personality, humour and an appetite for hard work, there's no war service more enjoyable or worthwhile. Apply for further details to your local Labour Exchange or Bus Depot.

The Board of Trade tells you How to Treat Wooden-soled Shoes

You'll soon be seeing more and more wooden-soled shoes about the place. They save rubber and leather—both badly needed for direct war purposes—and are snug, well-fitting and waterproof.

It's said that the factory and mill workers of the North, who wear wooden-soled clogs, seldom suffer from colds and weak chests, so wooden-solers will be welcome when the winter comes again. When you first put on a pair of these shoes, you'll feel at once how solid and comfortable they are—but you may have to adjust yourself by a little practice to the rolling tread of the rigid wooden sole. It's naturally different from the flexible leather or rubber sole. Experts tell us that the right way to do the "Wood-n-Sole-Walk" is this. From the moment the heel touches the ground, the shoe should be allowed to "roll forward till the top of the toe is reached."

Like all shoes, wooden-soled shoes should never be dried too quickly and too near a fire or radiator. And—this is most important—the leather or composition reinforcements at the toe and heel must be replaced as soon as they are worn through. The wooden sole itself can't be repaired once it has begun to splinter.

Are YOUR Children Immunised?

—if not, have them done NOW, urges the Ministry of Health

Thanks to immunisation, diphtheria is already less deadly. For instance, in 1938 there were 64,937 cases and 2,931 deaths, while in 1942, after free immunisation had got going (it was launched in December 1940), the figures were down to 41,436 cases and 1,825 deaths. The disease would become much less virulent still if the four million odd children not yet immunised (more than half the child population) were given this safeguard.

Other countries realise the value of immunisation; for example, in Canadian cities where most of the children are immunised, infection is rare. This year Sweden has introduced immunisation for all children, and in Italy, where immunisation is being carried out at an increasing rate, the diphtheria case and death rate are falling appreciably.

Your children should be immunised as soon as possible after their first birthday. The process is simple and free and does not upset babies. Your doctor or clinic will give you details, but if in difficulty write to the Local Medical Officer of Health at your Town Hall.

Give up all the rubber you can and outwit the Japs.
Make "SALVAGE" your war-cry.

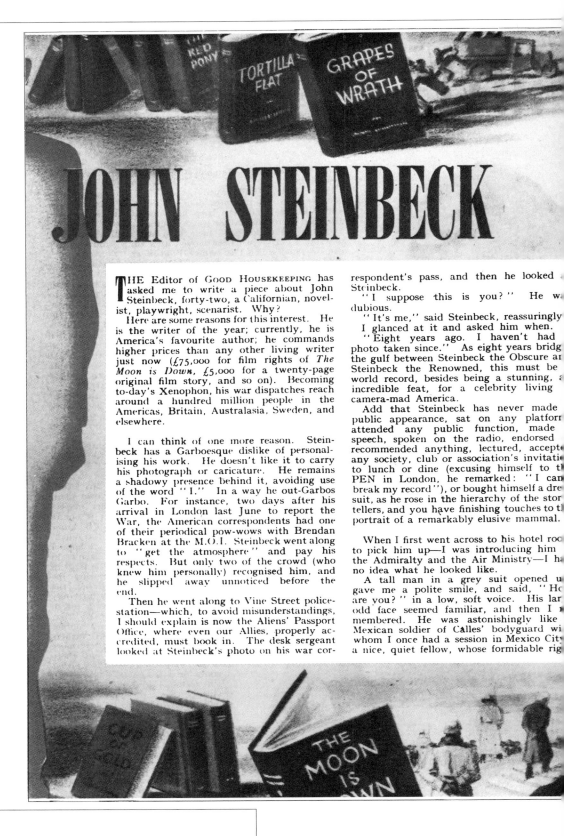

JOHN STEINBECK

THE Editor of GOOD HOUSEKEEPING has asked me to write a piece about John Steinbeck, forty-two, a Californian, novelist, playwright, scenarist. Why?

Here are some reasons for this interest. He is the writer of the year; currently, he is America's favourite author; he commands higher prices than any other living writer just now (£75,000 for film rights of *The Moon is Down*, £5,000 for a twenty-page original film story, and so on). Becoming to-day's Xenophon, his war dispatches reach around a hundred million people in the Americas, Britain, Australasia, Sweden, and elsewhere.

I can think of one more reason. Steinbeck has a Garboesque dislike of personalising his work. He doesn't like it to carry his photograph or caricature. He remains a shadowy presence behind it, avoiding use of the word "I." In a way he out-Garbos Garbo. For instance, two days after his arrival in London last June to report the War, the American correspondents had one of their periodical pow-wows with Brendan Bracken at the M.O.I. Steinbeck went along to "get the atmosphere" and pay his respects. But only two of the crowd (who knew him personally) recognised him, and he slipped away unnoticed before the end.

Then he went along to Vine Street police-station—which, to avoid misunderstandings, I should explain is now the Aliens' Passport Office, where even our Allies, properly accredited, must book in. The desk sergeant looked at Steinbeck's photo on his war cor-respondent's pass, and then he looked [at] Steinbeck.

"I suppose this is you?" He w[as] dubious.

"It's me," said Steinbeck, reassuringly[.]

I glanced at it and asked him when.

"Eight years ago. I haven't had [a] photo taken since." As eight years bridg[e] the gulf between Steinbeck the Obscure a[nd] Steinbeck the Renowned, this must be [a] world record, besides being a stunning, [an] incredible feat, for a celebrity living [in] camera-mad America.

Add that Steinbeck has never made [a] public appearance, sat on any platfor[m,] attended any public function, made [a] speech, spoken on the radio, endorsed [or] recommended anything, lectured, accept[ed] any society, club or association's invitati[on] to lunch or dine (excusing himself to t[he] PEN in London, he remarked: "I can[']t break my record"), or bought himself a dre[ss] suit, as he rose in the hierarchy of the stor[y] tellers, and you have finishing touches to t[he] portrait of a remarkably elusive mammal.

When I first went across to his hotel roo[m] to pick him up—I was introducing him [to] the Admiralty and the Air Ministry—I h[ad] no idea what he looked like.

A tall man in a grey suit opened u[p,] gave me a polite smile, and said, "Ho[w] are you?" in a low, soft voice. His lar[ge,] odd face seemed familiar, and then I [re]membered. He was astonishingly like [a] Mexican soldier of Calles' bodyguard wi[th] whom I once had a session in Mexico Cit[y,] a nice, quiet fellow, whose formidable rig[ht]

Peg away at Paper Salvage – it's more important than ever.

Don't have waste charged to your account.

The writer of the year—introduced by the man who saw most of him during his recent trip to this country

hand his more voluble colleague held up for me to inspect—the legend was that it had dropped a berserk mule in its tracks.

But the impression faded rapidly and then went away and never returned. Physically, the two could have exchanged skins, and the fit would have been good—both over six feet high, weighing maybe fifteen stone, with notably heavy shoulders, ears, nose, hands, narrow grey eyes, clipped hair on the upper lip, tousled dark hair thinning from a high forehead and rounded jaw. But Steinbeck was as quick as the other had been slow—quick in movement, decision, speech, quick in the uptake, very quick.

And when we began to talk about where he'd go and what he'd do, he explained that he got his stuff very quickly, and then he wrote two or three thousand words in a day. He worked any time and all the time. I thought he underestimated the difficulties of doing that kind of thing in war, and just before he left for Africa, at the end of August, he told me that what with fighting the authorities to get what he wanted and getting his stories done and out on time, he was glad to be flying away. Actually he had let himself in for doing a daily "Steinbeck story," running 600–1,000 words. Tough, very tough, even for a Steinbeck, who has a technique in these things.

He got into war reporting in this way. One day the New York *Herald Tribune's* literary critic, Lewis Gannett, and his wife, came to dine with the Steinbecks in their Manhattan apartment. (Mrs. Gannett illustrated his *Tortilla Flat* book.) Steinbeck said he'd like to go war reporting. He thought the real stories of the war were not being written. He wanted to do the little stories, the stories of the "common men" in the war. The 'plane-gunner—not the pilot. The submarine cook—not the skipper at the periscope. No generals, politics, or tactics. Gannett apprised the *Herald Tribune* editors, who immediately grabbed Steinbeck—the first top-flight writer to go out war reporting.

He arrived in London with no set programme. His first visit was to a Fortress station. It was largely chance. Visiting U.S. Fighter Command headquarters to write an article for the *Herald Tribune's* Sunday magazine, I mentioned to Captain Arthur Gordon, who arranges these things, that I had cable news Steinbeck was coming over. It might be a good idea to have something ready on the line for him. Gordon agreed. So as Steinbeck and I talked in his bedroom, I asked him if he would like to make a start on the bombers.

"Yes." A single, precisely enunciated word. I picked up the 'phone, got Gordon at a station. He said he'd come right up. He arrived two hours later, and the visit was fixed in three minutes. Steinbeck would bunk and eat with the men.

I was writing a naval story, and I asked Steinbeck if he'd like to take a look at the British Navy. The Clyde was closed to newspaper men, but there was Dover, with mine-sweepers, M.T.B.s, sea-rescue patrol. He could take in a local anti-aircraft mixed battery and a neighbouring train-busting 'plane squadron.

"Yes," said Steinbeck.

I told the Admiralty folk something about Steinbeck. They greeted him with genial smiles. He was to stay with Commander Eykyn, at Dover. Then they got on the telephone at once to Dover. "I've got somebody coming down to see you—Mr. Steinbeck—yes, a Big Shot." Steinbeck, who had been taking it all in with his

(Continued on page 112)

Illustration by Tim

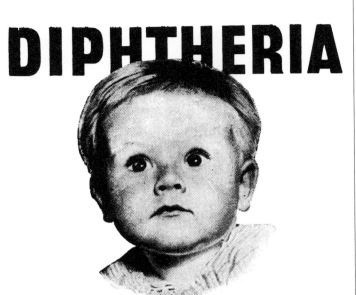

DIPHTHERIA

IS DEADLY—

Give your child the protection medical science now offers. Read the facts below and apply at once to your Council Offices or Welfare Centre—treatment is free.

IMMUNISATION IS THE SAFEGUARD

FACTS ABOUT DIPHTHERIA

Over 50,000 cases occur yearly in Great Britain. Between 2,000 and 3,000 of these die.

Even the best-cared-for child can get Diphtheria—it is not due to dirt or drains—and there are no "safe" areas.

Diphtheria is one of the worst dangers to children. It is particularly deadly to children under six years of age.

Even when not fatal, it may leave ill effects which last a lifetime.

FACTS ABOUT IMMUNISATION

There is nothing to be feared from immunisation. It is SAFE and simple. Merely a "pin prick" which is over and forgotten in a moment. If an immunised child gets Diphtheria it is usually in a mild form. Immunisation gives almost certain protection against death from Diphtheria. Only two treatments are necessary. The best time is soon after the first birthday. Protection takes three months to develop so get your child treated NOW—it is dangerous to delay.

Issued by the Ministry of Health & the Central Council for Health Education

D7a/1

John Steinbeck
(Continued from page 111)

(Continued from page 111)

bat's ear and unobtrusively observant grey eye, took his pipe out of his mouth at that. "Big shot?" he growled. "We'll soon change that idea."

He had moved out of the hotel ("This place is a mad-house, everybody talks and drinks too much"), and rented a little top flat with a glass front overlooking the Green Park. He came back from his expeditions with his notes and impressions. He sat, dressing-gown falling off his hairy chest, hunched over his typewriter, banging out his taut sentences (he's a bad typist), making stories. His words began to flow across the transatlantic 'phone.

The first article sent, his story of the troopship he had come over in, electrified America. There had been so many troopship stories that editors had long since said that there is and can be no story now about soldiers' routine sailing to the wars. Yet, lo! here was the first real story of a troopship ever written. The sophisticated editor of a digest got so excited about it that he offered $2,500, which is £625, for the mere right to reprint it, although most of America had already read it.

And as more stories came in, the hard-boiled managing editor of the *Herald Tribune* picked up a pencil and wrote a private memorandum: "They (the Steinbeck articles) are even better than we had hoped. In fact, I haven't read anything better about the war—anything to equal them in graphic description or in beauty of writing."

The first editor Steinbeck worked for had not thought so highly of his stuff. Fired from the New York *American* reporting staff seventeen years ago, Steinbeck decided to write the way he wanted, and not the way editors seemed to want. Meantime, as he had to eat, he went down the street to where gangs were building a new sports arena, Madison Square Garden, and got a job, humping a hod. One winter he had a better job for his purpose—he was caretaker on a property. As he was practically snowed and frozen in, he had plenty of time and energy to study and experiment with writing.

For those interested in the man and his writing processes, there are two clues. One is contained in the four stories comprised in *The Red*

Pony. That book is autobiographical. I suspected it when I read it, and Steinbeck confirmed it. There is still something of the lonely farm boy in Steinbeck. He is still capable of poignant emotions—indeed, his emotional content is very high, its flash-point low.

The other clue is to be found in his passion for vertebratology. He got interested in it at college, hadn't enough money to pursue the study, and picked it up again later.

You know the *vertebrata,* that comprehensive division of animals which contains all those with a backbone or segmented spinal cord; the main nerve cord always tubular and enlarged inside the head to form the brain; and with never more than two pairs of limbs.

Steinbeck and a partner have a research station and laboratory on the Pacific coast. Steinbeck selects his vertebrate and goes out on an expedition. The expedition examines the bird, reptile, fish in its special environment. Besides scientific notes, Steinbeck brings back specimens, has them prepared in the laboratory, and sells them to museums and colleges. Revenue from sales about covers the cost of expeditions.

You can see in this the genesis of *Tortilla Flat*—even more, of *The Grapes of Wrath.* The Californian notes the migratory labour flow to the sunny fruit lands of the Pacific coast. A vertebrate is involved. Man. Trace it back to its source in the Oklahoma dust-bowl. Trace it again from source out along its seasonal migratory path. But instead of writing a report on the expedition, *Sea of Cortez* fashion, make a story of it. An epic of the under-privileged, a saga of the victims of an inexorable machine civilisation.

Steinbeck has a scientist's trained observational powers and detailiousness. Away from first-hand observation, he builds a competent story, for he's a natural story-teller, and a good craftsman; but he's unconvincing and his stuff smells synthetic. *The Moon is Down* is merely a propagandish product by a skilled technician. Steinbeck himself doesn't like it (he thinks his best book is the non-fiction *Sea of Cortez,* the story of one of his expeditions).

In *The Moon is Down* he tried to write a novel which could be put on the stage as a play just as it stood, with no rewriting. It's a technical trick he's been trying to bring off for years. He failed, again. You may notice he tried the same thing with *Of Mice and Men,* which is built up stage-play fashion, each action taking place within the confines of a glade, bunkhouse, barn, etcetera, so that the story is ready for the theatre, in seven acts.

Wanting to write a play-novel, or a novel-play, may rather suggest a man trying to bring off the trick of swimming while playing golf. However, there it is, a Steinbeck aspiration.

He has been more successful in retaining his integrity while compromising adroitly with the facts of a mass-production, utilise-your-by-products, mechanised civilisation. He writes what he likes, as, how and when he likes. Having satisfied himself, he is through. His work is on record, and anyone who wants it can buy it as it stands.

But if the film factories want to churn his product around to make it palatable to the masses, he won't always argue with mass human nature, with its longing for illusions, dreams, and happy endings (compare the book and the film versions of *Tortilla Flat!*). And if periodicals cannot run his work at length, all right again—he'll take the money for cut versions, but ignore them. He was asked to send an approving message to a British magazine running a cut—the film—version of *The Moon is Down.* He refused. "I don't object to cut versions, but why should I approve them? I don't. I haven't approved a cut version in my life, and I won't start now." All this business and exploitation side he leaves to his agents.

Once he's done a thing he wants to get on to something else. It's work done, life lived, why go back? He's the despair of the crowd who want a personal appearance. He has never made one.

When he arrived in London, his *Moon is Down* play was running, the film was coming on. All news to him. Told of it, he showed no interest at all. He was invited to attend a performance of the play, invited to attend the première of the film at which the King of Norway would be present. He declined both invitations.

Two departments of the B.B.C. wanted him to come on the air. He said, no. He's allergic to the radio. Invitations to lunch and

(Continued on page 115)

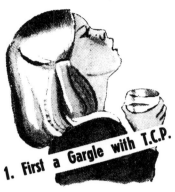

Until then . . . When toffee apples are two-a-penny and little Tommy's only danger is a sisterly smack for being greedy, the whole world will be at peace to enjoy the fruits of the earth. Until then, if we follow the advice of those who are in charge of supplies the foods and fruits in Britain will last longer and go further. If by eating more potatoes we can save more bread then let's all feel delighted to do so. And if we don't get any fatter we *are* becoming a healthier nation.

FORD MOTOR COMPANY LIMITED, DAGENHAM, ESSEX. LONDON SHOWROOMS : 88, REGENT STREET, W.I

Save, oh Save.
Develop an "eagle eye" for Salvage.

John Steinbeck

(Continued from page 113)

dine poured in from peers and politicians and moguls of all kinds. " Thanks, I don't think I'll be able to. I've come to work. Besides, I'll be away." He was invited to meet Bernard Shaw. No. He was invited to join H. G. Wells on the platform of an anti-Fascist meeting. Oh, no.

One evening it was the M.O.I. Would Steinbeck dine with the Minister there that evening? Steinbeck said he feared he couldn't, he had a very definite engagement. A compatriot who was present said, " Churchill will be there, you ought to go." Steinbeck said he'd ring back. He returned to his drink and looked undecided. " I've got this date. I can't go."

The compatriot looked at him and suddenly made up his mind for him. " It's something you *have* to do," he said, and rang the M.O.I. and said Mr. Steinbeck had got free from his other engagement —which he hadn't—and would be very happy to dine that evening. Steinbeck glared at him. " It'll take my last clean white shirt," he said. It was a last despairing, rebellious gesture. The other shrugged.

Mr. Churchill did not make the party. The shirt was expended in vain.

Likeable himself, Steinbeck is a man of strong likes and dislikes. Sometimes his dislikes seem irrational, but they mean much to him, and he cherishes them.

He was going to dine one night with General Eaker, C.-in-C. the 8th Air Force. He seemed uneasy— " I don't much want to go.

" I'm afraid he wants me to write something about fighter 'planes. I don't *like* fighters."

He's allergic to plutocrats. He said of one: " He's an evil little creature—he's not even complex." He likes to know what makes people " tick "—why, rather than how, they do the things they do.

Bums are one branch of *homo sapiens* he loves. The true bum has reduced life to its bare essentials, and achieved a profound philosophy. So long as he can get a spot of tobacco, a drop of wine (it would be beer here: this was California), he has all he wants. I suggested that the problem of the next meal must worry them, too. " Not the great bums," Steinbeck laughed. " The little bums maybe, not the great bums. A great bum can always rustle a meal. No trouble at all. They have great tact."

He sees things resolutely his own way. We were talking of where the real stories of the War lie. I said I couldn't find them in battle action, but maybe I was spoiled for that—this was my second war, and I had been through the first from start to finish, on foot and in tanks. He suddenly said: " The story of the War is right here—it's in the people's faces, and in those fireplaces hanging on a broken wall three stories up."

He has a sense of the incongruous. One story idea which made him eager was that concerning the Beefeaters. He wanted to be in the Tower of London during an air raid and see the Beefeaters swop their pancake hats for tin helmets. " I suppose they *do* wear tin hats? " He had me there.

In the end he had to make do with a second-best story about a castle built by a king for his mistress—neither of whom may be identified, because mention of that ancient scandal would give away the castle's location—now inhabited by American soldiers, armoured cars, and jeeps. His strong imagination made him see that the old place is not outraged by the new thing. Soldiery and wars don't change, only accoutrements change; and the ghosts of the king and his lady would find the new helmeted soldiers and their equipment quite in place on those lawns once paced by men-at-arms in troubled times.

There is nothing more to say about Steinbeck, the man, except possibly that he adores his wife, the second Mrs. Steinbeck, and in London cursed the tardy air-mail which failed to deliver her letters daily.

But the last word about Steinbeck, the story-teller, has not been said. He is in his full tide. We don't know how far off the ebb is. I recall a heated quarrel—it led to a divorce—between a man and a woman over the question of whether the work of the peasant Rodin changed for the worse when he made money and won acclaim. The same question-mark hangs over Steinbeck now.

Not that the two are quite alike. Rodin was absorbed in sculpture. Steinbeck is more interested in his study of the vertebrates.

If he made enough money to secure his preferred way of life (which is not inexpensive) he might retire from fiction-writing as decisively as Gene Tunney retired from professional boxing; and after that the only tales the world would get from Steinbeck would be the detailed and illustrated stories of his scientific expeditions.

Ransack the house for Rubber.

Lay in stocks of winter fuel NOW — offer your neighbour storage space.

MINISTRY NOTICE BOARD

Topical advice from the Ministries of Health and Home Security and the National Savings Committee

DON'T LET HOLIDAYS CAUSE A SAVINGS SLUMP!

It is natural to want as much spending money as possible for the rare week's holiday, when it comes round, but if every one of us stopped saving for a week, the loss to the country would be terrific. Whatever you do, when the holiday is over, switch back into the regular routine of so much to your savings account each week, and do not be tempted to let things slide. A little and often is the safest method to follow.

P.S.—If you are not a member of a Street Savings Group merely because nobody has asked you, what about trying to get one going yourself? There is still room for a great many more of these Savings Groups. Full details of how to form a group can be obtained from the National Savings Committee, Bouverie House, Fleet Street, London, E.C.4.

More Blood Donors are wanted!

Blood transfusion is saving lives all over the world, and it is important that the supply of blood should never run short. Look out for public announcements in your area asking for volunteers, and if you are reasonably fit, do your bit by offering your services. The giving of blood for transfusion is a quick, painless and simple operation, and a piece of valuable war service open to almost everyone.

Blood received from donors can now be dried and divided into plasma and serum, ready to be sent thousands of miles, if necessary, to wherever our Fighting Forces are in action. Quite apart from those on active service, blood transfusion saves many lives in this country, especially those of young babies and their mothers. The particular form of jaundice and anæmia that sometimes occurs in tiny babies can be beaten by a transfusion of the specially tested Rh negative blood, a new discovery. Remember, there is no need to apply specially to your hospital, but just keep your eyes open for any notice asking for volunteers to enrol.

Beware of Fires

It is important to be a fire guard and know what to do when the fire bombs fall, but it is equally important never to start a fire yourself, for more loss is caused in this country by fires due to carelessness than to the enemy fire blitzes. Be particularly careful when you are out of doors; if you are having a picnic, take great care to see that the fire you use to boil the kettle is really extinguished, and never, never throw away cigarette ends and matches without being sure they are quite "dead"!

—and don't forget the ever-present need to make-do and mend!

Our Rubber supplies have been severely cut – Salvage helps fill the gap.
Fine extravagance in your household and invest the proceeds in War Savings.

LAST autumn I asked the women of Britain to help me to balance the " Fuel Budget " by saving coal, coke, gas, electricity and paraffin. The success which attended their efforts is now history, and a striking tribute to what the voluntary system, backed by the determination of the people, can do.

Despite all the wartime difficulties with which they have to contend, women cheerfully found time, and put up with inconvenience, to help in the vital task of winning the " Battle for Fuel." No praise can be too high for what they did.

Now, almost a year later, I am renewing my request to you all to save fuel in every form. I ask you particularly to husband your reserves of solid fuel, and to accept, whenever possible, coke and anthracite in place of house coal.

Your fuel savings are a direct contribution to the war effort. Coal is, after all, the essential munition of war. Without it, our factories could not operate ; not a 'plane, gun, tank or ship could be turned out, and Britain would lie open to the enemy.

I am confident that you, the housewives of Britain, will respond to my appeal in the sure knowledge that by doing so you are helping to speed Victory.

G. Lloyd George.

Minister of Fuel and Power.

Keep on saving Paper zealously – it is needed more urgently than ever.

Avoid travel whenever possible.

How to get on

THE technique of managing the great American male is not as difficult as might at first be supposed. After all, several million American women do it constantly, so there's no reason to suppose their English sisters cannot do likewise—with a little practice.

Still, with more and more Americans appearing on the English scene, there is bound to be a certain amount of confusion and agitation (at first) among the ladies of this sceptred isle who, one way or another, find themselves faced with this new and rather bewildering problem.

For the guidance of those, therefore, who lack confidence in their own ability to entertain, attract, pacify, subdue or otherwise handle Americans, the following information has been compiled to fit almost any given set of circumstances. The advice offered may not be infallible, but the research has been as reliable and extensive as the war effort will permit. We have interviewed housekeepers, week-end hostesses, Red Cross workers, Army staff-car drivers and nightclub singers. For a balanced diet, we also included one barmaid, two W.A.A.F.s, a W.R.E.N. and an ex-A.T.S. girl—all of whom had much to say on the subject. In addition we had our own rich experience—nigh on thirty years, man and boy—in the U.S.A. to draw upon.

So here, as they say in Brooklyn, is the dope. If you don't take too much of it, it won't hurt you.

The average American is a changeable fellow and at any given moment is likely to be hilarious, depressed, energetic, homesick, hungry, fatalistic, talkative, moody or affectionate. This calls for a certain mental agility on the part of his companion. But what he is usually depends, to a large degree, on the time, the place and the companion. The housekeeper we interviewed, for example, was inclined to think of Americans as mainly hungry and homesick. The barmaid was sure they were all hilarious and generous. The staff-car drivers were inclined to regard them as energetic — and affectionate. The

W.R.E.N. said rather sniffily that they lacked discipline. The ex-A.T.S. thought they were wonderful; in fact, they were the main reason she *was* ex.

All of these ladies were more or less right. Be that as it may, let's get down to brass tacks (if they're not an essential war metal) and examine these characteristics in more detail.

If you are a nice motherly soul with an Ameri-

WE'RE delighted to have expert advice, we've encountered here, it would be our fault and warm interest melt traditional

can lodger under your wing, you probably won't have many problems. Americans are fairly well housebroken and like to be petted. Up to a point, they can stand a lot of mothering.

But if you are not the motherly type—if, on the contrary, you are likely to be having what is known in America as a "date" with an American—ah, then things may be different. Quite different!

Suppose you find yourself trapped at the beginning of an evening with an American who is suffering, let's assume, from both hunger and homesickness. Since one is a state of body and the other a state of mind, it is well to deal briskly with each in turn. The only known remedy for hunger is food, so if you are not in a position to feed the American—preferably with a thick slice of ham and six or eight eggs—the correct thing to suggest is that he feed you. Choose a place where the food is as good as Lord Woolton will

British housewives can command Victory by their Salvage efforts.

Be British to the bone and save your Bones.

with Americans

By One of Them

Drawings by The Harts

permit. Your escort will moan gently about it and make invidious comparisons with the kind of steaks they have in Texas. But pay no attention. Smile sweetly and listen attentively, and as soon as the edge is off his appetite, begin working on his homesickness.

The best way to do this is to sympathise heartily with him and tell him constantly that the war is almost over, and that it's just a matter

though we must say that, from the Americans

if we didn't get on. Their friendly good manners

British shyness like magic !

of minutes—practically—before he is shaking hands with the Statue of Liberty. He won't believe this and neither will you, but it does wonderful things for his morale. And pretty soon, if all goes well, you will have an entirely different problem on your hands—an American who is now hilarious and energetic.

One way to cope with this type is to dance with him. The average American enjoys dancing far more than the average Briton and—damaging though this statement may be to Anglo-American relations—is usually a much better dancer. So why not take advantage of this fact? Besides, if he's inclined to talk too much, as most Americans are (this squares the international account), this form of entertainment will keep him relatively quiet.

By this time, if you have been observing your American closely, you will have come to certain general conclusions about him and his fellow-countrymen which are probably as true as generalisations ever are: that his sense of humour is different—more wise-cracking, perhaps, less subtle than good British humour; that he has an eager, puppy-like friendliness that makes him call people by their first names on sight; that he is patriotic to the point of actual small-boy boasting about his country; that he has a vitality so tremendous that it can be both frightening and wearying at times; that, like men of any nation, he likes to talk about himself.

As for love and such stuff, you will find him considerably less—shall we say—reticent than his British counterpart. Preliminaries are reduced to a minimum. It may have something to do with the mechanised age in which we live. But contrary to rumour, the average American is not a very good philanderer. He frightens too easily. If you are a happily married woman with a husband in the Middle East, you can control any situation at any time with a short, two-letter word.

If, however, you are (happily) unmarried, you might as well be prepared for quite a variety of snares and delusions. The approach is standardised up to a point. The first question is usually: "What's your first name?" The second, about two minutes later, is: "Are you married? No? Good. . . ."

From there on, however, there seem to be dozens of techniques. We wouldn't know much about them, of course, if it weren't for our recent enquiries. But our notes seem to be full of revealing little paragraphs like these:

(*a*) The "Life-is-short-to-morrow-we-may-all-be-dead" approach. Particularly favoured by airmen. Can be quite effective under certain circumstances. Recommendations: don't let your sympathies run away with you.

(*b*) The "I'm-so-lonely-you're-the-only-one-who-cares" angle. Dangerous because it's so flattering. Best antidote: reflect sternly upon the number of times he has probably used this hoary device and suggest forcibly that he think up something more original.

(*c*) The spider-web technique.

(Continued on page 121)

"DRIED EGGS
are _my_ eggs—
my _whole_ eggs
and
nothing but my eggs"

Dried eggs are the complete hen's eggs, both the white and the yolk, dried to a powder. Nothing is added. Nothing but moisture and the shell taken away, leaving the eggs themselves as wholesome, as digestible and as full of nourishment and health-protecting value as if you had just taken the eggs new laid from the nest. So put the eggs back into your breakfast menus. And what about a big, creamy omelette for supper? You can have it savoury; or sweet, now that you get extra jam.

DRIED EGGS build you up!

In war-time, the most difficult foods for us to get are the body-builders. Dried eggs build muscle and repair tissue in just the same way as do chops and steaks; and are better for health-protection. So we are particularly lucky to be able to get dried eggs to make up for any shortage of other body-builders such as meat, fish, cheese, milk.

Your allowance of DRIED EGG is equal to 3 eggs a week

You can now get one 12-egg packet (price 1/3) per 4-week rationing period — three fine fresh eggs a week, at the astonishingly low price of

1¼d. each. Children (holders of green ration books) get two packets each rationing period. You buy your dried eggs at the shop where you are registered for shell eggs; poultry keepers can buy anywhere.

Don't hoard your dried eggs; use them up — there are plenty more coming!

Note. _Don't make up dried eggs until you are ready to use them; they should not be allowed to stand after they've been mixed with water or other liquid. Use dry when making cakes and so on, and add a little more moisture when mixing._

FREE — **DRIED EGG LEAFLET** containing many interesting recipes, will be sent on receipt of a postcard addressed to Dept. 627E, Food Advice Service, Ministry of Food, London, W.1.

ISSUED BY THE MINISTRY OF FOOD (S.74)

Have you bought your weekly National Savings ration?

Our Allies suffer great privations – make our voluntary fuel cut worthy of them.

How to get on with Americans

(Continued from page 119)

Employed only by a few patient souls who expect a long war and think they can go in for long-range planning. This type favours strategy over tactics. Danger lies in becoming slowly and imperceptibly involved. Solution is to fly away before the web is fully spun.

And so forth and so on.

Actually, we ran across a few highly individual cases. For instance, one of the W.A.A.F.s—a pretty one with upswept blonde hair—told us with a happy, far-away look in her eye of an attractive young American soldier who could not resist gently biting her ear upon occasion.

" Indeed! " we said interestedly. ' And what did you do—take evasive action? "

She gave us a demure glance. ' When *he* gets to that point," she said primly, " I always feel it's time to let my hair down."

Then there was the staff-car driver who remarked sadly that the most dangerous approach was really the fatherly act, the " I've-got-a-daughter-just-like-you-at-home " refrain.

" What? " we said, horrified, naturally. " Do you mean to say that the *married* ones . . ."

" The worst wolf I ever met," said this Red Riding Hood darkly, ' was happily married and had a lot of cubs! "

To be serious, for a moment, the truth of the matter is that Americans in Britain are like Britons in America—somewhat out of their element, but most of the time on their best behaviour. And their best behaviour is pretty good. ' Managing " them may seem like a hazardous occupation, but it isn't, really. Try it some time—it is possible you may be agreeably surprised.

One thing we can positively guarantee you, lady—you won't be bored.

PEOPLE COULD WASTE A LOT MORE MONEY... WE SHALL HAVE TO WORK OVERTIME

TOUGH JOB, TOO, NOW THAT PEOPLE ARE GETTING KEENER ON SAVING !

DANGER - Men a

THROUGH force of circumstances men are to-day having to do housework. They do it ponderously and reluctantly, but still they do quite a lot of housework.

Ask any of these male victims of circumstances what he thinks of housework, and he will be politely evasive. His mind obviously wanders nostalgically to camps and barracks, where the housework was all done by man power and was " unpretentious but organised and effective."

Press him to be candid, assure him he can't hurt your feminine feelings. He will then revert to the callous male you suspected all the time, and say:

" Well, take the expression ' What a wonderful housekeeper she is.' One used to hear it—er—occasionally long ago. Well, that in itself was an admission that the vast majority of housewives were *not* wonderful housekeepers. In fact, looking back on the situation as it was in those happy days, most housewives were terrible housekeepers—simply *terrible*. The class which was called the backbone of England (or of Scotland if you lived in Scotland) evaded housekeeping by employing servants ; and these human beings were ' kept in their place,' which was called the kitchen."

At this point the narrator's expression will be overcast by fast-approaching cynicism. Playing for time, *you* can interject brightly that there were, no doubt, a chauffeur and a Nannie as well. But the critic will only repeat, mournfully, " The kitchen." This is your cue to ask, very, very tactfully, " Was there something wrong with the kitchen ? "

" Pretty well everything," he will reply. " We men have to help in kitchens now. And perhaps it's all the fault of the men anyhow—we let it all happen. Once upon a time you women rocked lots of cradles ; but you tired of that. To give you something to occupy your minds, the men took you into offices, hoping you would make the tea instead of the office boy. But as all intelligent women are born organisers, you simply organised the office boy into going on making the tea."

You can ask pretty briskly if he means that women haven't been a success in business, and he will weakly admit that business would " never be the same again without them." And then, overcome with pious frankness, he will blurt out, " Haven't the women in Britain's factories been a tremendous success ? It

was a stroke of genius putting them there. Look[...] Hitler. He said woman's place was in the hom[...] The home . . . The fool ! It's cost him [...] war ! "

Abruptly your male critic will revert to the subj[...] of kitchens, and the remark you have long be[...] expecting will be trotted out.

" Well, take my own case," he will say with gr[...] personal interest. " We have shared four differe[...] households with four different families in three o[...] years. This was first-hand insight into four differe[...] kitchens, varying from a glittering 1938 model in [...] ultra-modern house built by a progressive you[...] architect, to an ' olde cottage ' kitchen, seventy yea[...] olde and still in its original state, except for a Bo[...] war-era gas stove. ' A doctor and his wife liv[...] there,' the house agent said, adding : ' But th[...] are both dead now.'

" In between those two experiences came [...] fifteen-year-old ' builder's spec ' owned by a wid[...] lady who ' gardened a lot '—so much so that, belie[...] it or not, the death-watch beetle had established [...] firm penetration of the draining-board in the [...] called kitchen. The other home was a nondescr[...] house where everything just happened, and t[...] grocer's boy and the baker's boy (that was early in [...] war) tried for a pleasant ten minutes to get a cheer[...] but scatterbrained housewife to make up her m[...] about books and orders and invariably got on th[...] way by tactfully suggesting ' Why not have the sa[...] as last week ? '"

At this point you can interject : " Ah, but y[...] have been unlucky in meeting exceptions. A[...] anyhow, why did you leave the ultra-mod[...] house ? "

" Well—that one was potentially all right, c[...] tainly. But, you see, the lady of the house—a v[...] intellectual sort of person, she was, too—had no i[...] how to co-operate with the servants. The servar[...] in turn, had no idea how to work the scientific kitch[...] which everybody looked upon as a sort of sh[...] window display where nothing could be displac[...] The nervous tension resulting was too much [...] everybody, and very shortly the head of the hou[...] hold got himself called up to darkest Africa, where[...] has spent some adventurous and happy years."

" Well," you say (for by this time you will h[...] caught his frightful ' Well ' habit yourself), " w[...] does all this prove, if anything ? What do y[...] really object to ? "

Vork

By
Caroline Berkeley

Housework and men are like petrol and flame—put them together and anything may happen at any time. Here are some drifts of comment overheard recently.

The kitchens themselves, to begin with. women take them on trust as the architect builder leaves them. You never dream of ving the dresser or the gas stove to more venient positions, or raising the kitchen , or indeed of having any system about thing. You don't work out the shorter better way of doing a job. Your general s on furnishing, too, seem designed in the n to create as much unnecessary and futile k as possible. You hoard and won't get rid seless junk that only gets in the way; you ire the Royal Navy, but you won't clear the red decks of your own homes. And, worst l, you put up with things. What man, faced a lifetime of washing-up, would just put up its drudgery? We would jolly well invent ething and simplify the shapes of cups and es, forks and things, so they could be easily ned."

eeing the look in your eye, he will go on kly, "We men understand all these things . After the war, when Mr. Bevin's Young ly in the kitchen complains about a door g draughty, or no ventilation for the cooking es, we are not going to have her smash kery for the humane purpose of relieving feelings. If it's a choice between the lady he house having a new hat or a new fur coat, he kitchen having a draughtproof door (we will invent some), I expect Mr. Bevin will t his young lady to come first."

ursting to exercise the famous freedom d speech, you will be thwarted with the ning: "But don't you women rush at purely ntific housekeeping after the war! Try to at it with the balanced mind of a man. You ember the scatterbrained housewife I men- ed? Well, hers was the best house to live hough she knew nothing of scientific house- ing. You see, the science of housekeeping e thing, and the art of living another. Both necessities every housewife should carry in intellectual haversack."

nd then, beaming, he will murmur, "Well know it isn't every woman one could talk to ankly. You are all such exceptions to rules. will you make a cup of tea or shall I show ?"

hat can you do but make the tea?

Brilliant woman doctor, reproached by husband for haphazard method of table-laying: "Well, if I can't be an amateur in my own home . . ."

Young Naval Officer (unmarried): "I'd rather have a charming wife than a perfect housekeeper. There are too many drearily efficient people about."

Husband: "The trouble is you will do things too well. When we are short-staffed in the office we cut down unnecessary work." *Wife*: "Of course, we could have dinner on a trolley every night." *Husband*—very hastily: "No, that's much too uncomfortable."

Bright Young Thing: "The only men I know who do any housework are Canadians—they're marvellous."

Fascinating, blue-eyed stockbroker of our acquaintance: "The thing to do, when asked to wash up, is imme- diately to drop several plates. Then you're never asked again."

Middle-aged D.S.O. who spends three days weekly training his lawn: "I'll do a bit of coal-humping if it's absolutely necessary, but there it ends."

Harassed mother of three: "My husband's just finished his holiday at home. He *said* he was doing it to help, but you know what it means. . . ."

Magnificent middle-aged lady on a bus: "I tell him I simply cannot even boil an egg—that is if one had an egg, of course."

War-workers MUST travel; must YOU?
Show your will to win by saving whenever and wherever you can.

ISSUED BY THE BOARD OF TRADE

NEW LIFE FOR OLD SHEETS

FIRST STEP — TEAR YOUR WORN SHEET DOWN THE CENTRE

Watch for signs of wear and deal with a sheet that needs it before there's a hole. Tear or cut it in half lengthwise and join the selvedges in a flat seam by hand. Then machine-hem the outer edges. These thin parts will go under the mattress where there's little strain on them, so your re-made sheet is almost as strong as when new.

NOT only sheets but *all* your household things must be made the very most of. These hints will help you to put off buying new.

USE SHEETS AND PILLOWCASES TURN AND TURN ABOUT, so that each gets its fair share of wear. Put newly laundered ones on top of the pile and take them out from underneath. Things not in constant use should not be stored in a hot cupboard as heat weakens the material. Save wear and tear by mending things that need it before they are washed, or at least by giving them " first-aid tacking." When the washing is done at home, avoid bleaching (which is an expert's job) or you may damage your things. Dry in the sun instead wherever possible. In ironing, take care the iron isn't too hot and never iron over the folds. Air everything thoroughly.

See to Stains at once.
Practically all stains will come out if treated at once. Pour boiling water through tea and coffee stains while wet, then wash in the usual way—do the same with fruit stains. Don't forget that egg stains and blood stains should be soaked in *cold* water.

Things you can turn into Towels.
A most serviceable bath towel can be made out of an old honeycomb bedspread that you are no longer using. Tea towels can often be made out of worn table runners, table mats, doyleys, etc., otherwise they should be put by for the duration to save laundering and mending. Never let things get too dirty before washing them : the extra rubbing is harmful and you use more soap in the end. Watch your towels for thin places and mend before holes come and before washing. When patches are needed, use old material—a new patch on a worn towel is apt to tear away. Two thin towels diamond-stitched together will make one strong one. Towels don't need to be ironed—rough drying will save time and wear.

● JOIN A MAKE-DO & MEND CLASS
Sewing and household jobbery classes and mending parties are being formed all over the country. Already there are hundreds of them in full swing. Any Citizens' Advice Bureau will be glad to tell you where and when your nearest class or party meets, and how you can join or help to form one in your own district.

**Mend and Make-do
to save buying new**

Make sure your children know and practise Road Safety rules.

Give up your Rubber to win the final Rubber.

Travel as little as possible, and then outside rush hours.

Good Housekeeping

OCTOBER

Vol. XLIV   No. 4

" *Good Housekeeping* " *Editorial
Offices, Good Housekeeping Institute,
Good Housekeeping Centre, and Good
Housekeeping School of Cookery : 28-
30 Grosvenor Gardens, London, S.W.1.*
   *The Editor will not hold himself
responsible for the safety of any MSS.,
but when stamps are enclosed he will
make every effort to ensure their safe
return.*
   *The Editor begs to inform the readers
of GOOD HOUSEKEEPING that
the characters in the stories in this
number are purely imaginary, and that
no reference or allusion is intended to
apply to any living person or persons.*

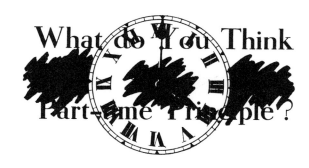

What do You Think Part-time Principle?

RECENTLY, enquiring of one of our senior colleagues how his wife managed with her part-time factory work, we were told " She likes it—though she thought she wouldn't." Pursuing the subject, it transpired that the lady was not so much enamoured of assembling nuts at the bench, but that she enjoyed the extraordinary variety of human contacts and getting away from the house, where incidentally she does a full-size job in raising live-stock and garden produce, as well as running the home.

We found this specially interesting, as it dovetailed very nicely with a theory we've been turning over in our minds. The theory is briefly that the " part-time principle " is one of the good things that has come out of the war; too good, in fact, to be lost when peace comes.

You may remember that when the demand for labour first became acute and it was suggested that factories, and shops and offices, too, should try a short-shift system so that house-wives could work part-time, the great mass of employers obstinately set their faces against it. Later, pressure of events made them think again. After the preliminary organisation was done, they found to their surprise that not only did the part-time system work well, but it increased output, as the amount of work done per hour over a short shift was sub-stantially more than when full hours were worked.

In this last sentence lies the whole core of the matter. If short working hours mean more output per hour, as they can and do if workers go " all out " while they are at it, cannot we reorganise our whole system so that everyone puts in less hours at his main job, and so has time and energy for taking on some contrasting part-time occupation?

How would this work out? Let's take the case of the house-wife. With better housing and improved domestic appliances, household work could be speeded up, though not perhaps in all cases, quite enough to free her for outside part-time work, paid or voluntary. However, to even things out, the house-wife would rely on the part-time work in the home put in by her husband, whose shorter main-job working hours would leave him sufficient time and energy for it. Thus, while the wife would enjoy outside contacts and the stimulus of a dif-ferent kind of work, whether it might be serving on the local Council, or selling hats in the local store, helping in a Nursery School or in one of the new Continuation Schools, the husband would be able to spend more time in enjoying and taking an active part in the upbringing of his children, in exercising his creative skill at the kitchen stove or in putting down for winter the fruits of his husbandry in the garden. Isn't there the basis of a truer and therefore happier married partnership here, than when the wife gets housebound and circumscribed in outlook, and the husband comes home from long hours outside the home to relax like an oriental pasha, while wondering what has happened that his wife has grown so dull?

WORK AFTER A WOMAN'

They're training now, those Britis
war-scarred Europe a home again. No le
and disciplined, yet full of sympathy an

AFTER the war. . . . It would be impossible, and unnatural, not to think of it sometimes. To daydream of fruit out of season, and blinding neon lights, and husbands who come home punctually every night to dinner. But what can we really expect?

The one thing to realise is that the things we are fighting for will be ours after we have won the peace, but not immediately after we have won the war. Men fight wars and women help them. Women are expected to win the peace, with the men as assistants.

So the question to debate is not "What shall we get?" but rather "What can we do?" when the lead is given back to us again.

It may very well be necessary to put in order the house next door before we can start in on our own. Europe is the house next door. And Europe's probable condition was summed up very well, back in 1942, by an American, who said:

"With victory achieved, our first concern must be for those whose sufferings have been almost beyond human endurance. When the armies of our enemies are beaten, the people of many countries will be starving and without means of procuring food; homeless and without means of building shelter; their fields scorched; their cattle slaughtered; their tools gone; their factories and mines destroyed; their roads and transport wrecked. Unknown millions will be far from their homes—prisoners of war, inmates of concentration camps, forced labourers in alien hands, refugees from battle, from cruelty, from starvation. Disease and danger of disease will lurk everywhere. In some countries confusion and chaos will follow the cessation of hostilities. Victory must be followed by effective action to meet these pressing needs."

European countries may be liberated piecemeal, in which case war will have to be waged alongside relief. But even if Europe falls as a whole, there will probably still be war, requiring transport and food and clothing, in the Far East. So the only things going to freed Europe will have to be priority necessities. But among those priority necessities must be women with a knowledge and ability to help the women freed from domination who will, for some time, be too weak and exhausted to help themselves.

The basic machinery for relief after the war is, mercifully, already in existence. Agricultural seed, livestock and implements, clothes, medicine and dehydrated foods, transport and industries are all being considered now. So is the rôle relief workers must play.

After the last war it was possible for a lot

Illustrated by Jack Matthew

of unqualified people to go to Europe. Reli
work was very largely a free for all. You and
might decide, on a sudden whim, to dress u
smartly, buy a canteen, and trundle over to son
nice warm place like the Riviera with it. On
there we might be useful or we might get badly i
the way of some other, seriously qualified reli
workers.

This possibility will not exist again. The co
trolling Leith-Ross Committee is in touch wit
all the big organisations like the Red Cross, th
Y.M.C.A., the Quakers, who will provide many
the right type of volunteers. Even the Allie
Governments in England are putting through ve
severe tests their women over here who hope
go back with the vanguard to organise relief
their own countries.

Many women, British and Continental, are a
ready training for the work they hope they ma
be allowed to do. The rest of us, behind t
lines, will be required to support them by exampl
encouragement and self-denial. And on the
success or failure will depend our immedia
security, and the future peace of our children
lives.

Recently I went to meet some of these wome
I found twenty-four of them in a large classroo
overlooking the levelled bomb-scars of Centr
London. They represented every Allied Eur
pean country, and they were waiting to hear a
English doctor talk about starvation.

The first woman I talked with there was

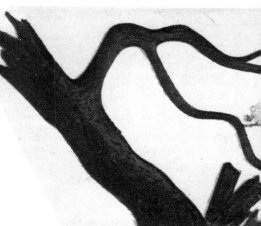

WN HEART   By Jeanne Heal

Allied Women who are pledged to do their part in making
the fighting men who lead the way, they must be tough
ng-kindness.   Theirs will be an exacting, but rewarding task

Force uniform with POLAND on the sleeve.
told me she had been a concert pianist,
by the time war cracked over her head,
was organising the military hospital in
rsaw. She ran it right through the siege
, as a prisoner, for eight months after the
nan occupation. She knows what death
starvation can do. She will not be sur-
ed by anything she finds when she goes
e. She talked about the terrible transport
culties there will be in a Poland from
h already the Germans have taken every
and bicycle and train and horse.

hen there was a Czech girl. She was a
lent when the war broke, but she walked
Prague right through Yugoslavia, Greece,
a to Marseilles and the last boat out of
ope and a government job in London. I
d her if she resented the idea of English
en, who know so comparatively little of
suffering, going to help "organise" the
hs. On the contrary, she felt the British
-balanced outlook would be a godsend to
e x h a u s t e d
trywomen, she
the British
t go if relief is
ucceed.   Only

she hoped that relief would remain neutral and not get mixed
up with politics the way it did
last time. "Vote for me and
I'll give you an extra loaf of
bread" kind of thing. As soon
as possible after the elections,
administration should be trans-
ferred to the people of each
country.   These views were
shared by all the women with
whom I talked.

With a Belgian social welfare
assistant I talked about the
children.   They will probably
present the biggest problem of
all. Little children without
schooling; children over nine
who have been taken from their
families to forced labour in Germany · where they are being
brought up as good little Nazis;
over one hundred and fifty

(Continued on page 129)

Rubber is needed for Salvage – stoppers and caps are not too small to save.

Help Britain's wheat stocks by eating more Potatoes.

Work After a Woman's Own-Heart

(Continued from page 127)

...usand orphan children in Poland ...ne; children who must populate ... new Europe we will build.

...hese women, and many others, ... taking a course, between war ...s, organised by the British Coun-... They have been specially ...ected by their governments, and ...ey are learning about specific ...eases and famine relief; how to ...k maternity services under emer-...ncy conditions and how to trace ... wounded and help illegitimate ...ldren. In addition they help ...k and nurse, delouse and ad-...ister, over here.

...hey are studying such things as ... probable mental effects home-...sness and the Nazi regime may ...ve on group psychology, learning ...w to protect themselves against ...min and epidemics, and having ...up discussions on the mental at-...ude successful workers must adopt. ...hen there are the many British ...men who will be needed. I met ...t a few of these too.

...any Quakers are taking corre-...ndence courses in social practice ...d the economic, political and reli-...us history of special parts of ...rope in which they may work. ...eir work will have a definite reli-...us aspect and reconciliatory aim. ...e Red Cross are lecturing doctors ...d nurses on malnutrition, insect-...ne diseases and epidemics, and ...nt welfare. Many similar organi-...ions are preparing spare-time ...tures. Perhaps the most in-...esting of these, as a sample, are ... Girl Guides.

...hey have never done relief work ...ore, but this time they hope to ...d trained Rangers and Guiders ...r twenty-one. They are very ...l suited to the work, used to ...d conditions and team-work, and ...h a direct entrée, through the ...des in the countries in which ...y will work. Very sensibly, they ... paying a lot of attention to the ...kground of the countries they ...ect to visit. The Chief Guide ...Poland is here—Guides were an ...ortant influence in Poland; they ...n ran their own hospital. She ... told them a lot about the ...l customs and superstitions they ...y meet in her country . . . cer-... days, for example, on which ... new project started would be ...sidered foredoomed to failure. ...tain foods which must not be ...en except on feast days. Colours ...ch might be considered unlucky.

These fears must continually be al-lowed for and respected if the work is to succeed.

When I went to meet some of these Guides they were spending a Yugoslav week-end at their head-quarters. Lectures on the religious outlook, cookery and history of the country were being given by ex-perts, and Yugoslav girls in costume were teaching them folk dances and songs. Other week-ends are spent working in the special air-raid shel-ters for people too verminous to be allowed in the ordinary public places, or cleaning and scrubbing in feeding centres, or at a typhus dis-infection station—just to see if they can stand it.

These women intend to face the diseases and dangers of work in Europe. Any two of them may well meet, in some crowded French railway station among pitifully re-turning exiles, or on some battered, ruined plateau that once was a proud Greek city. But what of those of us who stay at home? We shall have to help too. Now, we are one of the best-fed countries in Europe. After the war we may have to accept reduced rations so that others, whose sufferings have been greater, may live at all.

We may have to send them much of our food, our raw materials, even our labour. But quite apart from humanitarian reasons, we should do well to remember that in helping them we help ourselves. By giving them back their health so they can work, and their in-dustries so they can trade again, we enable them to produce the things we need. And, above all, by associating ourselves with an entirely international body, freed from political prejudice and aiming only at helping the helpless, re-lieving the suffering, we can take part in the only movement which can assure peace for all time and bring friendship through under-standing without concern for race, religion or social standing. That big movement has begun, now, among the cosmopolitan gatherings taking place in this country. May it go forward to freedom everywhere.

Lunch-time Cookery Demonstrations, Wednesdays and Thursdays; new series start October 27. Afternoon demonstrations, Tuesdays, from November 2. Details from the Good Housekeeping Institute.

Keep your Paper Salvage flag flying.
There is still too much waste in Britain – don't be a guilty party.
Remember to keep paper salvage separate and clean.

pocket plan

Regd Design Nos 839672 and 839709

LOOK FOR THE REGISTERED EAR-PIECE

Encourage the children to start their own War Savings Group.

Rags are very versatile – give yours a chance to prove their worth.

Good Housekeeping Activities

*The illustrations show the exterior and interior of Good House-
keeping's new Wartime Meals Centre in Grosvenor Gardens Mews*

Good Housekeeping Wartime Meals Centre

A Good Housekeeping Wartime Meals Centre for
the general public, organised on British Restaurant
lines, is now open on the premises (entrance,
Grosvenor Gardens Mews, North). It is run by
the Canteen School senior students, under fully
qualified supervision, as part of their training.

Readers are cordially invited to visit us when they
are in the neighbourhood—just beside Victoria
Station.

Address all Canteen Cookery enquiries to Mrs.
M. R. Murphy, Principal, Good Housekeeping
School of Canteen Cookery, 30 Grosvenor
Gardens, London, S.W.1. Telephone : Sloane
4591.

A Career for Now and the Future—Canteen Cookery

Good Housekeeping School of Canteen Cookery
offers training for a career of first national importance in war and peace time.

The school is constantly notified of openings for
trained canteen personnel in schools, hospitals, industrial canteens and British restaurants, and
successful students receive full co-operation in
finding positions.

The twelve weeks' intensive course consists of six
weeks' household cookery and six weeks' advanced
training in adapting this to large-scale work. Dietetics, staff management, book-keeping, large-scale
ordering and food and fuel economy are among the
subjects covered. A period of this training is spent
in running the newly opened Good Housekeeping
Wartime Meals Centre.

Domestic Science Teachers and others holding a
recognised certificate for cookery, or those who can
satisfy the Principal that they have sufficient knowledge on which to base advanced training, may
now take the six weeks' Senior Course only.

The " Make-do and Mend " Advice Centre

This is an important new department of the
Institute. Housewives, whose time is limited, can
receive quick replies to the many " Make-do and
Mend " problems which confront us all to-day.

Household " jobbery " is a speciality, and the
many years of experience of Good Housekeeping
Institute is available to enquirers in the Centre.

This month and next, the problem of " Winter
Woollies " is being dealt with. Miss Garbutt, the
Principal, recommends that woollen clothing for
next winter's use should be thoroughly overhauled,
demothed and made good NOW. It is too late to
make a good job of repairs and readjustments when
the cold weather is already with us. " Be Prepared "
is a good motto to adopt in all branches of " Make-do
and Mend." Call, write or 'phone with all your
Make-do and Mend problems to Good Housekeeping Institute.

Good Housekeeping Institute Lecture Hall

Both " Make-do and Mend " and Cookery Lecture
Demonstrations are suspended during August, but
they will recommence in September. For full
particulars and syllabuses of forthcoming lectures
write or telephone to Miss P. L. Garbutt, Principal,
Good Housekeeping Institute, 28–30 Grosvenor
Gardens, London, S.W.1. Telephone : Sloane 4591.

*Never light fires with clean paper.
Tanks and 'planes need fuel more than you do.*

A little BOVRIL helps the Vegetables along

Delicious—that's always the word for vegetables cooked with Bovril. For a little Bovril does wonders for tastiness — it adds the highly concentrated flavour of prime lean beef. Regular supplies of Bovril are available even in these days.

Keep the family up to scratch about Salvage.
Will the Pattern of Victory be cut from your Paper?
Wastefulness puts a weapon into Hitler's hands.

Wisdom & Stature

By
Joyce Barton

Boys.
  Whistling—
    Hallooing—
      Catcalling.
Banging big-booted feet,
Kicking all things movable,
And many that are not.
Testing their welling strength,
Their untried limbs,
On trees, walls, bannisters,
—And on their kind.

Boys mouthing rude noises :
Laughing with uncontrolled hilarity
At jokes of a practical nature ;
Sniggering subduedly
When they perceive the point
Of a subtle shaft, sex-tinged.
Saturated with male pride :
And simultaneously
Shamed by the down on lip,
Shocked and secret in the new knowledge
Of the mating stir.

Boys. Scornful of all women but mothers—
Who are no women, but infinite and sexless.
Vocally, actively scornful,
Derisively pulling pigtails.
Scornful : except for one, generally adult,
For whom they entertain the purest of all
          adoration ;
She is accorded dog-like devotion,
Before her they are inarticulate.
Sometimes they avoid her for weeks.

  Clean boys, uneasy in new clothes,
  Unhappily restricted ; the butt of comrades'
          jokes.
Of a community—the only one—where rags
          speak no shame and dirt may
          direct.
  Slouching boys, hands pocketed, hair awry ;
  Feeling no shame for a rotten tooth,
  But brought low by a too-blue pullover
  With stripes.

Boys. Mulish and unapproachable,
Lazing through lessons
With a self-imposed labour limit,
Beyond which no adult can drive.
Receiving chastisement with a well-feigned in-
          difference,
Or hard-fought tears.
Momentarily abject—
But resilient as rubber,
And innocent of rancour :
Winning an audience with a display of those
          same weals.

  Boys, feet dragging, despising the dance,
Destroying its tempo ;
Yet of all humanity romantic :
Awake, alive, bewitched
By a bomber, or a barrage balloon,
Or even a man with a winch.
Deliberately dull to distraction ;
Yet all their senses hungrily aware—
Projecting themselves entire into bodies astral,
          mechanical, heroic,
Without the confines of logic.
They are the bomb that bursts,
    The wolf that howls,
        The helmsman,
          The Great One.

  Boys. Shouting coarse catchwords ;
  Savouring horrid oaths with relish :
Singing psalms on Sundays with passionless
          clarity.
  Greedy to revulsion—
Albeit gentle with kittens and babe sisters.

Spirits of the Primeval. Animals with a soul
That betrays them to tears of shame at reproof,
That produces strange loyalties even to
          suffering ;
The while they will torture or ostracise another,
          who by misfortune is beyond the
          pale of gangship.
              Men.

Emergency *Beauty*

For the Morning after a Sleepless Night.

There are those who can fire-watch or dance until the wee sma' hours, snatch an hour or two of sleep, and face the new day as fresh as a daisy; but if you belong to the other (and far larger) group—those who drag themselves up looking as bad as they feel—I recommend the " three-S " treatment—salts, stimulation and suggestion.

Sleep as long as you can, but get up the moment you awake, and take a glass of alkaline salts. Next, stand in a few inches of warm water, sponge your body with cold, and dry as usual, then use a second, dry towel, or a friction brush, to scrub the body, continuing until your arms are aching and your body is in a pink glow.

Extend the stimulating treatment to the scalp and face, brushing up from the hair-lines, and giving the face a two-minute massage. This brings the blood to the surface to re-animate the tired skin. When it comes to make-up, resist the temptation to pile on the rouge. Try using a smaller quantity of a brighter shade. Pat on a warm-tinted powder, groom lashes and brows more carefully than usual, and apply a gay lipstick.

In a Heat Wave.

Change your diet to fit the weather. Cut out oatmeal, fried foods, heavy puddings and pastries, and eat more salads, etc., take plenty of liquids, but avoid iced drinks.

Wear loose-fitting clothes, light colours rather than dark; cool blues, greens and pastels rather than reds, yellows and browns; lawn, linen and cellular fabrics rather than wools and silks.

If perspiration is a problem, switch to another form of deodorant, cream instead of liquid, liquid instead of cream, and add a little boracic powder to your talc.

Have your hair thinned out and tapered, and choose a hair-style which keeps the hair off the neck and forehead—the new " Maria " style, for example. Start the day with a tepid bath, but yourself dry and apply plenty of talc, allowing plenty of time to dress. Hurrying will make you hot.

Wear a light make-up, and do your face more often than usual during the day. It's a good plan to lighten your beauty preparations, adding a little rose or distilled water to foundation lotion and complexion milk, and a few drops of Eau de Cologne to your creams. Pinky shades of rouge and lipstick are cooler-looking than vermilion shades.

At night, bathe hot, tired feet in cold salt water, remove the under-blanket and all but a firm flat pillow from your bed, and arrange door and window to secure a draught.

In Dusty Weather.

Keep your hair covered with hat or scarf, and brush it thoroughly at bedtime to remove all dust. Shampoo it more frequently than usual.

A complexion milk or foundation lotion is the best powder-base at such times, for, unlike creams, they don't attract the dust. Failing one of these, use calamine lotion, but counteract its slightly drying effect with plenty of skin food.

Bathe the eyes, morning and evening, with a strengthening eye lotion, and if irritated by dust, soothe them by resting them for at least ten minutes under buttermuslin sachets filled with used tea-leaves and wrung out in very hot water.

Blow the nose thoroughly at least twice a day, wash the hands more often, and gargle at bedtime with a mild antiseptic or salt and water.

Any bones, rags, paper, metal or rubber to-day?

Your fuel cuts will help to free our friends.

**By
Susan Drake**

In a Drought. Dry, dusty weather makes the daily bath more essential than ever, but if water is scarce, a full bath is out of the question, and a bath on the instalment plan is the only solution. You will need a kettleful of hot water, a jug of cold, a wash-hand basin, a foot-bath or bowl, flannel and a rough towel. Now stand in the foot-bath and wash the entire body from the hand-basin.

Perhaps you long for a bath and all that you've got is a bowl of tepid water. Well, you can still have a refreshing bowl-bath. Put a handful of kitchen salt in the bowl, dip a softish brush in the salt-and-water solution—a well-soaked nail brush will do—and go over the whole body. Now plunge each foot in the bowl and finish by towelling yourself briskly. This treatment is excellent for gooseflesh, and makes the skin satin-smooth.

Another plan is to add two tablespoonfuls of vinegar to your bowl of water, wring out a small towel in this, and wet-friction the body. This is a grand freshen-up treatment on a hot day.

If the water supply should fail completely, dust yourself thickly with talc, leave for a moment, then give yourself a friction with a rough towel. This gives a pleasant feeling of freshness.

For an Attack of the Jitters. Like most of us, you get nervy once in a while. You find yourself jumping sky-high at any sudden noise, or even at the sound of the telephone. You sit at your desk with one leg wound tightly round the other, sit nervously erect in bus or taxi, and clench your hands even in sleep. Yes, you've got the jitters, and here's the cure.

Diet first : make sure you are getting sufficient nourishing food—nervousness is often traced to malnutrition—and don't eat large meals when you are over-tired or emotionally upset ; instead, take a small quantity of easily digested food. Eat plenty of raw young vegetables, and lots and lots of lettuce, for lettuce soothes the nerves and a bowl of lettuce soup for supper will enable you to sleep like a healthy child. Another good plan is to get some lime tea from the herbalist and take this instead of tea or coffee. Above all, don't bolt your food, or eat on the wing. Make your lunch-hour sacrosanct, and relax while you eat.

Remember the pigs and poultry – they enjoy kitchen waste.

Your salvage has already freed many ships – keep it up.

HARD-HITTING ULSTER

**GAIL RICHMOND takes ship for her latest
" rediscovering Britain " journey, and gives us a lively
and thought-provoking sketch of Northern Ireland**

WHAT'S going on over the water in Northern Ireland? A lot of people on this side asked me this question, and so I went across to find out.

The sea trip, the Customs sheds, all added up to the illusion that I was experiencing the almost forgotten event of a journey "abroad." But, when I landed up in Belfast, just as the streets were filled with workers hurrying home, I knew I was still in the United Kingdom, and it was a very good thing to know.

These workers gave me my first and strongest impression that, although there is no conscription in Ulster, the people are right up to their hair-line in war. An atmosphere of intense effort hits you, as it does in any of the great industrial cities on this side; the workers come out of their jobs in the shipyards, the factories, the government offices, with the same strain of tiredness over their faces and the same set of the jaw. The streets are packed and the stations crammed with men and women in uniform and in civilian working kit.

Their vitality reaches you within the first five minutes of being among them. Here is a race of go-getters, determined, pushful. A great many are of Scottish descent, which accounts for the intonation of their voices, more Scottish than the popular conception of Irish brogue. They also use phrases associated with Americans, but in reality America must have adopted them from settlers. Most notable is the pleasant "You're welcome," given in exchange for thanks for a service.

Let's take a quick look at the set-up of Northern Ireland. Its normal population is just a shade more than one and a quarter million, and there are only two main cities, Belfast and Londonderry. The chief industry is agriculture, yet apart from sending us food products to the value of over eleven million pounds a year, the people of Ulster have supplied us with an immense number of ships, aeroplanes, transport vehicles and, in fact, every weapon of war, and thousands of her men and women are serving with all branches of the Forces.

And she needn't have done a thing—there has been no compulsion for one Ulster man or woman to work or fight.

Yet with that tiny population and with slender defences, she has swung her whole weight in with us, suffered with us in raids, submitted to all our forms of rationing, including food, although with her agricultural output she could, if she chose, be living on the "fat of the land."

This is something pretty big for all of us to remember for all time about Ulster and its people.

Belfast had two smackin[g] raids and lost seven thousan[d] houses. So the housing ques[-] tion, never very satisfactory[,] has become acute. It is est[i-] mated that the whole provinc[e] could do with a minimum [of] fifty thousand houses, wit[h] half this number for the cap[i-] tal. It has not been settle[d] yet where the new city house[s] will be built. So far it ha[s] been Belfast's excellent polic[y] to encourage people to liv[e] outside the city, which prob[-] ably accounts for the fe[w] slum areas. There are very cheap street-car fare[s,] a network of bus routes and a good train servic[e.]

Ulster has an important brick industry, and[,] for this reason, houses constructed by a syste[m] known as simplified brick building look as if the[y] will be one good emergency answer. Briefly, thi[s] is a method wher[e]by bricks are put together int[o] sections, slotted through with steel rods an[d] sprayed with cement. The houses are then erecte[d] by cranes, and ten can be built in a week.

But whether this type of house, or a prefabri[-] cated one, will finally be chosen, Belfast house[-] wives are keen on more colour in their home[s.] They ask: "Why black grates and boilers?["] Why, indeed!

I was interested to hear that there are thre[e] women on the housing committee, because I wa[s] struck with the very quiet rôle women seem t[o] play in Ulster. Before the war, the main bod[y]

Illustrated by Xenia

women industrial workers was concentrated in
the linen industry. Another big group, of course,
worked on the farms owned by their menfolk
through a State scheme of land purchase, by
which farmers paid a small annuity for a limited
number of years.

But, in the main, Ulster women seem comparable to Canadian women in city areas, who also
before the war were content to marry young and
keep house.

However, as the war years have gone, so the
scene has changed. Thousands of women who
have never worked before are now in industry
and commerce. And they're making a grand
show, proving themselves as adaptable as the old-
timers of the linen trade, who also changed their
line of effort when the fine linen industry col-

lapsed as a result of being largely sustained by
imported flax. Now home-grown flax is used for
war purposes, and workers accustomed to delicate
weaving are turning their deft fingers to other
tasks, such as making parachutes and harness
or fuel tanks for aircraft, and assembling aircraft
parts.

It seems to me that those concerned are getting
more than a little worried about what policy
should be adopted for encouraging women to
return to their homes after the war is over! Perhaps the new houses will do the trick!

The invasion of industry by young workers has,
incidentally, brought about the first need Ulster
has ever felt up to now for Youth Welfare organisations. These were practically non-existent before
the war, but now there are almost ninety young
people's clubs, and a total of forty-five thousand
girls and boys in the various movements, including pre-Service training corps.

The clubs have lectures and discussion groups,
as well as handicraft classes and physical training.
"You have to be a first-rate lecturer," the head
of the youth services told me, "or the youngsters
soon find it out and you're for it! Youth wants
the best." Sport, literature, aviation, radio engineering are a few of the subjects which seem
to have a special attraction.

It's in Your Hands

THE impression you make upo your circle is, often quite lite ally, in your hands. Too ofte they tell a story quite different fro the one your lips are speaking. I this psychological age our gesture and mannerisms tell secrets abou our souls.

● The actress is taught that ever gesture has a meaning. Th woman playing the part of poised and charming woman ho her body as well as face and voic under control. Her every move ment builds up the impression o charm and ease. If, however, sh wishes to suggest inferiority, sh slumps, squeezes her arms, cover her mouth and fiddles with he hair. Check your gestures. Mos of us have at least one which should be pruned away. Get friend to pull you up every tim you pinch your cheeks, gnaw you nails or scratch your head. Don twiddle away your charm.

● If you don't know what to d with your hands, have a few postur lessons. When standing, keep erec but relaxed, and vary the position of your arms. When sitting, fol the hands lightly in your lap palms upward, or let one lie on th arm of your chair. Hold—don clutch—your handbag.

Read your meters regularly – SAVE FUEL.

Salvage bones – don't expect our ships to import them.

Just a gesture—but what impression does it make?

- Large sketch: the woman who screws up her face and gesticulates wildly in the name of animation forms premature wrinkles and reveals her state of jitters

- Work counter-clockwise round the small sketches: scratching the head is ugly and insanitary— leave it to the typical stage yokel

- Nail-biting denotes nerve trouble. Take calcium-rich foods, have professional manicures, and if necessary, consult a psychiatrist

- This face-pushing act causes ugly lines and reveals apathy and acute boredom. Even if you do feel weary, try not to show it so plainly

- Fussing with the hair betrays inner distress, and it's a mannerism which infuriates men. Do your hair and then forget it

- Face-picking is an unattractive mannerism to you, and those who see you, but to the psychologist it tells of a sense of frustration

- " Men never make passes at girls who wear glasses " is true only when they twiddle, bite or fidget with them continuously

- According to our pet psychologist, nose-rubbing means subconscious dissatisfaction. In any case, it's neither pretty nor polite

- A mouth-covering habit betrays a lurking inferiority complex and tends to give the impression that you're ashamed of your teeth

- Chewing your beads shows a need for reassurance. Incidentally, it destroys their decorative value and also distorts your face

Salvage dead wood from your garden to keep the home fires burning.
War Savings are War Weapons.
Dig now and prepare for a bumper crop next year.

Save FUEL FOR BATTLE

says
FUEL WATCHER

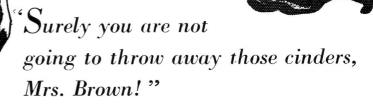

"Surely you are not going to throw away those cinders, Mrs. Brown!"

"Oh no — I have always found them better than coal for lighting the fire."

"It isn't only that — it's also a question of saving burnable fuel. Do you know that if cinders were properly used in every household the home coal consumption of the country would be *750,000 tons less each year?"

"Good gracious! I had no idea that it was so important. Now I really am glad that I have always saved cinders."

*REMEMBER that 750,000 tons of coal are used in producing the steel for making 10 battleships.

ISSUED BY THE MINISTRY OF FUEL AND POWER

Rubber, Paper and Metal should be the Big Three on your Salvage List.

Reach your Fuel Target by constant vigilance.

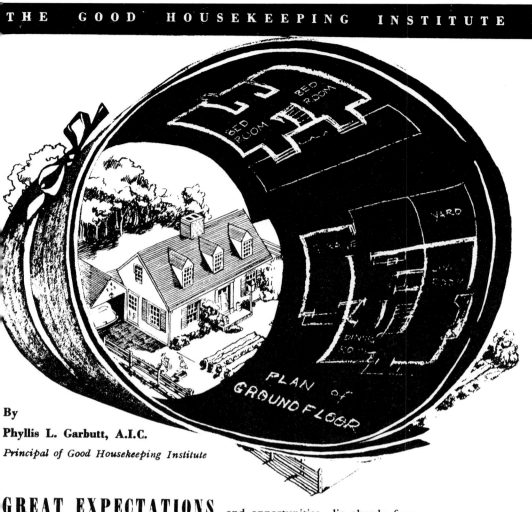

By

Phyllis L. Garbutt, A.I.C.

Principal of Good Housekeeping Institute

GREAT EXPECTATIONS—and opportunities—lie ahead : for you

as a woman, for us as Good Housekeeping Institute. The next few years must necessarily contain decisions—domestic decisions as well as international and political ones. And who shall say that the domestic decisions, in the long run, will prove the less important ?

Women's views, and women's needs in their homes, are being considered more to-day than they have ever been before. The post-war kitchen is discussed everywhere. Women begin to make their opinions heard and felt—they criticise the Portal house, offer suggestions to the Scottish Housing Advisory Committee, write in dozens to the Royal Commission on Population.

But women are still, in the main, inarticulate. They endure endless discomforts, maddeningly monotonous work, rather than " make a fuss." Their views have to be sought and encouraged : they have to be invited to say boldly what they timorously think. Government departments, committees and councils—the people who are making these decisions—must

Don't forget that your Clothing Coupons have to last until April.

What about National Savings Certificates for Christmas presents ?

be told what the women are really thinking ; so must the manufacturers and agents who can materialise certain of the committee's plans in terms of actual cookers and refrigerators, curtains and carpets and chairs.

Then, too, there is the very important matter of design— design not only for efficiency but for beauty. Many of the most " modern " fittings, particularly for bathrooms, are still hovering, so to speak, in the just-before-the-war era when fitness gave way to sumptuousness, no-colour gave way to too much colour, and white, unless it was that nebulous "off-white," was considered the last word in dullness. The best artistic brains in the country, the most sensitive tastes in colour and line and fitness for purpose, are not too good for designing the surroundings in which women must spend so much of their time. Committees and manufacturers must link with the artist-designers. We wish that British manufacturers would mention in their advertising the designers they employ for *your* benefit. Too many designs in the past had a very vague air of compromise about them— an air of something one had seen done a little better abroad— a suggestion in some cases that the people who did the designing had no considerable education and were too often only copyists. This leads to everything looking much of a muchness, a standard which Mr. D. S. MacColl has recently called " manufacturers' taste." After all these years of monotony there will be an appetite for variety and, if we are to deserve a share in the world's markets, a need for brilliant artist-designers. Living must be made as lovely and as gay as it can be for all of us. In this work—the work of liaison between the women in the home and the people who plan her home for her—Good Housekeeping Institute is determined to play its part.

This is the collective side of our work. But we want to serve the individual housewife as well. The young women of to-day have made a first-class job of their war work ; they are equally determined to make a first-class job of their home-making. We are sure of this, from the many letters we receive from women in the Services or on war jobs. And we want to help them. We want to help *you*.

When your post-war home begins to turn from a dream to reality, how will you know, amid all the bewildering claims, which cooker or hot-water system to choose ?

How will you choose your wall finishes, your floorings, your bathroom fittings and (most important of all, you may think) the right equipment for your kitchen ? How will you be sure of spending your money to best advantage, buying the really efficient and rejecting the shoddy and worthless ? This is, perhaps, where the Good Housekeeping Institute advice service to our readers—free, of course—will prove to be your standby.

The advice we give is not guesswork. Nor does the Institute accept manufacturers' claims for products (whether they be vacuum cleaners or packet dyes, oil stoves or washing machines) until those products have been submitted to rigid test. Our consulting board of advisory experts contains some of the finest scientific brains in the country : we have access to information that no other magazine can tap. And we give our advice without fear or favour—recommending

Homes overseas are open to our Service-men – try to return that hospitality.

The Services are always in need of reading matter.

the article that you most need to meet the conditions of your purse and your home.

Your purse and your home . . . we like to help here if we can. Because every sort of good housekeeping (whether it be grand or humble or in-between) must begin with a plan of spending and a plan of work, we specialise in budgeting. Money budgeting, of course, and time budgeting, too. Can we help you, when you have planned your home, and reality has emerged from the blue-print, to plan your time to enjoy an intelligent and comfortable life in it ?

Come and visit us at the Institute if you can : we are delighted to welcome visitors at any time, and shall be more so than ever when peace comes and our depleted staff can be brought up to full strength again. Or write to us with your problem. Write as fully as you can—explain clearly your needs, say what your budget is, mention the size of your household and any other details that will help us to help you. We want full particulars, not from curiosity, but so that we may suggest the right appliance, plan the right budget, choose the right gadget (for we are interested in the small things of the home, remember, as well as the big ones) and generally come to the wise decision that will make you the grateful, friendly, satisfied reader we want.

WE ADVISE ON :

HOUSING ; BUDGETING ;

FOOD & NUTRITION ;

HOME MANAGEMENT

& EQUIPMENT

Wartime

By

Christine Palmer

*(Combined Domestic Science
Diploma, Leicester)*

MANY dauntless brides are setting up house now, in spite of the difficulties. Many more are determined to have a home of their own as soon as they leave the Services or have their husbands with them. But furnishing materials are difficult to find and prices fantastically high; although furniture and domestic goods will be mass-produced as soon as the war is over, there will still be limited supplies and a necessary uniformity of design.

How can the bride prepare now to give gaiety and elegance to her home? The battle is to the imaginative and to the clever-fingered.

Utility furniture, austerity materials, standardised fittings, can all be used wisely and subordinated to the more decorative accessories which can be collected now. The war bride can make a virtue of necessity by buying very slowly and choosing only things she really likes. She can experiment with cheap or makeshift furniture and then be really sure of her taste before she buys more permanent pieces. Meanwhile, she can concentrate on the smaller details.

No one could pretend that she has an easy job ahead of her—the wartime bride setting out to make a home. She will need all the energy and persistence she can command, but if she applies her imagination and a great deal of thought to the limited and often unpromising materials she finds, she may create a more beautiful background than the often carelessly assembled homes of pre-war brides.

PICTURES

Some wedding-present money might be wisely invested in one or two good modern paintings, drawings or woodcuts. But they should be chosen very carefully and should be the kind of pictures you really wish to live with.

Old prints, etchings and book illustrations can be collected now and framed after the war, as the choice of framing is very limited now—but there may be curious old frames in a family attic or junk shop which would be perfect for them. Old prints of some of the places to which we are taken by the disturbances of war will have a life-long interest.

If in your search through the attics you find a large, heavy picture frame, consider its possibilities as a frame for a shelf for flowers or a still life group, or a display of china on two narrow shelves.

CHINA

Most of the utility china is of beautiful design, and some may well become period pieces. White utility coffee cups on a pale pink tray look lovely, and all the white utility ware blends well with old pieces of colourful china.

From market stalls and antique shops or from kind relations you can often get part of a tea service, or a lovely old teapot which will look most distinctive combined with white cups of a similar shape. Search, too, for odd jugs or sugar bowls which will serve a double purpose—they are often perfect for flowers. In village shops you may find little white china shoes or baskets which would make enchanting table decorations filled with spring flowers.

" *Hope* Chest "

SECOND-HAND FURNITURE

Second-hand furniture presents all kinds of exciting possibilities. Freed from ugly mouldings and clumsy handles, it can be given new beauty by stripping and painting with flat white paint. Decorate, if you wish, with simple designs, using artists' colours and a good camel-hair brush. Victorian what-nots can be converted easily into bedside tables or dumb waiters. Ornate Victorian mirrors, which can often be bought for a song, stripped and painted white or any pastel colour, can be hung over a low table or shelf to make most attractive " dressing-tables."

A closely-fitting cover of light-coloured felt with an over-hanging scalloped edge can transform an ugly table and bring it into harmony with the decoration of a modern room.

Cutting down the height of tables and chairs is often useful—a charming low tea table or coffee table can be made from an out-of-date occasional table ; a chair can sometimes be made much more comfortable by cutting the back legs a little shorter than the front. Box mattresses removed from old beds and put on to four blocks make good divan beds.

Don't, however, pay absurd prices for second-hand furniture. Collect and use any cast-off family pieces, or search for real bargains in junk shops. Prices of much second-hand furniture have never been so high, and auction fever can attack even the most balanced of individuals, so beware the second-hand " bargain " that may prove more of a worry than an asset.

LINENS

Beautiful linens are missing from wartime trousseaux, but a minimum of utility sheets, pillow cases and towels can be put into stock, and their value enhanced by carefully marking with embroidery or cross stitch. A series of French mottoes, for instance, cross-stitched along the borders in scarlet, makes a set of utility hand towels look very distinguished.

Unrationed net and lace can be made into elegant table mats and frilled slip covers for small cushions.

BOOKS

Prices of books are not exorbitant, and they always have a decorative as well as an interest value when you furnish. Attractively shelved to display to good effect the colours of their bindings, they can form the chief decoration of a room. Books on furnishing, interior decoration and home management are particularly good purchases for the bride, and the collection of old or unusual cookery books is a fascinating hobby.

KITCHEN EQUIPMENT

Kitchen equipment should be collected gradually as and when it is available. Buy the best you can find, because for cookery, as for all crafts, good tools are necessary. There are good earthenware dishes and oven glassware in the shops from time to time, and cooking equipment of very good quality can often be found at sales and market stalls.

Turn off that light, unless it's really necessary.

Salvage is essential to the Battle for Freedom.

By SUSAN DRAKE

Thirty-one Kitchen Beauty Hints
One for Each Day of the Month

1. The next time you prepare tomatoes for the table, wash your hands with some of the parts you normally throw away. Tomato juice whitens the skin.

2. Washing dishes or clothes? Then take time off to wipe off your make-up and cream your face. The cream will prevent the steam from enlarging the pores, the cream-plus-steam will give the skin a pore-deep cleansing. Steamy work over, remove the cream and wipe the face with skin tonic, rose water or complexion milk.

3. A bout of cooking often spells ruin to an attractive hair-do, unless you decide to use the steam as an ally by carefully pinning your curls and tying them up in a scarf.

4. A few minutes to spare and half a pound of prunes in the cupboard? Then make this Swedish complexion drink. Split and stone the prunes, put them in a saucepan with a quart of water, an ounce of sugar and the rind of an orange or lemon. Boil rapidly for two minutes, simmer for half an hour, strain, and, if possible, add the juice of an orange or lemon. Serve cold.

5. When peeling potatoes, set aside a piece of peeled potato and rub this over the fingers when work is finished. It will remove stains.

6. Here's a tip for glossy hair. Add a heaped tablespoon of oatmeal to a glass of water. Leave overnight, strain off the milky liquid and drink it down. Try this every day for a month.

7. Sour milk may be a domestic tragedy, but it is also a beauty find. Strain off the lumpy curds and use the clear liquid which remains to wipe over face, neck and hands. The lactic acid it contains will bleach the skin and whiten a sallow neck. Keep the face wet with the liquid for five minutes.

8. For the sake of your teeth, finish every meal with something hard and tooth-cleansing—a piece of raw carrot or celery, or a hard crust.

9. Your ankles are swollen after a long day on your feet? Then soak the feet for fifteen minutes in hot water to which you have added a cupful of vinegar.

10. For hot, tired feet, use a handful of kitchen salt and cold water.

11. *Do* eat the skins of apples, cucumbers and potatoes, and the green as well as the white parts of celery and leeks. Eat all the raw and lightly cooked vegetables you can.

12. *Don't* eat more than you must of fried and twice-cooked foods, starchy puddings and pastries. Avoid strong tea and strong coffee.

13. The next time you have cucumber salad, save the end piece and rub the cut surface over face, neck and hands, allowing the juice to dry on the skin. Cucumber juice is whitening and astringent.

14. Perhaps you are making a batch of rolls tea cakes? Save some of the yeast for your look A couple of teaspoonfuls dissolved in a cupful milk makes a pore-cleansing, skin-refining fac mask.

15. If you've got to watch your figure, remem ber that a pint of beer contains 225 calories (th fuel equivalent of 2½ slices of bread), and that or ounce toffee or two small biscuits equal 1c calories.

16. For rough hands, try rubbing with ra mutton suet. A little of this rubbed over th hands before doing "wet" work will protec them.

17. Apple juice is said to prevent wrinkles. Ru the cut side of a piece of apple over face an neck and allow the juice to dry on.

18. A pinch of kitchen salt on your toothbrus night and morning, will tone up spongy gums an whiten and preserve the teeth.

19. If your skin is oily, try adding one part fir oatmeal to four parts of your face powder. paste of oatmeal and milk used in place of soa will chase away blackheads.

20. A little vinegar in the rinsing water on wash ing day will prevent your hands from becomir rough or puffy.

21. Use a little household ammonia when wasl ing your hair-brush and comb, to keep them swee and clean.

22. A paste of flour and water will discipli unruly eyebrows. Spread the paste over the ey brows in the direction you want them to li Leave on as long *(Continued on page* **10**

Good-night My Son

GOOD-NIGHT, my son; sweet waking in the morn!
Sleep softly in your narrow, rocky bed.
I go with unbowed head as you would wish—
Life's laughter was your legacy to me.

But I shall always feel poignant regret
That ere I saw the pattern of your life
Unfold to show the man I knew could be,
The book was closed; your pattern changed—and mine!

For nineteen lovely years I watched you grow
Through passing phases from the child to youth.
I heard the breaking timbre of your voice,
And marked the keen maturing of your mind.

Then just as comradeship between us throve
Came war. You went—so gay and confident
Of life, of future years. Now I recall
How I sewed buttons on your battledress

And that first stripe you had. As I stitched it,
You bade me wait (I did, with fear) until
The day you came, so young, so proud, to show
That one brave star upon your shoulder-strap.

Then swift time did excel itself to race
Through weeks, faith holding fast to hope, until
Those last brief days, each hour remembered now!
And after waiting—silence—and the end.

How true the lovely thought, conceived in grief,
That you and life are one. That life in you
Can never die, but lives serene and gay
Beyond my falt'ring gaze. For life is His

Who gave us life. And in encircling time
In other guise, in other climes, we shall
Give greeting each to each. I think that I
Shall always feel that old familiar tug

That my heart gave when you came hast'ning home
From school—from Army camps! And know your laugh—
The careless, loving jests you flung at me—
Shall recognise your kisses on my cheek!

Good-night, my dear. Your manhood here is o'er.
Its cup of life drained dry to the last drop
Almost before the cup itself was formed!
Good-night, my son. You will awake with Dawn!
                    E. Wheatland.

Back the Attack – through War Savings.

Coughs and sneezes must be prevented from spreading diseases.

How's your Fuel Conscience?

Forever Walking Free

Written by an American,
a story of London with a twist that
may come as a shock

by
MacKinlay Kantor

THEN the lights twisted across the clouds, fighting to find something and hold it, and guns started up in the nearest park; resentful bright flashes reflected behind cardboard buildings across the way. Joan felt bereft and vulnerable, there in Wycombe Road—the roadway itself was so wide it seemed like a moorland, unroofed and exposed.

Ahead of her the little witch-lights of pocket torches carried in other people's hands began to blink and bob more rapidly; other people were running, and Joan thought she'd better run, too.

She left the bus stop where she had been vainly waiting, and sought the shelter of shops and boarded-up, bombed-out hotels in her flight. She held close to the shadow of buildings; already, as the defiant battery in the park barked and slammed, flak was raining on roofs and in the street itself. Joan wondered about a shelter—she'd better find the nearest shelter, though she hated being down there in dankness with frightened children and heavy-breathing old ladies.

Between the crash of guns and the remoter, hollower *pak-pak-pak* of shell-bursts in the sky, she heard people laughing nervously across the road. A boy and a girl, both laughing and fleeing as the artillery banged more rapidly and defiantly. That distant girl was crying, "Oooh, Billy—Billy, Billy, *Billy!*" and Joan heard the rush of other frightened feet above the scuffle of her own running.

She heard someone else cry, "Next turning—it's in *there*," and they must mean that there was a shelter nearby, and so she should bend her path across that open road, though she feared to leave the comfort of the buildings.

It started squealing in the wet clouds, a piercing whistle. *Fooooo . . .* the squealing was aiming right at her, and she felt one of her stockings jerk below the suspender—oh, another ladder!—and the next stockings she bought would necessarily be of that awful utility kind.

She was worrying more about her stockings than about anything else in the world—more than she worried about the whistling sound that stung her ears.

Everything became bright. She couldn't believe there was such brightness anywhere; it was like a thousand lightning flashes rolled into one. Joan imagined that she was away off somewhere on a balcony in a stage-set, and from that high post of observation she saw her thin little figure in Wycombe Road still running stubbornly, throwing out her legs in that funny way that all women ran, skipping and sliding.

In the next second she knew, "That was bomb. It fell. It went off right *here*," and in wide-awake understanding she recognised the enormous noise that had smothered her, smothered all Bloomsbury and all London. She thought again, "Never touched me. It never did! All you have to do is not be frightened; then you'll be all right, you see," and she nodded at her own wisdom as she kept rushing on.

An avenging flash from the park guns showed her a turning at the left. She remembered that—sometimes she had crossed along that narrow roadway, but always in broad daylight, when she was on her way to her job at the M.O.I. There was an archway—a very old archway, part of an ancient building, curved and protecting. The lane went underneath like a tunnel twisting through a mountain, and below that arch anyone could find safety from shrapnel.

She skidded into the alley; the blackness of the tunnel loomed ahead. Shrapnel came down; in the last look she had at Wycombe Road, she saw dazzling little fragments spattering amid the metal sparks of their impact on the pavement. Bombs couldn't hurt her—Joan Warrock had demonstrated that; but flak was something else.

She tripped over a kerb just under the archway, and went down on her knee, and certainly that fall must have finished the other stocking. A voice said to her, "Hey, sister! What gives?" and a man was there. Through the winking, gasping exhaustion which claimed her Joan looked up and saw (Continued on page 150)

The noise and brightness smothered her. She ran. Under an archway she met him. That's how it began

Illustrated by Phil Dorman

Home Food is the stuff to give the Troops – entertain our Allies.
Keep the Home Fires burning – but don't put on too much coal!
Give your children the gargle habit – "cold" weather is here.

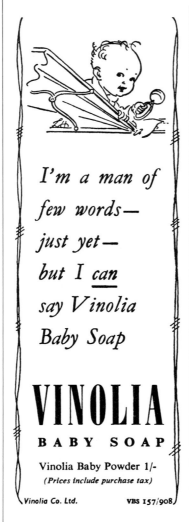

Forever Walking Free
(Continued from page 148)

him bending down—she saw the orange dot of a cigarette.

"I'm all right, thank you."

"Here. Let me help you up."

He drew her to her feet; he could have dragged her away, this strange young man, he could have done anything to her right then, and she would have been unable to resist.

"Quite a show, sister! I've been here watching it."

She realised that the nearest guns had ceased firing; faintly the realm beneath the heavy old archway showed in greenish-white; she knew what that meant. A giant flare hung in the sky somewhere at hand. Night-fighters—R.A.F. night-fighters—were up.

Joan saw a gleam of brass on the dark coat beside her. "What are you—R.A.F.?" she asked, and that was rather silly, because already he had called her "sister" in a good American voice.

"Hell, no—U.S.A."

"I should have known," she said, and giggled.

"Why?" He was laughing, too. "I mean—how come you should have known I was an American?"

"Well, naturally. Your voice."

"Bet you can't tell what part of the States I'm from."

And she felt a cigarette pressed between her fingers.

"Let me see, now. You're not ——" she hesitated. "You're not from below the Mason and Dixon Line, are you?"

He chuckled. She liked his chuckle. It sounded light and merry and childish; he might be a lot of fun, this chap.

"Mason and Dixon line? Say, where'd you ever pick that up?"

"You're not the first American I've met," said Joan flippantly. . . . See what his face was like now. In the gloom she thrust the cigarette between her lips and lifted her head questioningly.

His lighter flared. In the bright wash of rosy flame, before her exploring cigarette half poked it out, she saw his face. He was young— not much older than she—he couldn't be more than twenty or twenty-one.

He was staring at Joan seriously, examining her face just as attentively as she had looked at his, and she wondered if he liked it.

"Well, well! A blonde." The lighter snapped shut.

Joan drew in the smoke eagerly. "Thank you. I like American cigarettes ever so much!"

"I like you—ever so much," he said boldly.

Guns in the park started up again; for a few minutes it was so noisy you could scarcely hear yourself think. The American had his hand around Joan's arm, drawing her back against the wall.

"Why did you do that?"

"Just to comfort you," he said simply. "I was afraid you'd be scared at all the shooting."

"Oh, I've heard ever so much shooting. You should have been here," she told him pityingly, "during the blitz."

"I'll bet that was something." He still held her arm. She didn't mind, really. Something about his slim, quiet, ruddy-browed face . . . maybe he wouldn't start pawing— not right away, at least.

"What's your name, honey?"

"Joan Warrock. What's yours?"

"Menton—Staff-Sergeant J. A. —Buster to you."

"Buster? That's your nickname?"

"Everybody always called me that. But you know how it is, in the Army—everybody always calls you by your last name."

Now all the firing, bombs and shell explosions alike, seemed moving fatefully away to the east— east and south, down the Thames.

"There goes Jerry," said Joan. "Hope he doesn't come back. What a noisy night!"

"A couple fell close to here," said S/Sgt. Menton.

"Quite so. That big one nearly got me."

He took a fresh cigarette for himself and lighted it deliberately. Again she saw his ruddy face; the jaunty, humorous eyebrows, and well-moulded mouth. . . . "Oh, not half bad," she thought, and wanted to giggle again. Suddenly she was selfishly glad that Jerry had come over early this night, while she was on her way home. "On leave?" she asked.

"Well," he told her, "you can say that I'm off ops, at least."

"How many missions have you done?"

"Eleven."

"Are you a pilot?"

He explained, "Look here, I'm not British; I'm not R.A.F. We don't have sergeant-pilots in the

American heavy bombers. I'm just a waist-gunner."

"Waist-gunner. . . . Just what does that mean?"

"Means I'm good with waists," said S/Sgt. Menton, and he put his arm firmly around her waist.

Joan turned her face hurriedly away, though he hadn't struggled to reach it—not yet, anyway. "Come, now," she cried severely, and she let her body stiffen. "You're really quite nice, you know."

Immediately he relaxed his arm. "The lady," he said, "is always the doctor—or ought to be. Where I come from."

"And where's that?"

"Call me Buster," he said softly. "I haven't heard anyone call me Buster for a long time."

"Okay, Buster. Where do you come from, Buster?"

"Quincy, Illinois. Gee," he said, "that sure sounds swell. Your calling me Buster." He took a deep breath. "Look. You in a hurry? I mean—were you going anywhere, or anything?"

Joan said, "Going home."

"Well, look. How about our stopping and maybe having a drink and something to eat?"

She cried in amazement, "Why, this must be the very first time you've been up to London!"

"Oh, I've been here scads of times."

"Well, then, you should know that it's past closing-time. All the pubs were closed two hours ago; and supper clubs can't serve drink after eleven."

He sighed. "Sister, I know your town better than you do."

"Then—you know a place?"

"I'll say so. Swell place. It's run just for folks like us. They're still open; they're open all night. The liquor's swell, the food's A-1 and they've got a swell band."

She was weakening. Swell liquor, swell food—and a band. . . .

"I say—is it far?"

"Over here in Stokemore Place. The Blue Polly, they call it."

In faint-echoing darkness, Joan felt her forehead wrinkle as she attempted recollection. Seemed as if she—"The Blue Polly," she whispered. "I've heard of it."

He was tall and slender and demanding, standing beside her in the midnight. "Come on, Joan. Let's go. You'll like it, I promise you."

He swung her around and marched her rapidly away. His feet seemed very certain and assured.

The court swung right towards Black Bush Square and something must have fallen here, too—or else maybe it was only the impact of the great bomb which had dropped in Wycombe Road, the bomb which sought to blot Joan Warrock into nothingness. Glass was thick underfoot; long silver slivers, fine dust and cornered fragments.

"Go easy," the girl kept saying to Buster Menton. "I shan't have a shoe to wear if I cut these!"

"You'll be all right," Buster assured her. He gave her arm a little squeeze, and Joan didn't mind.

Air-raid wardens and policemen and other people were poking all around and over a big mound of rubble that half blocked the road opposite one corner of Black Bush Square. Men called orders and directions to one another; they didn't pay any attention to Buster and Joan as they went past.

"Those flats!" Joan gasped to Buster Menton. "Remember? You should, if you know this district so well. That big block of flats, right there—the whole corner's gone. A lot of people must have been killed!"

"I know," said Buster. "Folks do get killed in a war."

It might have seemed callous, the way he marshalled her past. Still, what could the two of them have done? Nothing. The Civil Defence Service had people especially trained for jobs like that.

A short, squat man wavered on the pavement ahead of them. He didn't seem to want to move . . . . a man in a dressing-gown or something like that, and he was bareheaded. "I was inside," he said coolly to Buster and Joan. "In that flat. Second storey up." He pointed. "Inside there. . . ."

Buster halted, and dragged Joan to a stop beside him. "Anything we can do for you, Mister?"

"Sorry," said the other. "Not a thing. I'm waiting around for awhile. That's all, thank you—waiting around——" He drifted behind them, a squat, grey shape.

"Poor fellow," said Joan. "A bit balmy, maybe."

"Flak happy, I guess," Buster muttered. "That's what they call it in the Eighth Air Force. Well,

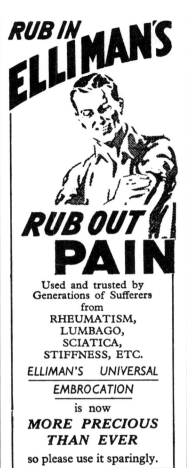

Take full advantage of the nation's Immunisation services.

Save rubber – pump your cycle tyres.

Save a pound of coal, put a Hun in a hole.

Forever Walking Free
(Continued from page 151)

come on. Here's Stokemore Place."

Joan shrilled with excitement. Buster broke into a bright peal of laughter. He turned quickly, as if delighted beyond words at her enthusiasm, and bending down, he kissed her full on the mouth. Then, before she could protest through the immediate astonishment of it all, he had pulled her along to the door of the Blue Polly. Faintly, they could hear the beat of jazz.

"Buster, boy!" Joan Warrock heard herself exclaiming. "I've never seen the like, really! And I thought Stokemore Place was practically all bombed out!"

A long room beyond the vestibule was choked with people, and others were lined up three-deep in front of the Blue Polly's bar. Such a bar Joan had not seen for years—not since early in the war. Bottles shimmered, in translucent yellows and browns and reds before the mirror; believe it or not, there was even a gigantic pyramid of champagne bottles.

There was a preponderance of R.A.F. and other British Services at the tables; very few Americans. Still, the beaming waiter who came towards them seemed to know Buster Menton, for he smiled and nodded and bowed an extra time or two.

Stowed behind their little table, Joan turned to look quizzically at Buster. She saw that he was as neat as a charm; just from his face and his voice, she had known he would look like that. His blouse was well pressed and well fitting; he had his Eighth Air Force patch and his combat wings, and the inevitable row of medal ribbons which all these American fliers wore.

"Like it, Joan?"

"It's heaven," she said. "I didn't know there was a place like this in all London."

"I'm glad you like it. Remember—I prophesied you would?"

"Righto. And won't you call that waiter back? I'm famished."

The waiter gave them a menu which they studied. No jugged hare or Spam—not an ounce of such stuff listed. There was chicken and salad, and cold sliced lamb, and shrimps—actually a shrimp salad. "In season," said Joan Warrock, completely awed, "they'd have oysters, too, wouldn't they?"

"Absolutely. But I wouldn't eat them, even for a bet."

"I thought," said she, "that all Americans loved oysters."

"Not me. I'm from the Middle West. We don't have them out there. But "—he spoke as if with all assurance—"one of the very next meals I have, it's going to be sweet corn."

"But you can't get any here, can you?"

"Certainly not. But *I* can get roasting ears."

Joan persisted in wonderment. "Where? At your Base? Where are you stationed?"

He looked at her for a moment. "Brookwood," he said.

Somehow the word placed a chill on her heart; she didn't know quite why. "I suppose," she said, "I shouldn't have asked that, should I? 'A slip of the lip may sink a ship.'"

"Ever hear of my place?"

"Oh, yes . . . Brookwood. I must have known someone stationed there before." She frowned a little. "It's in Surrey, isn't it?"

"That's right." He grew more expansive. "Lots of Eighth Air Force fellows down there. R.A.F., too. R.C.A.F. and Australians—some Poles and Czechs, too."

Politely she put her slender fingers against his mouth. "Now, now, darling. Mustn't talk about your Base."

He grinned; he kissed her fingers before she took them away. "Let's talk about you, Joan Warrock. Where do you work?"

"M.O.I. I'm on the telephones."

He asked, "Night shift?"

"Oh, no. I was at a party tonight. A girl-friend's flat. A great lot of boys there—from the Services, you know. But they—well, I'll be perfectly honest; the chap I was supposed to be with—he got fresh, you see. I didn't care much for the party, anyway. So I just slipped out to catch a bus, and then the sirens went. . . . Then I met you."

Buster Menton asked, "Sorry?"

"Not a bit of it. I like you."

"I love you," he said calmly.

She threw him a quick glance, and opened her mouth to say something pert and cynical. But—somehow, the way he was looking at her——

"Buster," she whispered. "You shouldn't say things like that."

"Why not?"

"Because it's——"

Assurance now
. and for tomorrow

The Dorothy Gray preparations you are using today
such care . . . are identical with those you used before.
The same fine quality ingredients are blended with
meticulous care, to exactly the same formulas.
Dorothy Gray skin-care is such that had we not been able
in any particular to maintain our standards, we should have
withdrawn the preparations.

Dorothy Gray

Dorothy Gray is a Registered Trade Mark

Saving each day helps the war on its way.
Sow now for winter needs.

DORVILLE

FOR THE WELL-DRESSED WOMAN

*Tailored Suits &
Dresses, Pullovers*

Dorville models are at most first-class stores
(in the Knightsbridge area at Harvey Nichols)

ROSE & BLAIRMAN LTD. DORVILLE HOUSE MARGARET ST. LONDON W1

TO PUT THE FLAVOUR
INTO THAT MEAT PIE
USE . . .

FOSTER CLARK'S SOUPS

Forever Walking Fre[e]

(Continued from page 152)

"I do love you, Joan. I've be[en] looking for you, I guess."

"Where?" she whispered; a[s] the coloured orchestra was mak[ing] a great deal of noise with its tru[m]pets, yet somehow her whis[per] reached his ears.

He said, "All over Britain. I[I] walked around in blackout a[nd] daylight, and I didn't find any[one] like you."

She wanted to know what [he] liked especially about her.

"Well, first it was the way y[ou] came towards me—there in t[he] alley, kind of—and then your voi[ce] I've always liked blondes. A[nd] you've got a kind of funny lit[tle] cute way; your voice is sort [of] warm and—I guess I could ta[lk] baby-talk to you without mu[ch] trouble. I like your legs," [he] added.

The way he said it all—she w[as] very near to tears. "Buster, [I] swear you've never really seen [my] legs."

"Yes, I have. On the way ov[er] here to this table. I walked [be]hind you, and I liked everythi[ng] about you. That suit is sort [of] worn, but I liked the way that [it] hung—and—well, the way it sort [of] swung when you walked." His fa[ce] was red, but he seemed determin[ed] to tell her how much she was [at]tracting him.

Joan waited a minute; then, fe[el]ing as if she had made one [of] the greatest decisions of her exi[st]ence, she reached over with [her] left hand and let him kiss [her] lightly on the fingers again.

"I'll eat them," he said.

"No," she giggled, seeming [to] feel that she actually loved hi[m] too, just as he declared that [he] loved her. "Here comes our fo[od] . . . ham, Buster; honestly[—I] couldn't have believed it!" S[he] spoke quite loudly; the orche[stra] had stopped playing for a seco[nd] and people at the nearer tab[les] up and wander? I remember so[me]times when I was a kid—I me[an] a little kid back in Quincy—I'd [see] the sunrise on the old Mississippi, pink and blue and kind of colou[rs] like soft candy or precious sto[ne] or something, and I'd want to [go] places."

She cried, in misty delight, "C[h] say some more, Buster dear—s[ay] some more things like that! [I]

Forever Walking Free

ke poetry. Where would you like
wander?"

"I'll take you," he said, "side
y side with me . . . we will
ander. Just over rooftops—we
uld start right now, and forget
bout the war and everything,'and
st keep walking. Go right on
st—go out there in all that pink
d mist—and we could walk on
e ocean—you know," he looked
wn at her blissfully, "like Jesus
the Bible. I remember that,
Sunday school, how He walked
the water. . . . Then we could
rn around again, and go any-
here we took a notion. Quincy;
d sure like to show you Quincy.
bet ten bucks you never saw any-
ing that remotely resembled the
ississippi River! We could have
cnics in the brush over on the
issouri side, and then just keep
going . . . Yellowstone Park,
d geysers and painted rocks and
ings—I always did want to go
ere——"

A man was coming towards
em; a police-constable—he came
ght towards them; he lifted
rough the dawn, he didn't step
t of their way or anything; he
emed to go right between them,
d yet his body never brushed
an Warrock's.

She felt dizzy. "Buster," she
ied softly, after the policeman
as past, "that bobby—he didn't
ven see you!"

"Didn't see you, either," said
uster. "How's about it, babe?
re you coming with me to Quincy
d Yellowstone National?"

She stopped abruptly. She didn't
now why, quite . . . that mention
Brookwood was haunting her
emory; now it began to come
earer—she had gone there, she
d been there once, Sylvia Wil-
ams had taken her.

She saw in her mind a wide place
grass and rhododendrons, with
e train running on a Surrey hill-
de up above that valley——

"Where——?" The words were
rd for her; she fought them out
ere smiling at her, but not un-
ndly.

"Okay," said S/Sgt. Menton.
We eat!"

"Buster," she asked, in the
rest whisper this time, "you said
at the Blue Polly was open prac-
cally all night. Well, does the
orchestra stay on and play—till
dawn, maybe?"

He said; with his mouth full of
cold ham, "Absolutely!" and nodded his head violently.

"Well—let's actually stay all
night, shall we? And eat—and
drink—and be merry?"

It was close to dawn indeed,
when they crept past the thick
blast wall into Stokemore Place,
and moved contentedly east to
Marston Street.

Buster walked close against Joan
Warrock, his hip tight to hers, her
hand snuggled in the angle of his
arm, as he told her about his last
mission with the U.S. bombers. It
was over the Ruhr, he said, and
the flak was bad that day. They
got a burst right alongside the
waist of his B-17 before they
crossed the Dutch coastline, coming back, and that was why the
other fellows had to lift Buster out
of the Fortress when they came
back to their Base.

"But you look all right, darling.
You don't look as though you were
wounded, or anything."

He said, honestly, "I feel swell,
too. I really never felt so well before. Not ever. And now especially, having found you——"

They turned up Marston Street,
and saw a far-away cluster of fire-
engines and dark-bodied workers,
toiling around wreckage through
the first colour of a smoky sunrise.

"Now, especially," he said, "I
want to keep you with me, just
like this, and keep walking. Always."

"I'd like to," she said, happily
and sleepily. "But I can still catch
a bit of shut-eye before work, if
I hurry back to my room. War's
got to be won!"

Buster said, "Sure, but not by us."

Even through the indolent dream
that possessed her, his words had a
certain angry impact. She drew
her yellow head away and looked
up seriously. "Why so? We're
all in it, you know."

"Look," he said, with the dawn
growing paler and pinker on his
lean face, "I want to take you
everywhere. Didn't you ever feel
like that—like you wanted to get
of her mouth; the question came
as a faint scream. "Where did
you say you were—stationed?"

The same kind face, the same
jaunty eyebrows; he was there; he
hadn't faded, he was still adoring
her with all his youth and strength.
"Brookwood, in Surrey."

"Yes. I know." She managed
to say the rest: "*Let go my
arm!*"

He said, "Darling. Don't be
afraid! There's nothing to be afraid
of. I mean that—honestly."

"Brookwood's a—a——" She
couldn't look at him any more.
"A military cemetery."

She began to whisper her accusa-
tion—the discovery, the incredible
mystery of it all—her tongue was
running on and on, and later he
told her that people often found it
like that. "O God," she said,
"it's a cemetery! I remember now;
I was there with Sylvia Williams
—her fiancé was killed in the
R.A.F., he's buried there——"

The short, squat man who mur-
mured that he had been in the
wrecked flats; how well, how terribly she knew what manner of
man he must have been . . . the
Blue Polly itself; now she remembered that, too. It went when
most of Stokemore Place went, in
May, 1941. All those people in it,
scores of boys and girls and other
folks, when the bomb came down.
. . . And that other bomb—this
night in Wycombe Road—she kept
running, she ran and ran, she said
it never touched her, and then she
sped into the turning under the
archway, and Buster helped her to
her feet after she fell.

"Oh, heaven and earth, oh, oh,
oh, I can't believe it; that man,
that policeman never saw you, he
never saw me either—now here are
more people coming towards us; ah,
they don't see us, they will never
see us, they will walk through us
as if we were air——"

"Joan," he whispered, "you're
frightened, aren't you, hon? Hold
tight to me. You'll soon be—you
won't be scared any longer. And
then—we start wandering off, just
anywhere in God's green world
that you want to go. It doesn't
matter. Anywhere."

Presently he asked, "Feel better
now?"

"Yes," she whispered. "Buster,
put your arms around me."

"Always," he said, "always,"
and they started on again.

Youthful frills and deep pleats from shoulder to hem on an attractive floral rayon dress, which Maxlim makes in a wide variety of colours. 7 coupons. £6 3s. 6d. from Bourne & Hollingsworth

Maxlim's Utility finger-length smock and adjustable side-pleated skirt in many lovely colours. 8 coupons. £3 1s. 5d. from Bourne & Hollingsworth

In dull turquoise crêpe, a Hanovia Utility dress has a wrap-over front which ties with a bow at the back. 7 coupons. £2 18s. 11d.

The less you spend, the sooner the end.

Don't waste the smallest thing – there's a use for everything.

More paper needed! Won't YOU help?

FOR THE MOTHER-TO-BE

In dull tartan checks, a well-cut Utility tweed coat (below, right) can be worn slimly belted or as a concealing swagger. Treasure Cot. 18 coupons. £4 10s. 6d. The little boy wears a Buster Utility suit from Treasure Cot, blue and white striped shirt and lined trousers in butcher blue. 4 coupons. 10s. 2d. Size 16.

Chalk-stripes are used in an interesting way on this pleated woollen frock and its matching jacket in red, navy, brown or green. Individually made to measure by Du Barry. 19 coupons. £12 14s. 10d.

Spend on Savings.

Rubber saved helps erase the Axis.

It's an all-in war ; save more paper.

in the road, on the bus, the shops, with "Have y¢ news of Martin?" . . . Sue happy at her hospital? . . . "Where's Tim?— don't you know?" . . . Su¢ denly—or it seems sudd once it hits you in the face¢ we in this banned area a¢ with all leave stopped, are little world of the midd aged and the elderly. . . .

But this is not all. In¢ these placid valleys, drowsi¢ villages, small country tow¢ the roaring tide of the N¢ World has surged—and ho¢ The scene is dense with oliv¢ drab or greenish-khaki u¢ forms, the switchback cou¢ try roads are streaked by jee¢ and lorries (and, believe m¢ streak is the word), and the¢ is the sound of transatlant¢ voices mingling with the slo¢ soft voices of the west cou¢ try now. California, he¢ they come. . . .

Now, I have the happy f¢ tune to possess a vast cl¢ of American cousins, thr¢ generations of them, in fa¢

KATHLEEN WALLACE surveys the America

in the West Country, and decides th¢

the Funny Thing is US

A TRANSFORMATION scene has taken place in our part of the west country. It is as visible and startling as a landslide; at least, if you come to it suddenly, as I did, after an autumn and winter in town. When first we came to Mid-somer Gabriel, the village and the whole neigh-bourhood were full of young people of under-Service age, and gay good times they had together while sharing the local war-effort in all its forms and branches. The stream has been dwindling, of course, drawn off gradually, but now time has caught up with us.

The young people have gone. It is we, the parents, who are left; and who greet one another

and in the by-gone times of easy travelling, ¢ shared one another's lives frequently and co¢ siderably, and with never-ending enjoyment. S¢ it was merely natural that before I came ba¢ to the west country I should get into touch wi¢ the London headquarters of the American R¢ Cross and offer my services in any capacity whi¢ they could use down here. The warm thanks a¢ friendliness with which a voice at the oth¢ end of the wire answered me, made me feel almo¢ ashamed.

But I didn't need to get into touch with hea¢ quarters here: I hadn't unpacked before someo¢ rushed at me with:

Illustrated by Emett

"They say you have a lot of American relations—you'll work at the American Canteen, won't you?"

"Yes, rather!"

The next thing is the news that an official of the American Red Cross will meet a representative number of us and give us some idea of what is wanted. Three of us go from Midsomer, and as the meeting is at a house many miles inland and well off bus-routes, a voluntary worker is detailed to scoop us all up in her car.

We arrive rather late, to find ourselves in the great billiard-room of a country house, where a half-circle of British women are established in the curved window-seat, and the young representative of the American Red Cross, in her neat uniform, faces us. She explains to us the working of this vast, new club, and what is expected of us. She speaks in a very soft, southern voice, and as she speaks, I look round the semicircle of listening faces, and wonder whether it is all more comic or more dismaying? . . . Timid, shrinking faces, which are only too evidently visualising These Americans as something seen through zoo-bars, and my dear, don't go too near—they bite, you know! . . . Staunch, battle-axe faces, alert, eager and energetic—but ye gods! how forbidding . . . I wonder, not for the first time, why your true British matron must wear hand-knitted woollen jumpers when she is a solid 44 (measurement, please, not age), why she

affects a beret, a form of headgear which I, personally, feel only becomes the troops, and the younger troops at that. And why, because you live in the country, you need let your figure get completely out of hand and disdain the use of cold cream when available? Why, in short, you should represent, in all honesty and alacrity, the will to serve your fellow-men, and necessarily look like something drawn by the pen of Sillince or Pont? . . .

I am roused from these unseemly and straying reflections by the voice of one of the workers:

"We shall never understand what the men are saying," she announced with a whinnying giggle. "Their accent . . ."

She does not mean to be offensive. She is merely exhibiting that supreme obtuseness to the existence of tact which is one of our national traits. The American woman smiles and says:

"I know. It is difficult at first, but I think you'll get used to it. Have you," she adds with that simplicity which, in itself, constitutes dignity, "any difficulty in understanding *me*?"

There is a shocked murmur of assurance, but the original speaker sticks to her guns with:

"But they don't all talk like *you*! . . ."

Finally, the Red Cross superintendent tries to make one thing clear. I feel acutely that she is dismayed by the sight of the material offered her (us, in fact), and is making the best of it.

"Our boys are a long way from home," she says simply. "You may think them rather rough . . . but don't mind that. Think of yourselves as their hostesses. They—our boys—appreciate the motherly touch. . . ." (In her soft drawl, the words come out as "the murtherly turch.")

I look round the circle once more, and think, as I wrote to Martin that night, "My heart sure bleeds for the boys, buddy! . . ."

Each village in this district is to send one shift of voluntary canteen workers a week; and the night for Midsomer Gabriel comes round. An army lorry swoops round the village and collects us all and we go rocketing and swaying over the long main road.

I have worked among a good many groups of women in two wars, and I know most of the small tribulations and teacup-storms which are supposed to belong exclusively to Women at War. So I will put it on record that I have never met a group who could laugh at themselves as can the group in which I now find myself.

Paper is needed more than ever; turn out your desks.

Every little bit of tin tells in the total — for Victory.

Preserve All Paper Extra Rigorously.

NOW that new ideas and hopes for education are in the air, it is time for us all to consider the kind of teachers we want for our children. We think of teachers, in England at any rate, with a rather queer mixture of respect and contempt. We need to sort out our ideas a little more and consider whether the conditions we are offering in the schools are good enough to attract the kind of people that will be best for the children.

On the whole I think we all realise that it isn't, largely, a question of money. We don't want people going in for teaching chiefly because it's a well-paid job, although it ought to be paid well enough to allow a civilised and unworried life. Teachers ought, I believe, to be paid rather more than they are now, in order to compensate for the late start they have at earning their living, and the expense their training involves. However, money is, definitely, a secondary consideration. What is important, I believe, is that every teacher should have the chance of training, regardless of the family's ability to afford a college education. A great many good teachers are lost owing to the fact that they can't afford the years of preparation involved.

Another extremely important point to be discussed is the question of marriage. Wartime has altered things, but in peace it is usual for women teachers to be obliged to resign on marriage. This does seem extremely unwise, partly because it prevents a great many people who would be good parents from marrying at all, and partly because it deprives the children of some good teachers. There are, certainly, some adjustments needed where married teachers are concerned, but on the whole it is not a good plan to try to keep the teaching profession celibate. Of the young teachers who trained with me, a great many married and gave up their work (some married secretly and kept on, but found it very worrying!), while others decided to keep their work, and later on regretted this. Surely it is unreasonable to expect such sacrifices, especially when they may react harmfully on the pupils. Certainly marriage is by no means a necessity for happiness, and many spinsters lead full and satisfactory lives, but generally it does tend to broaden the outlook and sympathies and to help towards a balanced life.

Then there are the questions of permanence in the

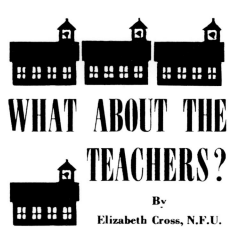

WHAT ABOUT THE TEACHERS?

By

Elizabeth Cross, N.F.U.

profession, the entry of teachers straight from college with no other experience, and the carrying on unt the day of retirement. As a general rule teacher are chosen, almost automatically, from the studiou and academic pupils, who pass their exams, go t college and then return as teachers. They live in world of school, and ar often extremely ignorar of any circles outsid their own particular one which may be culture but is sometimes narrow This tendency to remai in the groove is fostere by the pension system which necessitates teacher putting in s many years at certai approved schools in orde to earn the retiremen pension. In some privat schools where no pensio scheme exists you com across more enterprisin; teachers who have give; up school work for a fev years and tried some othe jobs, so broadening thei outlook, but generall once a teacher, always teacher. Or, conversely once you leave a teachin; post and try your luck elsewhere, it is very hard to go back again.

This seems a great pity from the children's poin of view, because it means that they are losing th chance of being taught by many lively and know ledgeable people. To give an example from m own case, I am a far better person now, after severa different jobs that have taken me to different coun tries and among all kinds of people (jobs that hav included manual labour as well as brainwork), thar I was when I first left my training college, yet think it unlikely that I should get half such a goo post as a similarly trained teacher who has gone on teaching without a break, and I should stand no chance of a pension. Yet I guarantee to interest a sorts of children, to teach with practically no apparatus, and to see that a good time is hac by all !

There is a cruel old saying, " Those that can, do Those that can't, teach." Now, it is time that we invited some of those doers into the schools—we can

Parents

MOTHERS' ENQUIRY SERVICE: The Good Housekeeping Children's Doctor answers by letter questions on mothers' and children's general health, diet, etc., and a selection of letters is published in the magazine. Replies cannot be sent by return. The Doctor cannot, of course, deal with queries on the treatment or diagnosis of disease, which must be referred to your own doctor, nor does she answer questions not concerned with mothers and children. Address your letters to the Children's Doctor, c/o Good Housekeeping, 28-30 Grosvenor Gardens, London, S.W.1, and please remember to enclose a stamped addressed envelope.

d room for real carpenters to teach their craft (and range things so that they have time to get on with eir own work, too), room for real painters, practising writers, men and women who have travelled and ne all kinds of commercial jobs. I don't know ny we value permanence so much in a school, why achers must stay for years and years. Some may d this permanence to their taste, but many others ow lamentably stale. In any case, it would surely nefit the children to have different people with fferent talents.

Parents might well consider whether we shouldn't more to encourage a variety of interesting people take up teaching or school work from time to ne, and try to arrange things so that different types e attracted into each school community, giving the ildren the benefit of varied experiences. In the nools themselves there are jobs for many kinds of ople, from the woman who is interested in catering and housewifery, to the one who cares for rdening and animals, in addition to teachers of the ore usual subjects. A certain amount has been ne about exchanging teachers with those from other untries, and this should be encouraged, while we ght also consider exchanging teachers from school school on occasions. The whole programme uld become far more flexible, particularly if we anaged to get rid of some of the examination gies.

Teachers, as a general rule, tend to stick together. ey often take their holidays together, lodge gether, go about in little gangs talking shop, and ogether live in a world of their own. This is tting it very rudely and in a sweeping manner, but s, largely, a fact. Consequently, teachers lose a , they are often unable to view their pupils' probns, or their home circumstances, from an unofessional, *human* standpoint. They tend to get off from the vulgar, commercial, up-and-down uggle of life, and their teaching suffers in consequence. We need to do everything we can to help chers to keep in touch, to get them really mixed with the everyday affairs of the village or town in ich they work, and to enjoy being people in their n right. There is still too much flavour of the ister clinging to the profession!
Teaching is one of the most important and worthile jobs in the world, and most teachers are tremely unselfish people, so it is up to the community to make the best conditions possible for ir work.

THE GOOD HOUSEKEEPING CHILDREN'S DOCTOR ADVISES:

I have a baby now 5 weeks old, and should very much like to continue with breast feeding until the weaning period. Can you make any suggestions?

If you have carried on breast feeding successfully so far, there is no reason why you should not continue to do so until baby is 7 or 8 months old.
There are a few simple rules which will help you: (1) Try to get an hour's rest during the day. Start the 2 p.m. feed in good time, and when it is finished, lie down and rest for at least half an hour. (2) Don't forget to have plenty of drinks; especially remember that the pint of milk allowed is for you to *drink*. A glass of water taken half an hour before feeds is a grand help. (3) Your diet should be as full as present conditions allow, and if you take the orange juice and cod-liver oil, you need not give baby any till he is 3 months old. (4) Keep the breasts well supported in a well-fitting brassière, and wash them once a day at least.

I am rather worried about my baby girl, aged 10 months, as she appears to have a slight " shake " in her head. In every way she appears healthy and normal. About a month ago I noticed that when sitting up in her pram watching the other children at play, she wagged her head from side to side, and I also noticed a very slight unsteadiness of the left eyeball. But when playing with some object in her own hands and while looking intently at it, or closely watching some object while in my arms, she keeps her head quite steady. I'm not sure if it is that her neck is not quite strong enough, or whether it's the beginning of some disease. Do you think it will wear away, or should I take her to a doctor?

I do not think you need worry about your little daughter at present. She is probably cutting her teeth, and thus she is conscious that all is not quite well with her head, and so moves it round.
If you find that the movements persist for more than two months, or become worse, then I advise you to get a children's specialist to see her. For the moment I should just pay special attention to her diet, making sure that she has a good supply of vitamins, and avoid too much excitement or over-stimulation.

5 lbs. OF COAL SAVED IN ONE DAY
BY 1,500,000 HOMES WILL PROVIDE
ENOUGH FUEL TO BUILD A DESTROYER

*NOTE : 5 lbs. of coal are used in 2
hours by a gas fire or electric oven.*

Is YOUR home helping to build
a destroyer?

Save FUEL for BATTLE

ISSUED BY THE MINISTRY OF FUEL AND POWE

The stitch in time that saves nine is more important than ever.
Keep health up and fuel consumption down — eat raw vegetables.
Invest in your country — buy National Savings.

New ways with the new SALT FISH

THE salt fish we get now is proving very popular. Are you serving it often? You should; because salt fish is every bit as nourishing as fresh fish—a really first-class body-builder, as good in this respect as a meat meal. Grand for children as well as grown-ups, and what a bargain at only 10d. a pound!

As you know, this fish has to be soaked for at least 24 hours to get the salt out. Ask the fishmonger, and if he hasn't soaked it for long, finish the soaking at home. To do this, put the fish, skin side up, in plenty of cold water. Then cook it the same day.

HOW TO BOIL SALT FISH. Drain off the soaking water and rinse the fish under the cold tap. Cut in convenient pieces; put in a pan with cold water to cover and bring slowly to the boil. Cook until tender, about ten minutes. Drain well, and use as required.

You can use any of your favourite recipes calling for fresh fish. But, to give you something new, here are some special recipes:

COD PANCAKES. ½ lb. salt cod, cooked and flaked in small pieces, 1 level tablespoon chopped parsley, salt and pepper, 2 level tablespoons mixed herbs, 6 oz. mashed carrots. **Batter:** 4 oz. flour, 1 level tablespoon dried egg (dry), 2 level teaspoons baking powder, salt, ½ pint water. (Makes 4 helpings.)

Make the batter by mixing together all the dry ingredients, adding sufficient water to make a stiff batter. Beat well and add the remainder of the water. Add to the batter the flaked cod, parsley, seasoning, herbs and carrots. Melt some fat in a pan and when smoking hot drop in large spoonfuls of the mixture. Brown the pancakes on one side and then turn over and brown the other.

SALT FISH LYONNAISE. 1 medium-sized onion, sliced, fat for frying, 3 medium-sized potatoes, cooked and sliced, 1 lb. soaked salt fish, cooked and flaked, 1 teaspoon vinegar, pepper, chopped parsley.

Fry onion in a little fat till tender, add potato and fish and fry until brown. Sprinkle over vinegar, pepper and parsley. If liked, serve with a sauce and salad, or with vegetables coated with sauce and extra potatoes.

Baked Cod with Parsnip Balls and Piquant Sauce

2 lb. parsnips, salt, pepper, browned crumbs, 1 lb. soaked salt cod, 4 tablespoons dripping. SAUCE: ½ oz. margarine, 2 level tablespoons flour, ½ pint vegetable stock, salt, pepper, mustard, 1 tablespoon vinegar. QUANTITY: 4 helpings.

Cook the parsnips till quite soft. Drain and mash well with seasonings. Form into balls and coat in browned crumbs. Skin and bone fish, place in baking tin and spread with dripping. Bake in a quick oven for 5 minutes, then add parsnip balls and bake together for 20 minutes.

Sauce: Melt margarine, add flour, cook 3 minutes. Add liquid gradually, stirring well, and cook for another 5 minutes. Season and stir in vinegar. Serve with fish in centre of dish, the parsnip balls round and the sauce over the fish.

TASTY FISH-PASTE SANDWICH FILLING

3 oz. finely chopped cooked salt fish, 3 oz. well mashed potato, 1 tablespoon chopped parsley, 2 tablespoons chopped raw onion, 2 dessertspoons vinegar, 1 teaspoon made mustard, pepper, ½ oz. melted margarine. Mix all ingredients together very thoroughly to give a smooth paste.

Road casualties are still high: keep your family cautious.

Wise housewives economise – to buy National Savings.

Mend and make old clothes do for the duration.

What we housewives know about rations fades into insig

Here is the authoritat

the Allied Invasion Army, told by t

WHEN Marshal Rommel gave a curtain-raiser warning to Atlantic Wall commanders that " this is going to be the m modern battle that has ever been fought," it is pretty cert that one of the Anglo-American invasion army's ultra-mod resources which most worried him was outside the weapon equipment list.

I mean the Second Front soldier's fuel—rations.

Montgomery in Africa gave Hitler's pet general his first prise taste of what dynamic and scientific rationing can me The British commander's success in keeping his troops fully e gised and nourished by a balanced battle ration, coupled w new-type supply methods, all planned for and meshed with high-velocity campaign, was a potent factor in the victory wh drove the Afrika Korps back whence it came, and brought Eighth Army to fight with undiminished vigour alongside Gene Eisenhower's invasion force, a thousand miles west of its Alamein starting-point.

Rommel knows that the integrated Anglo-American Seco Front army under General Eisenhower's supreme command even better serviced on the man-fuel side than was the Brit Eighth, which so disconcerted him by holding its vigour h and its sick-rate low—curves exactly the reverse of those recor by his own army in its eastward drive to the gateway of Egy

Break down the Second Front army to its ultimate compone and you come to an individual soldier. Call him Bill. Bill m be your son, sweetheart, brother or husband. He may be d or fair, and any shape, size or weight. I don't know whether swam, waded, duck-rushed, glider-landed or 'chuted down into on to Fortress Europe—but he's over there now. Average he's a male organism, 22–24 years old, 66–70 inches high, 130– pounds in weight.

That is Bill from Bolton, Lancs., the average British soldi Joe from Boston, Mass., the average American soldier, runs 68- inches high, and 150–170 pounds, and he eats differently, a rather more. Joe or Bill is geared to the highest-performar war engine yet evolved. This means that besides being wh Nature made him—a nutritional process—he is also what hi speed, winged-armoured-motorised war across sea and oce has made him—a nutritional problem.

Hard-trained, Bill or Joe can walk-and-run 10 miles in 2 hou sprint 100 yards in 16 seconds, carry a man his own weight 2 yards to cover in 90 seconds, jump 10 feet, climb a 12-foot v tical rope and traverse a 20-foot span of horizontal rope. Th and sundry other feats, necessary for his own safety and t enemy's discomfort, he does in battle order, under fire, often w

MENU *for*

Prepare your ground to double its last year's production.

How does your garden grow? Sow now for your winter larder.

Take pride in your patchwork.

nce beside the work of the Army Catering chiefs.

etailed story of the ration recipe of

rilliant correspondent C. PATRICK THOMPSON

nd cold, with the ground to sleep on (if he's lucky), and
-morrow probably harder going than to-day.

In normal army training, Bolton Bill burnt off about 3,600
lories of energy a day, his bigger American comrade nearer
,000. Their commanders put those lost calories back by
scientific diet so balanced that Bill or Joe gets 15 per cent.
f his total calories from protein, 35 per cent. from fats, and
) per cent. from carbohydrates, along with an adequate
osage of essential food factors like vitamins in every ration.

Protein comes in meat, fish, offals, sausage; fat in mar-
arine; carbohydrate in bread, jam, vegetables, cereals, sugar,
ried fruit, slab cake, fresh fruit; protein-and-fat in cheese and
acon; protein-fat-and-carbohydrate in milk; vitamin A in
rtified margarine, vegetables and liver; vitamin B_1 in bread,
our and vegetables; vitamin B_2 in milk, cheese, offals, meat
nd fish; nicotinic acid in meat, offals and fish; vitamin C in
egetables and fresh fruit; vitamin D in tinned fish, milk
nd fortified margarine (although Bill or Joe doesn't need
ore vitamin D than the sun's action produces in his skin).

Bill or Joe's digestive apparatus zestfully extracts the
tal stuff of life from about four pounds' weight of these
asic foods daily. That's a sizeable item: a division will
et through 76 tons of food a day; 350 cooks, six-weeks'
ained in schools run by Supplies and Transport under the
uartermaster-General, are kept busy preparing Bill's grub,
sing mostly petrol cookers in the field; 74 three-ton lorries
re needed to shift the food, unit transport picking up
here R.A.S.C. transport dumps at bulk breaking-point.

All this presented no tough problem while Bill and Joe
ved in a secure base, with all facilities. But whenever they
ossed the moat and started fighting, things changed. What-
ver communications lines and supply facilities our own
ombers and artillery left intact, the enemy could be counted
n to demolish if they looked like helping Bill and Joe's
upplies. The enemy also unkindly blasts bakeries, dumps,
eld-kitchens and cooks; and Bill and Joe, fighting, don't help
upply much by moving unpredictable distances at unpredict-
ble speeds, sometimes in unpredictable directions not marked
n the battle blue-print.

This complicates supply. It also causes Bill and Joe to
urn off calories at a rate which disturbs their medical officers
nless somehow those expended calories and that consumed
uman tissue can be replaced pretty regularly through the
perations of a digestive plant fed with the right foods, in
dequate quantities, and properly prepared.

Thus, months before D-day, *(Continued on page 167)*

BATTLE

Illustrated by Jack Matthews

PADDIS

Practical shoes for casual comfort

to bring joy to your walking hours.

Brown or navy suede, calf trimmed.

For personal shoppers only 51/11

Lilley & Skinner

356-360 OXFORD ST., W.1 · BRANCHES ALL OVER LONDON

Menu for Battle

(Continued from page 165)

hordes of specialist officers were working on Bill and Joe's Second Front ration. They examined field reports, checked statistics, experimented on troop units, added here, subtracted there, congratulated and cursed one another. In the process, rip-roaring transport men, used to thinking in terms of hundreds of tons and thousands of wheels, developed respect for more precise team-mates who argued about inches, fought over ounces, worked out vitamin contents in grammes and milligrammes, and attached importance to the fact that the riboflavin content of Bill and Joe's fresh ration, and that of the hard (tinned equivalent) ration, differs by one-tenth of a milligramme. These officers ranged down to two-pip technicians, but at the top were the respective Supply and Medical chiefs, jointly responsible for Bill and Joe's food.

Let me draw on a completed operation to illustrate the sort of team-work thing that has been happening, and is happening still.

When General Montgomery was getting ready for El Alamein, his supply and medical chiefs got together, studied the campaign plan, and agreed to scrap an existing low-calory, one-week battle ration. Medical produced a new battle ration that had everything—from Medical's viewpoint. It could be easily prepared without heat or water, had adequate A, B-series, and C vitamins, and 3,600 calories. Medical proudly brought its new

ration to Supply. Supply worked out bulk and weight, and checked on available transport, and claims thereon. Now, the purpose of an army is to fight: the more wings, wheels and tracked armour you give it, the more you boost its fire-power, speed and range, the more you increase its ration needs and complicate its ration problems. Machines and guns need rations, too. In priority, petrol and ammunition rank as Number One and Two. Cut them down, or off, and your war engine stalls and your men can't fight. Cut down Bill's normal ration to battle-ration size, and he can go on fighting hard for a long time. Cut him even below what Medical says he ought to have for proper nourishment, and he is still good for quite a time—he just calls on his reserves of fat and flesh, his stored-up vital forces.

Supply pointed out to Medical that its new battle ration was too heavy and bulky to fit the transport schedule. You can't have an unlimited number of wheels in a battle zone anyway, because of fuel supply, road capacity and like reasons. So Medical had to go to work all over again.

This time they pruned off 500 calories, but managed to retain variety of foods, and some bulk. Then they compromised with Supply by imposing a ten-day limit on this ration. This left it up to Supply so to arrange its affairs that inside ten days, at any and all stages of the advance, it could get

Our men—they joke

on the eve of battle.

They go forward

never faltering,

never dismayed,

on the road to victory.

They shall lack nothing

our support

can give them.

We are in duty bound—

each one of us

—to SALUTE

THE FIGHTING FORCES

with more

and yet more saving !

Issued by the National Savings Committee

Menu for Battle

the normal 3,800-calory desert field-service ration to the troops.

Supply managed it. A field bakery would run into a captured base through the dust of outgoing tanks, and start baking fresh bread to replace biscuit (in food priorities, bread is Number One, fresh meat is Number Two and fresh vegetables Number Three). A shipload of meat, flour and vegetables would dog the army's trail, put into port at a shore signal, dump its fresh-food cargo before the smoke of battle had dispersed. Worn out at the end of a long-day's running fight, the tank men formerly had eaten scrappily out of tins. Now petrol cookers, mounted on lorries, hung on to their tails, and the tank men got a hot meal during a lull or when they laagered for the night.

Thus the Eighth arrived at the end of its enormous drive fighting-fit instead of exhausted, and at peak strength instead of weakened by fall-outs. Its three-months' campaign sick-rate was under 2 per 1,000, which is remarkably low.

The Second Front army's dynamic rationing job has been necessarily more complex. One of the reasons is that General Eisenhower commands a two-nation force, and Boston Joe and Bolton Bill don't eat alike, and don't want to—although, on occasion, they must.

Each has a diet that suits him. Boston Joe consumes in his normal field-service diet more meat, milk products, fats, sugar, tomatoes and citrus fruits than Bolton Bill, but less potatoes and cereals. On the British base scale, Boston Joe's calories intake is 4,000 daily; Bolton Bill's 3,330 (cut from 3,700 pre-war). But on battle rations both eat about level, while resisting complete unification.

Boston Joe carries his K-ration (his one-day landing-rush battle food) in three rectangular water-proofed cartons, each 6 by 4 by 2 inches. These give him a 3¾-ounce block of veal-and-pork loaf for breakfast, another for supper and cheese product for dinner. On the side he has biscuit, chewing-gum, enough coffee product to make a pint, pure lemon-juice powder for a long drink, three sugar cubes, a fruit bar, cigarettes and a 2-ounce chocolate bar (the latter is the D-ration, which can be used alone in dire emergency, on the basis of three 4-ounce fortified bars to sustain Joe for twenty-four hours).

Send your waste paper to take part in the Second Front.

It need cost no more than a journey to the nearest Clinic to give your child immunity against Diphtheria – a journey that is really necessary!

There's also a 10-gm. pack of bouillon powder containing a vegetable protein derivative, salt, spices, flavourings and brewers' yeast. Yeast yields riboflavin, part of a ferment necessary for oxidation within the body cells. It also yields nicotinic acid, part of a ferment required for utilisation of sugars by the body cells. Normally these two come in milk, cheese, eggs, meat, liver, nuts, legumes and whole-grain cereals.

Bolton Bill takes his one-day landing-rush ration along in a single waterproofed squarish carton, 6 by 5 by 2 inches. He has no solid meal like Boston Joe's meat loaves, but the calory content ran higher than K, until lately Boston Joe's ration-planners produced a new-type 3,900-calories K. Cigarettes are not included, maybe on the argument that no British soldier moves into action without a packet of "fags" in his pocket, or one behind his ear.

Bolton Bill gets his main meals by breaking pieces off a block of compressed, dehydrated meat, and making soup or a stew with biscuit (he may find an onion or carrot around, too). He has about the same biscuit ration as Boston Joe, but his are larger and harder. He has two thick blocks of sweetened oatmeal for making hot porridge, although in emergency he can eat them as biscuit. Three bars of chocolate boost the total calory content. Two of the chocolate bars are vitaminised. The third replaces Boston Joe's fruit bar; it has raisins bedded in. Instead of bouillon powder, Bolton Bill has two meat-soup cubes. His sugar pieces equal Boston Joe's.

Surprisingly, Bill finds eight chewing-gum tablets in his ration, the lot approximating to Boston Joe's two sticks. He further has eight boiled sweets.

Eight cubes give Bolton Bill two pints of "Army-strength" tea. The British argue that a hot drink is a morale-sustainer; and, besides, the caffein in tea has a stimulant action on the higher centres of the brain. Not that there's much caffein in Bolton Bill's tea ration—or much tea, either. For actually Bolton Bill, while relishing his beloved tea in lulls between knocking off Nazis, is sustaining himself health-fully on sugar and milk. His eight whitish little tea cubes contain only 16 per cent. tea: the remaining 84 per cent. is sugar and full-cream dried milk, highly nourishing.

Both these landing-rush, high-calory, compact battle rations, any-way, are only part of the story of the solution of the Second Front battle-ration problem. That first ration had to conform to conditions created by the fact that we must fight our way in over contested beaches, or drop down from the sky. Thereafter, it was part of the team problem to get Bill and Joe off concentrates as quickly as possible.

Boston Joe has an intermediate individual-soldier ration. It comes in four tins, weighing a total of 4 pounds, and gives Joe more protein and bulk—our digestive apparatus needs bulk. On C, Joe's one-day sugar ration doubles; he gets four large dry biscuits, three "suckers," and three square meals—meat-and-beans for breakfast, meat-and-vegetable hash for dinner, meat-and-vegetable stew for supper. The K can be mixed in with C, and helps.

Boston Joe's third stage is the 10-in-1, still a battle ration—ten men's ration in a handy pack. Except that it is hard (biscuit instead of bread, canned meat and canned vegetables instead of fresh), the 10-in-1 starts to balance Joe's calory outgoings with his intake, and to do it in a balanced way, with plenty of variety.

There are five different menus in the 10-in-1. This variation is part of the science of dietetics we apply to the Second Front army. Give a man a varied diet, make it palatable, and his organism extracts maximum nourishment from his food. And the better he is nourished, the better he can endure, fight, stand shock of possible wounds and surgery, convalesce, and protect himself against assaults of all the bacteria, both Nazi and natural, which prey on weakened organisms.

Bolton Bill does not bother with an intermediate C. He jumps from his one-man battle concentrates direct to his composite pack. This is a 14-in-1. It contains less meat than Boston Joe's 10-in-1, but more of the things Bolton Bill likes and is used to. The calories value is about the same; the vitamin content varies. While Boston Joe eats a high-protein-content meat-and-vegetable meal thrice daily, Bolton Bill will breakfast on tea, sausage, biscuits and fat-rich margarine; dine on Irish stew and sultana pudding; tea (a meal) on biscuit, margarine, cheese, tea; and sup on soup and biscuit; and in between consume "suckers" and chocolate, and chew gum.

Always ready to serve ...

There's plenty of Heinz — in Italy, Sicily, Africa and elsewhere. That's why there is less in the shops. And who would have it otherwise? But don't think you cannot get Heinz at all. Keep a sharp eye open and you will still see the famous name about. And, as ever, it stands for goodness — goodness that stays good in store.

HEINZ

57
VARIETIES

Baked Beans — Soups — Salad Cream — Mayonnaise

H. J. HEINZ COMPANY LIMITED LONDON

Make time to help Farmers to bring in their Crops.

Don't give presents – give National Savings Certificates.

More children are killed by road accidents than by enemy action
– Drill road sense into YOUR child.

Menu for Battle

Bolton Bill's 14-in-1 weighs 66 pounds. Bill will hump it any place under any kind of fire: it contains his cigarettes.

Neither Americans nor British fool with vitamin C—claimed by some European scientists to boost a man's capacity for physical work if taken in large quantities. If Bill or Joe is in a parachute or some other special formation whose work calls for increased muscular activity, he gets the extra stuff his organism needs from food supplements to his normal ration.

One vitamin tablet he has, in reserve. It is a single compound-vitamin tablet which contains, besides ascorbic acid, the chief vitamins present in yeast—i.e. it is loaded with the B-group of vitamins, and vitamin C. Cases of the tablets go over with Joe's medical stores. They are an issue on the M.O.'s advice. Medical only recommends them to the Field Commander as an addition to rations when men are on a tinned hard ration for some time, without a chance to supplement it with fresh stuff. Prolonged lack of riboflavin causes degenerative changes in the membranes covering the tongue, lips and cornea, while deficiency of nicotinic acid leads to pellagra.

Incidentally, in the last war there was some nutritional disease, nutritional science being less advanced and less attention being paid to the composition of the last-war soldier's ration. Beriberi occurred at Gallipoli and in Mesopotamia, and at the siege of Kut-el-Amara beriberi and scurvy both broke out in epidemic form. In the present war, despite enormously greater complexity and rationing difficulties, there has been practically no nutritional-deficiency disease.

Weight for weight. the Second Front soldier's canned food ration runs higher than his fresh ration in proteins, carbohydrates, iron and calories, but lower in fat, vitamins and minerals.

What his food-fuellers toil to do is to get him on to fresh or part-fresh rations as quickly, as much and as often as possible. He needs butter as well as guns in battle, and hot meals even when he is busy pumping hot lead into the enemy. Nature approves that, and anything that Nature approves benefits Bill or Joe. And anything that benefits Bill or Joe is bad news for the Nazis.

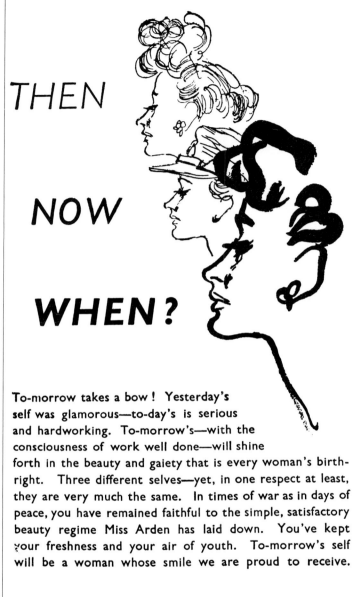
Blood Donors are still needed to keep up life-giving supplies on the Fighting Front.

Your child can't decide to be immunised against Diphtheria — that is YOUR responsibility.

Domestic Utop

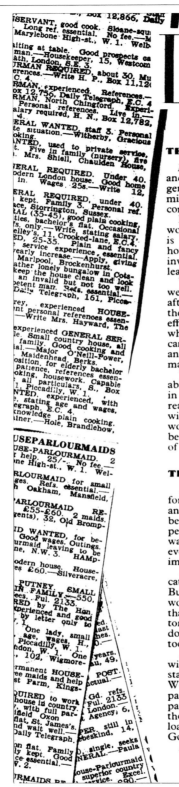

THE MISTRESS'S POINT OF VIEW

Most of us like housework, cooking and the care of children; we are genuinely happy to use our hands and minds on the job of making life comfortable for our families.

But at present the burden of housework is too much. Some recreation is essential to everybody; but in homes where there are children, invalids or old people, the day's routine leaves no time for recreation at all.

We bear this cheerfully now, but we do hope for more domestic help after the war; and we hope the "helps" themselves will be happier and more efficient. We do not want cleaners who cannot scrub a floor, cooks who cannot make a plain suet pudding, and general maids who cannot even manage the kitchen boiler.

We know many of us will not be able to compete with the wages offered in industry; we can only hope that reasonable wages and a good home will still have their appeal to some women. Older women who have been happy in domestic service most of their lives; young girls in need of the security of a home; these classes seem to hold out most hope for living-in domestic help, and if they turn to us for work after the war, we shall try to give them a fair return for their help.

Failing the living-in help? We hope there will be more and cheaper laundry services and good inexpensive restaurants. We know there will be a wider range of ready-prepared foods; we hope that as soon as possible the baker's and grocer's and greengrocer's delivery service will be restored, to save the endless, time-wasting calls on the shops.

And—we hope that part-time help, when we do need it, will not be too inflexible. We should like help in the evenings sometimes, to look after our children while we enjoy a cinema or concert. We should like a cook for an occasional dinner-party, a needle-woman for those last hectic days before the boys go back to school. In short, if we could have just the help we need, just at the moment we need it, we should be in Utopia indeed.

THE MAID'S POINT OF VIEW

Many of us left domestic work before the war for jobs with lower wages and worse conditions. We left, not because we disliked the work or the people we worked for, but because we wanted our independence, our free evenings, a life of our own and, most important of all, a higher status.

A great many of us are domesticated and like looking after a home. But we found even skilled domestic work was considered less important than any job in a shop, office or factory. There was a general idea that domestic work was only for the people too stupid for anything else.

If some training could be arranged, with certificates of efficiency, our status would be much improved. Workers could then be graded and paid accordingly. Some of us could pay a fee for this training, but for those who couldn't, surely grants or loans might be arranged by the Government?

Many of us, particularly in the towns, like daily work. It is pleasant to go back to a home of our own or to a hostel. But most emphatically we do not want hostels for domestic workers only. In our free time we want to meet people doing other kinds of work.

Hostels are not practicable in country districts. But many of us like living in a pleasant home with good food and few responsibilities. *We* should continue living-in—but with certain minimum standards. Those standards are set out opposite.

In the past, good mistresses deserved and got good maids. This was true whatever the "conditions of employment." And it may very well be true again after the war, for then there should be more good mistresses. So many women have had to do their own housekeeping, so many girls are learning domestic subjects at school, that perhaps in our Utopia there will be no more mistresses who don't understand the work themselves.

a

Mistresses and Maids in the Post-War World

THE INSTITUTE SUMS UP

The shortage of domestic help in private homes is acute now, but without good planning it may well become very much worse.

The Minister of Labour is fully alive to the problem and is already dealing with the subject of help for hospitals and institutions. The steps he has taken are big ones. He has not only brought home to women the vital need for this work; he has ensured for them fair conditions, reasonable pay and satisfactory living and transport facilities.

He has now set up a committee to enquire into private domestic work, but he emphasises that for the present there can be no hope of helping more than a few " exceptional hardship " cases. Meanwhile, the Sub-Committee of Domestic Workers of the T.U.C. have made their own recommendations to him. They include :

Training.—Adequate and uniform throughout the country, with some payment or maintenance grant.

Registration.—With certificates of efficiency after training.

Unemployment insurance for all domestic workers.

Hours of duty.—Eight hours a day for a six-day week, with reasonable time off for meals and extra payment for overtime.

Holidays.—A fortnight's paid holiday yearly for the first five years, after that three weeks' paid holiday.

Living accommodation if resident.—A separate bedroom which is light, airy, comfortably furnished and heated. If no sitting-room or " hall " is available, a comfortable chair to be provided in the kitchen. Every resident worker to have access to a bathroom.

Living accommodation if living out.—Provision of hostels or flatlets.

Pay.—This subject is still under discussion, but there is every indication that wages will be higher than before the war and comparable with those earned in industrial work demanding a similar standard of skill.

But even when all these plans are formulated, there remains the question of how many girls will be available and willing to take up the work. Thousands of women will be needed after the war for industries connected with building and equipping homes; thousands more for the making of fine-quality goods for export. How many will be left for domestic work?—how many will be willing to do it? If we could know these things now, then perhaps we could plan Utopia ourselves.

reflect a world ... is gone for ever

A PRIORITY WAR JOB

Domestic Work in Hospitals and Institutions

Can you give regular time each week, or even better, every day, to helping out your local hospital in its urgent need ? More desperate even than the call for nurses is that for capable, behind-the-scenes workers; public-spirited women who can cook or clean, or who, if without experience in their own homes, are willing to learn. It's unspectacular war service, but it's none the less truly vital, and something that lies particularly within the sphere of the practical housewife.

If you are due to be called up, you can opt for domestic duties in hospitals or institutions (instead of for factory work), while in some localities you may be directed to it.

Conditions of service and pay are safeguarded by law and, just as with industrial work, wages depend on skill and experience.

Minimum rate for non-resident domestic workers £2 10s. a week; for cooks, £3 5s. For resident workers the rates are respectively £60 and £100 a year. A 96-hour fortnight is recommended, and paid holidays are stipulated.

Your Labour Exchange has full particulars. Go and talk it over.

Turn out your rag bag : it may make a glad bag.

Start patching and mending instead of spending.

Mend for victory.

By Geoffrey Hutton

This is an important article that deserves to be read—and pondered—by each one of us. It is written by an Australian war correspondent who, before coming to this country to cover the Invasion, spent many months in the tough fighting in New Guinea

WHEN Montgomery with his Eighth Army crossed over from Sicily to Italy and began the long drive northward, the news came on the ship's radio, and the first whisper electrified everybody. We were a greasy, sweating crowd, jam-packed on a tank-landing ship just about 10,000 miles away, going to another landing on another shore and fighting another enemy.

But the men I was travelling with forgot the distance, forgot the burning tropical sun over Huon Gulf, forgot even the Japs they were to meet at the end of the journey on the swampy shore above Lae. As they yarned of Monty and his men, I realised that they were back with them at the break-through of El Alamein, back in the blitzed shambles of Tobruk, back in enticing, expensive Cairo. I was talking to the men of the Australian Ninth Division, who had fought through one-half of the war with honour, and were on the way to fight no less gallantly or efficiently in the other half. To them it was all one war, against German or Jap, in desert or jungle, and you may be sure it still is.

There is nothing easier than talking about One War; nothing harder, I think, than really imagining it. While the thoughts of England, America, Canada, focus on the men who are fighting their way through Northern France, it is hard enough to bear in mind the part that Patch's men are playing in Southern France, Alexander's men in Italy, the Red Army on the eastern plains, Tito's partisans in the Dalmatian mountains. Cast your mind half-way across the world to the monsoon-sodden jungles of Burma, then you must leap

another 3,000 miles to reach the nearest fringe of the world's second great battlefield—the Pacific.

How little the British people know about their war in this enormous battlefield has made me blink and gulp with embarrassed wonder. I know of a senior naval officer who blandly talked to an audience about the Japanese occupation of Midway Island. If I had told him how the Germans captured Malta, I suppose he would have been a trifle pained. Yet the battle of Midway was quite as important an air-sea victory to the

Allies as the battle of Malta. And both islands are in our hands for keeps. On the other hand, I find most people believe that the reconquest of New Guinea ended long ago, and that we have been cleaning up islands off the coast for the past few months. I am sorry to say that there are still several Japanese divisions at large in New Guinea and several Japanese bases still to be cracked.

There are several good reasons why we should know more about the other half of the war, the Pacific half. The Allied leaders who planned the distribution of the armed power of the United Nations were really globally minded. They decided on the Beat Hitler First policy, and they were correct. They decided that at the same time a holding and spoiling war should be fought against Japan, to prevent her entrenching herself and developing in strength in her enormous new "co-prosperity sphere." They decided that the moment Hitler was beaten, Britain and America should transfer every weapon possible to the second half of the job—beating Hirohito, or Tojo if you prefer it that way.

This means that a sizeable proportion of the British Army, a bigger proportion of the Air Force, and certainly the bulk of the Navy, will finish the war not when Berlin falls, but when Tokio falls. The rubber, tin and oil of south-east Asia are not the only reasons; there are much bigger ones.

China, struggling to set her foot on the path to

Pacific FRONT

Illustrated by Jack Matthew

ogress, is still held in a seven-years' bond of ffering and corruption. In south-east Asia a undred millions are being exploited, propagan-sed and prepared as fodder for the Japanese ar machine. A hundred thousand British and er thirty thousand Americans, defenders of ngapore, Hong Kong, the Philippines, are being arved and sweated in Japanese prison-camps. ustralia and New Zealand, the only two white mocracies of purely British stock in the Southern emisphere, escaped destruction by a miracle uite as great as the Battle of Britain, and they ll not be secure until the greedy militarists of okio have been sent packing. There will be no orld order until they have been destroyed as terly as the Nazis. And a big share of the b will be ours.

I think most people in England realise this, but fear there is some wishful thinking about the time and the cost it will take. Think over these simple facts: Japan is an industrial nation of about the same population as Germany. She holds a much bigger Empire, stretching over a radius of 3,000 miles from Tokio, all the way from Burma to the Central Pacific, and populated by at least 300 millions. Most of this she won from Britain, the Netherlands and America in about four months. This was the greatest single terri-torial expansion in history and makes even Hit-ler's look small. Her army cannot be compared with the Wehrmacht, but after seven years of un-broken fighting it is still substantially intact; it has suffered no blood-bath like Hitler's in Russia. Her Air Force and Navy have both been worn down in the last two years, but enough has been saved out of each of them for a decisive show-down in the "inner fortress." She knows now that she can never beat *(Continued on page 176)*

Mend and restore and you can lend more.

Patch for patriotism.

Do not spend! Make-do and mend.

Pacific Front

(Continued from page 175)

us, but she has one weapon left, and she is using it for all she is worth.

That weapon is space. The Pacific is almost half the globe; it could hold the North and South Atlantic twice over and still have room to spare. Pushing back along that 3,000-mile radius which the Japanese covered so quickly, we have gained a few hundred miles, here and there, in two years. The great victory of Kwajalein atoll in the Marshalls gave the American fleet an advance base just 2,500 miles from Tokio—approximately the width of the Atlantic away. Saipan, capital of the Marianas, now in American hands, is roughly 1,400 miles from both Japan and the Philippines. Pearl Harbour, main U.S. forward base, is nearly 3,500 miles away.

The push back to the Philippines is moving a little faster. Mac-Arthur's Australian-American team has leap-frogged up the north coast of New Guinea and is drawing within range. His landing on Byak Island last May brought the Philippines within 800 miles of American bombers; Davaos and Mindanao have since been raided. Since then, in July, there have been landings on Noemfoor Island, 100 miles west of Byak.

On the Indian Ocean side, distances are just as vast an obstacle. There is an enormous gap of blank ocean and enemy islands between Colombo and Freemantle, over 3,000 miles away in Western Australia. Right in the middle lies Singapore, the lynch-pin that was stolen. From one of our bases to the next is just about as far as from Southampton to New York. And can you imagine the Ameri-

cans invading Europe without the unsinkable stepping-stone of Britain?

There is no doubt that Japan has deliberately played space for time ever since she took her first beating at sea from the Americans in the Coral Sea battle of April 1942, and her first beating on land from the Australians at Milne Bay three months later. She seized Australia's last island barrier and hung like a cloud over the north, but she lacked the strength to go on. She pushed towards the vital American supply-line, and was checked in the Solomons. She drove east towards Midway Island and was beaten again. She never beat the supply problems of Burma thoroughly enough to make a real threat to India. She finally stalled on all fronts. Space had run her war-engine to a standstill: now it was to be her first line of defence.

It was not only the sheer expanse of water. I have flown the Pacific, and, as hour after hour reeled by, watched the maze of ribbon-like coral atolls and the steep volcanic islands rise out of the blue and recede into it. From the great fertile islands of equatorial East Asia to the tiny atolls of the Central Pacific, it is a maze of islands.

Approaching Japan from the east —Pearl Harbour way—you follow the widely scattered chain of little "unsinkable aircraft carriers" all the way to the Philippines or to Japan itself. It was made for amphibious war, and nothing else. But from the south, you strike other and greater obstacles. New Guinea, Borneo, Sumatra, the Celebes, Java, Luzon and Mindinao are great islands, each as large as a European country. Each of these, except only New Guinea, was taken in a quick canter and has been in Japanese hands for over two years. Each has to be won back.

You can see something of th[e] difficulty from the New Guine[a] campaign. Mercator was unkin[d] to New Guinea, lying almost plum[b] on the equator, it looks only ha[lf] its size. But apart from Greenlan[d] it is by far the biggest island i[n] the world.

It has other disadvantages fo[r] fighting. There are no roads at a[ll] worth mentioning, and no railway[s]. It is highly malarial, and rife wit[h] dysentery, gastric diseases, th[e] mysterious scrub typhus, yaws an[d] a score of other skin diseases. Th[e] rainfall in many areas is more tha[n] ten times London's, so that whe[n] you have laboriously scooped ou[t] an earth road with bulldozers, [a] few days of jeep traffic will turn i[t] into a morass. There are hardl[y] any port facilities or buildings ex[-] cept native grass huts. The whol[e] country is a mountainous tangle o[f] steep ridges, rainy forest, an[d] coastal swamp where the jungl[e] grows in a solid mat.

For many months we were fight[-] ing the war there on a shoestring and to beat the Japs in this terrai[n] we had to substitute the enduranc[e] and sheer guts of our men for th[e] mechanised aids we should hav[e] liked. Crawling through swamps sleeping in mud-holes, sniping an[d] being sniped, Australian, and later American soldiers, slowly gaine[d] the upper hand over the all-con[-] quering Nipponese jungle-fighters.

That phase of the war, fortun[-] ately, is over. It was slow an[d] costly, and it suited the Tokio war lords well enough, because at th[e] expense of a few armies of three o[r] four divisions each, they could kee[p] us edging through their outer de[-] fences for months. They wer[e] **more worried by the way our air[-]** craft and submarines were whittlin[g] down their merchant fleet and pick[-] ing off their naval task forces; b[y] the way our air forces were steadil[y] shooting Zeros and medium bomber[s] Bettys and Heiens, out of the sky[.] All the time we were storing u[p] knowledge—knowledge of how t[o] beat the Japanese when the heat i[s] on. I think we have that know[-] ledge now, but I think Britai[n] should be prepared for a real effor[t] to win a real war.

It will not be done solely by re[-] opening the Burma Road, or b[y] island-hopping, or by naval battles or "starving them out," thoug[h] these things will all have thei[r] place, and the pattern of victor[y] will be built out of them. The firs[t] problem is going to be supply, an[d] the time we take to beat Japan will depend largely on the time we take to organise it.

Consider the magnitude of this job. The supply line to northern France has a maximum sea length of about a hundred miles. To Japan it will have a minimum length, from San Francisco, of 4,500. From England it will be much greater. The most advanced ring of American bases from Dutch Harbour in the Aleutians southward is about the distance from Tokio that New York is from England. All our armies, all their weapons, ammunition and kit, must be carried over these vast distances, and maintained by an unbroken chain of ships and air transport.

Step by step the bases must be built to stage them forward. They must be built in equatorial islands without roads, with rudimentary harbours, with deadly climates. Thousands of tons of engineering equipment must go in to open up the way and prepare each stepping-stone, each airfield and store.

To seize these vital points means island-hopping, the despised but essential process of making our way back to Japan. The Americans have shown in recent months how effective this form of warfare can be. Instead of creeping from one island to the next, they have singled out the potential base from a whole archipelago and taken it in a single leap. From Kwajalein they blockaded the eastern Marshalls, from the Admiralties they blockaded Rabaul and Kavieng, from Green Island they blockaded Bougainville. The Americans call it " letting them die on the vine." To-day there are something like 50,000 Japs dying on the vine of

"REPAIR SQUAD, PLEASE!"

Mind you Make-do and Mend.

*Here's how your paper helps – one breakfast Cereal Carton makes
two Cut-out Targets.*

Making-over, Making-do – Saves supplies and money too.

4 WAYS TO

Go Windswept and Fluffy

At seventeen you can get away with a carelessly combed mane tossed back over your shoulders; you can even look glamorous with your hair blown all hither and thither as you come in from feeding the fowls. Over thirty, no.

You need a little more sophistication and a lot more satin sleekness. Choose your hair-style carefully—an easily managed style for preference, so that you can keep it always at peak of perfection yourself. Learn to be clever about pinning up at night. Treasure your hairpins and hair grips, cherish that fine hair net and wear it every night, whether you've pinned up or not. Experiment with scarves to keep your curls protected from blustery weather and sudden rain. There's bound to be one kind of scarf-turban that suits you; when you've found it you can keep a scarf in your pocket and be proof against the worst the weather can do.

*Illustrations
by
Tage
Werner*

Throw a Temperament a Day

Tantrums have a dual effect. They keep your mind juvenile, they make your complexion old. They cause frown lines and little tight creases at the corners of your mouth; they put an edge on your voice and a hardness in your eyes. . . .

If you'd stay young . . . cultivate serenity. The calm outlook, the masculine why-worry air, is the one to adopt. Life won't be any easier if you fuss and fume, and you'll certainly be less charming to see and know. So next time you find yourself ready to breathe fire—take a deep breath instead. Unclench your hands, count ten silently. Then put on your prettiest smile and ask *nicely* for what you want.

No paper scrap is too small for the big Scrap.

Have you ever studied the Highway Code?

We can't afford to relax our Salvage efforts.

LOOK YOUR AGE

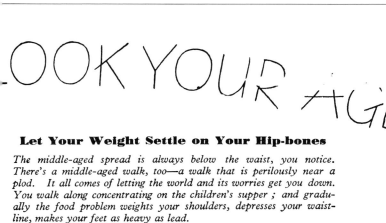

Let Your Weight Settle on Your Hip-bones

The middle-aged spread is always below the waist, you notice. There's a middle-aged walk, too—a walk that is perilously near a plod. It all comes of letting the world and its worries get you down. You walk along concentrating on the children's supper ; and gradually the food problem weights your shoulders, depresses your waistline, makes your feet as heavy as lead.

Rise above the food problem ; children need meals, but they also need an attractive mother. Lift up that surplus weight from the region of your hip-bones, put it back where it belongs. Hold yourself as tall as you can —not rigidly, but as if you were trying to get nearer the sun. Keep your shoulders back, your waist tucked in and your feet pointing straight ahead, and your posture will already be infinitely better. And " walk light "— you can do it, quite consciously, whatever your weight may be. Remember, when you get home, not to slouch or slump in your chair. You should be able to let yourself down into a chair gracefully, easily, slowly ; and if you can't, it's a clear case for a gentle daily dozen, with more bending-from-the-waist movements, and a regular daily walk.

Neglect Your Hands

" Show me a woman's hands and I'll tell you her age," said a famous man, and though war-work has been harder on our hands than on any other feature, there are still many unnecessarily old-looking pairs about. The easiest possible way to neglect your hands is to think that they are so bad they are not worth bothering about.

Even the most " hopeless " hands can be revived beyond imagination by just a little care. A face pack, bought from the chemist and thickly plastered on ; a twice-daily rub with an emollient tablet ; a course of creaming-and-sleeping-in-gloves (old cotton gloves for preference) ; and a good manicure, will take ten years off your fingertips in as many days.

By
Muriel Cox

Festive Fare for
CHRISTMAS

Don't you feel you and the family have earned the right to a little festivity this Christmas? To make the Christmas Pudding, the Christmas Cake and other seasonable things a little nearer to your memories of what such goodies should be? Well, the Ministry of Food has issued a leaflet containing some delightful suggestions and recipes. The leaflet is yours for the asking. Please see offer below.

Just to be going on with, here are a few extra suggestions you may like to try out now:

Braised Stuffed Veal Bird

2-3 lb. fillet or breast of veal. Other meat suitable instead of veal; breast of lamb, beef steak, pork. 1 *oz. fat for frying*, 1 *lb. mixed root vegetables (not potatoes).* STUFFING (*see below for recipe*). Bone breast or flatten fillet well with rolling-pin. Spread thin layer of the stuffing on and roll up. Tie tightly with string or tape. Make rest of stuffing into small balls. Heat fat in a large saucepan and brown the meat in it, both sides. Remove meat from pan. Pour off any remaining fat and add root vegetables cut in large pieces. Season well with salt and pepper and add 1 pint water or vegetable stock. Put meat on top of vegetables, place lid on. Bring liquid to boil, and boil gently; allow 40 minutes to each lb. meat. Fry or bake the stuffing balls separately. This takes 10-20 minutes. Dish up, arrange forcemeat balls round, serve with potatoes and sprouts. Instead of braising in saucepan, the meat can be baked in a covered dish in a slow oven if liked.

STUFFING. 4 *oz. stale bread-crumbs, 8 oz. finely chopped onion or leek, 2 tablespoons chopped parsley, 2 level teaspoons mixed dried herbs, salt, pepper, bacon rinds, 1 oz. fat, melted, hot water to mix.* Mix crumbs, onion or leek, parsley, herbs and seasoning together. Fry bacon rinds until crisp, and break in small pieces. Add dry ingredients with the melted fat. Mix to soft consistency with hot water.

Orange Flavour Whip

1 *lb. stewed or bottled plums, 2½ level tablespoons dried milk, 3 level tablespoons of the new sweet marmalade.* Strain the plums and keep the juice for a sauce or jelly. Mash the plums and mix with the milk and marmalade. Beat well. Serve in individual dishes topped with marmalade or custard.

Other delicious combinations are apples and plum jam; rhubarb and raspberry jam — and you can think of many others. When you use a somewhat colourless fruit it is best to combine it with a red jam. These fruit whips are very easy to make and great favourites at children's parties.

Macaroons

1 *tablespoon water, 1 oz. margarine, 1 teaspoon ratafia or almond essence, 2 oz. sugar, 2 oz. soya flour.* Melt margarine in water, add essence and sugar, then soya flour. Turn on to a board and knead well. Roll mixture into balls, flatten slightly and bake in a moderate oven for 20 minutes, till golden brown.

Do you save all bones for Salvage?

Keeping your wits when crossing the road, is your way of observing the Highway Code.

Turn your Newspapers into Paper News — make a Record contribution to Paper Salvage.

Miscellany of Verse

REBELLION

" What have you been doing ? "
People ask of me
Every time I see them,
Breakfast, dinner, tea.
Always must be doing,
Life is made for doing,
Must be ever busy,
Turn until you're dizzy.
Sometime I shall answer,
Shout it *loud* one day.
" Please, I have been being,"
That's what I shall say.

JUDY LAWLESS.

SPRING JOURNEY

I stood at a City bus-stop
On a blowy April day,
    A wind that smelled of the country
        Blew suddenly through my hair ;
e air was fluid as water,
The light was a glass-clear grey,
    And the muck and the folk and the chain-
        store
        Were indubitably there.

t my mind took a catapult caper
From the world of file and folder
    To a Northern kind of a landscape—
        Farm and furrow and fell.
lius looked in, too,
With the Cuckoo perched on his shoulder,
    Hedge-buds, fur-feel of catkins,
        Lambs' bleat and primrose smell

owded and jostled the mindscape,
Sending me daft for a minute. . . .
    When the 'bus came, I was in Eskdale—
        But before I was well aware,
abit, that excellent nursemaid,
Had stowed me efficiently in it,
    And back I came, in time to tender
        The right amount for the fare.

M. FARROW.

SUNSHINE ON MONDAY

Here I sit and take down letters
From men supposed to be my betters.
A smutty sunbeam, specked with spots,
Squeezes between the chimney-pots.
The slates are turned to cloth-of-gold,
And raindrops winking diamonds hold.
Clear shines the light through sparrows' wings
And glorifies the grimy things.
Across the tiny square of sky
Two golden gulls go drifting by.—
And yesterday the sodden clouds
Swathed the hills in dripping shrouds.
Ah! cruel, after such a Sunday,
The mockery of the sun on Monday !

JOAN CURL.

PROPOSAL

We boarded a tram ; it was pouring,
    Rain dripped from your hair.
A man slumped in front of us snoring,
    A boy sucked a pear.

Your mackintosh shoulder was warm,
    Though as wet as my own.
You looked out the window, and I
    Looked at you, dear, alone.

I said, " Mary, will you . . . ? "
    You turned ; there was no need to guess.
With your hand in my pocket on mine
    Just the pressure said " Yes."

W. Y. S. FITZGERALD.

REFUGEE DRESS

Lord, give my fingers speed and skill
To pile these needed garments high,
Another winter's aching cold
May thin the outstretched arms that fill
These waiting sleeves.   And if finesse
I lack, there lies beneath each fold
My veneration for your pluck,
And hope for all your wrongs' redress.

And may my boundless pity give
An added warmth to all I make,
Calming and softening the winds
Wherever you are forced to live
Outside your ravaged native lands.
And if some stitch is blundering,
Yet I have strengthened every seam
With prayers of one who understands.

BARBARA PALMER.

Don't be afraid of a "handyman" task, Your Make-Do and Mend
Centres will help if you ask.

Paper – Bundle – Salvage – Pulp – Gun Fuses !

DOVETAILING . .

. . . Slimma slacks in chalk-stripe blue suiting (£4 8s. 7d.; 8 coupons), with a Hart blouse in white and blue striped wool rayon with self-stiffened collar and cuffs (£3 19s. 6d.; 4 coupons).

. . . a black Meredith skirt in Royal Seal suiting with a knife pleat at the back and three more at the side of the diagonal yoke, worn with a Meredith blouse in love-in-a-mist blue moss crêpe. Skirt, 6 coupons. Blouse, 4 coupons.

Look over that old kitchen chair, YOUR hands can put it in repair.

Child cyclists are frequently injured in road accidents. Teach them their responsibility to themselves and other Road-users.

. . . a dirndl skirt in flame grey and black check with a black woollen blouse which buttons down the back. A two-piece from Jaeger. (Price £13 16s. 10d.; 12 coupons.)

. . . a Hart Utility blouse in honey-coloured wool with self-stiffened collar and cuffs (25s.; 6 coupons) with a Deréta skirt in honey and brown check tweed (£4 15s. 11d.; 6 coupons).

. . . a French pink Meredith shirt blouse in moss crêpe with a Meredith skirt in navy blue Royal Seal suiting. Blouse, 4 coupons. Skirt, 6 coupons.

Every little helps your Salvage pile.

Make "Digging, Saving, Reaping, Keeping" your gardening motto.

Y OU have undertaken to become an American
—just as millions of other people have done
before you. Getting to know your adopted
country will be an exciting adventure; the future
is before you.

You have no doubt heard a good deal from your
husband about the part of the United States
where you will probably live, but you may still
be wondering how you will get acquainted with
people, what they will be like, and how you will
manage your new home. This short guide cannot
answer all your questions, but it may help you in
making plans and in adjusting yourself to American ways of living.

Shyness: British and American

One thing you will notice when you meet people
in America is that most of them will start a conversation without much hesitation. But when
you think it over, you may feel that they have
not really said much to let you into their lives.
And perhaps you felt too shy to say much in
return. Actually, most Americans are shy below
the surface; they talk to cover it up and to make
you feel their friendly intentions while they gradually get to know you. They won't be surprised
if you are quiet. Smile, use your British habit of

thanking people for everything, ask questions, and
you will make people feel that you want to be
friendly, too. In America it is good manners to
praise anything you like, whether it is the food,
the furniture or the view from the window. Dress
your smartest for first interviews, and remember
that, except in the smallest villages, lipstick is
expected.

Listen, look around you, and take your time.
Arm yourself with a few items of "small talk"
—any odd fact about your voyage, what you have
seen, where you have been, to cover your thoughts
while you look about. Ask questions about simple
things, where to shop, what to buy, what to do
for entertainment. Everyone likes to lend a hand
to a stranger, and people who have done you a
small favour, and have been thanked with a smile,
will like you from then on.

American Humour

Don't mind if at first you feel left out of some
of the jokes that go by you in conversation.
For one thing, most jokes in any country depend
on some local topic or some peculiar twist of

slang—no one expects a newcomer to get them.
Just laugh and admit you don't.

A great deal of American written humour is
like your own, but there are some kinds of spoken
humour that you must learn to take calmly.
Exaggeration, of course, you know about, and
learning the American language includes recog-
nising what is true and what is too absurd to
believe. Kidding is perhaps harder to get used
to, but you have to learn. It may consist of
mimicking to see if you "can take it."

The American Language

The first lesson in "American" concerns the
names of things. You will learn these quickly, as
the Americans had to do in Britain. Some words
you will already have learned from your husband,
and the rest you will soon acquire. Use the
American names, so as not to be misunderstood.
You need not use American slang words that are
offensive in English, but if they are harmless in
America, don't be bothered by them. Change
your pronunciation if it causes misunderstanding
—otherwise don't.

Manners

American manners, as you know, are different
in various ways, some of which you may not like.
The Americans do not say "thank you" in as
many situations as the British, and they often
ask a question without begging pardon. In American the word "sorry" is not as polite as "excuse
me" or "I beg your pardon." A good rule is
to watch how people talk to one another in your
part of the country, and not to be surprised or
offended if they do the same to you.

Reading Can Help

The other part of the American language that you
need to learn is made up of facts about your part

Digest of a booklet prepared
Servicemen by Good
in conjunction with the Office of

Serve by Saving.

Make 1943 a bumper Savings year.

All out to win – save more paper.

r British brides of American

ousekeeping Magazine,

ar Information of the U.S.A.

the country and the life of the people around
ou. When you know something of the history
 your locality, where the people came from, and
hat they are interested in, you will begin to
now what they are talking about and why they
y such curious things.

The best way to start is by reading, because in
ading you can learn without being embarrassed
 not knowing what to ask. Take a local news-
per and read the local news until names and
cal events make sense in your mind. Go to the
blic Library and talk with the librarian, if it
 a small library, or the readers' adviser if it is
 big one. The best and most painless way to
arn about your new home from books is to read
vels about your state and region, and then
out America. At the library look over the
omen's household magazines. Subscribe to one

them to help you on styles and ways of doing
ings about the house.

aking Friends—in a Small Town

You may find yourself settled far from your
sband's family and surrounded entirely by
angers. In a small town the neighbours will
ll on you and try to be friendly. Neighbourli-
ss is highly valued in America. They will chat
th you when you are hanging out the laundry
 digging in your garden—which probably will
ve no hedges around it.

If your neighbours call on you, be sure to re-
rn the call in a few days. Then you can invite
em over for an evening. Home entertainment
 simple in America: people sit on the porch in
mmer or in the living-room in winter, six or
ght together, talking or playing cards. Light
reshments are served about ten o'clock—coffee
d cake or iced ginger-ale and sandwiches, per-
ps some candy or olives for decoration. Since
reshments are so simple, people often "drop
" without formality. For dinner, of course, in-
ations are necessary.

City Life

In a big city you can be as lonely as in any
strange city in Britain, and if you live in a flat
you won't have any neighbours.

But don't just sit down and die of home-sick-
ness. There are ways of making friends even in
New York or Chicago, but you have to be enter-
prising and self-reliant.

Wherever you find yourself, there are organisations that have open doors and expect strangers
to come in on their own feet. The churches are
still the principal ones. Then if you have belonged to the Red Cross or the Y.W.C.A. in
Britain, you will find its opposite number in
America. The church or the library can tell you
about welfare societies, young people's societies
and other groups or clubs catering for hobbies,
according to your tastes. These clubs and societies want enthusiastic members who will join and
do some of the work. You may as well find some
congenial organisation and work with it, for this is
one of the best ways to make real friends.

When you do get acquainted with people in a
big city, entertaining will be somewhat different
from what it is in a small town. People seldom
"drop in," but couples often meet friends by
arrangement for a dinner out, with a movie or
theatre or dance afterwards. Cocktail parties before dinner are more frequent. Sunday trips to
the country or the beach are a good excuse for
inviting new friends to go along.

Sports are especially good links with other
people. Incidentally, when you see American
sports or take part in them, don't expect them
to go by British rules. Sportsmanship is not a
matter of what the rules are, but consists in
playing by the rules and taking defeat gamely.
One unwritten rule is that spectators may properly
go quite wild and use violent language. Don't be
shocked, it is all in fun! Americans, like the
British, admire skill and pluck, and they particularly delight in anyone who can "take it" without showing any sign of distress.

Settling Down

Most Americans want more than anything else
to settle down and have a home with children
in it. But you will have to get used to what they
mean by "settling down." It does not mean
finding a secure job and a house and stopping
there for ever. It *(Continued on page 187)*

SORRY IT'S SCARCE

—but you'll be glad to find you get as many cups of good coffee from each bottle of 'Camp' as in pre-war days. It is therefore well worth waiting for—and your grocer is doing his best to distribute his limited supplies of 'Camp' fairly among his customers.

'CAMP' COFFEE

FULL STRENGTH
FINE FLAVOUR

Tired ?

Give your digestion " an evening off "

YOU can't digest a full meal when you're tired. Don't try to, or you're heading for gastric trouble. Instead, drink a cup of Benger's Food. It will soothe your stomach and give your digestion REST and a chance to build up its strength Benger's provides all the warmth and nourishment you need but in a form you can absorb without strain.

BENGER'S **— an essential factor in REST-THERAPY — the natural treatment for Indigestion**

For health's sake, grow more green vegetables.
National Savings are the MEANS of Victory.
Paper is a Weapon of War – save every scrap.

A Bride's Guide to the U.S.A.

(Continued from page 185)

means, first of all, finding a line of work with prospects of higher pay and a "future," rather than security. Love of home, also, is not necessarily connected with a house, for Americans move often.

Your social position will be what you and your husband make it. There are different social levels in America, and you will get placed in one of them, partly by your husband's job, partly by where you live, and partly by your own personality. Most British brides arrive in America entirely unknown. No one knows who you were at home, and in most places no one cares very much to dig into your past.

Homemaking

It is hard to give helpful information on housekeeping, because there are so many kinds of homes in America. You may be among that quarter of the population who live on farms, or the other quarter in small towns of 2,500 or less, or you may live in a city. The climate may be anything from that of New England, with snow all winter, to that of New Mexico, which is more like North Africa.

Your income may be small at first, and houses for people with small incomes in America are not Hollywood mansions. However, a girl can save a discouraging-looking house by a first-class job of homemaking at small cost. If you don't know how already, you can learn. Women's magazines are full of good suggestions, and many schools and colleges run evening classes in domestic science. If you live on a farm, be sure to ask about the Home Demonstration Meetings.

You may wish to take a job so as to increase your family income. If so, you will not be considered queer, nor will people look down on you. But do not waste your time. In America practically every housewife does her own work; your main job, therefore, will be running the house. Since your husband's prospects of promotion may be improved by an attractive home, you may add more to the family budget by homemaking than by a job.

Working out a budget is valuable whatever your income. To give you an idea of living costs, here is the budget of a family of four, living in Rochester, a fairly big city north of New York. The family income (pre-war) was $2,400 or about £600. Their expenditures were:

	£	s.
Food	175	0
House payments and taxes	80	0
Fuel and lighting	42	10
Telephone	10	0
Instalments on household equipment and upkeep	30	0
Clothes	45	0
Car (payments and depreciation)	37	10
Health (dentist, doctor and reserve)	30	0
Recreation and holidays	35	0
Insurance, savings	47	10
Miscellaneous	67	10
	£600	0

You will notice an item of £30 for health. In America there is no general health scheme, though locally there are good doctors and health services.

You will notice, too, the expense for the family car. Most families have cars, running all the way from luxury models down to ancient rattletraps costing about £5. People travel farther than in Britain to work, to school, to market and to social affairs, and vacations are often taken at great distances.

Another item is household equipment and upkeep. There are all sorts of gadgets, and there is terrific advertising pressure to make you think you cannot live without them. Americans have become fairly hardened to this pressure, and you should remember there is still a lot of comfort in having savings, rather than too many gadgets.

Go as slowly as you can in buying clothes until you know the markets and are familiar with what your friends wear.

Incidentally, don't try to outfit yourself on this side of the ocean. You will want to see what kind of climate you will be living in before building up a wardrobe. You will also need to experiment, because of central heating. Houses are warm inside, usually around 70 deg., so Americans dress lightly indoors and put on extra heavy overcoats when going out into the 20 deg. or lower winter weather. If you buy any clothes before leaving, use up your precious coupons on British-made woollen sweaters and tweeds.

In general, Americans eat three good-sized meals a day, with no regular tea, but often a snack at bedtime, and you will soon learn the usual types of menu.

Tinned and frozen foods and goods from delicatessen stores are generally good, and no one will think you are a lazy housewife if you use them. It is important not to make too much of a fuss about a dinner-party; your guests are more interested in you than in an elaborate meal.

No matter what your income is, it never pays to try to show off or live beyond your means. You and your husband will be judged not so much by what you spend, as by whether you are pleasant company and seem to be on the way up.

Americans are no Angels

Just as in all countries, the American ideal is often higher than common American practice. Americans believe in a friendly attitude to all kinds of people, which they call "being democratic." They often fail to live up to this standard, especially with people who seem "different." Less than half the American people are of British origin, and many of the others, chiefly from the European continent, are not entirely Americanised. There is some unfriendliness between people of different ancestry when they are settled in large groups still recognisable as "foreign." You will find that, although there are some groups who don't like the British, among the great majority such prejudice as there is about British girls is in your favour.

In spite of the mixture of peoples and the confusion of a new country, there is a large amount of agreement on the American ideals of freedom and goodwill. Americans do not like to be "pushed around" any more than British people do. Along with the feeling that everyone is "born free and equal" is a spirit of hope, with great expectations for the future.

You will be welcome in America, for you, too, have taken your chance and embarked on a great adventure. Americans admire courage. They will wish you good luck and happiness in your new life in the New World.

Dig, Plan, Grow and Preserve for Victory.

Paper saved is paper found – help to spread the word around.

Your country needs those old letters.

"Holidays at Home"

. . . but fun's FUN wherever you are!

Like angels entranced, they restfully rejoice in the antics of Mr. Punch. But soon they'll be "little devils"—running, jumping, skylarking about. To sustain their energy and offset strain, Mother should give them foods of utmost nourishment value. Weetabix is just such a food. And if you are fortunate enough to live in a Weetabix area where you can get this delicious cereal, your family will be as "pleased as punch!"

Weetabix

MORE than a Breakfast Food

SMALL SIZE **2 POINTS 7½d**. LARGE SIZE **4 POINTS 1/1d**.

Weetabix Ltd., Burton Latimer, Northants.

WX46

Rover curls up on

the chair . . . while you write to

Master—he, too, always loved that deep leather seat. Keep it in good trim for him with an occasional quick rub-up with O-Cedar Polish. O-Cedar is as successful with leather as it is with fine furniture; it protects and preserves as it polishes. You may need a little patience to get O-Cedar nowadays, but once you do, it will last you a very long time.

✳ *Your O-Cedar Mop (now so very difficult to replace) can be made to last longer if you shake it well each time after using and occasionally moisten the pad with a little O-Cedar Polish.*

STILL ACTIVE ON HOME SERVICE O-Cedar

Think! Can you save more paper?

*Help the Ministry of Health to destroy "Social Enemy No. 1" —
Keep to the fore in the National Paper Chase.*

Save – and pave the way to Peace.

NAGGING away in the heart of thousands of women are two questions : " Will they come back ? " and " When they come home again, will they be changed ? "

Whether their loved ones are in the Services, evacuated, directed to war jobs or prisoners of war, there is a constant dread of change. To us women change is always unwelcome, since for us it so often means loss—of youth, of looks, of love. We must realise, however, that this question can have only one answer—a ringing, emphatic " Yes." All those who have been away from home will have changed, changed radically. But change can be the harbinger of a greatly enriched relationship, if we are prepared for it.

Repatriated prisoners of war and civilian internees have already shown some of the problems that can arise, and when demobilisation and the re-orientation of industry really start, we shall meet many more. However, a difficulty understood is a difficulty half-conquered, and things will be much easier if we women who have remained at home try to realise what has happened to the character of those who have been away for years, with only a few brief, unreal leaves or holidays.

The fighting man will present the worst problem. There is no getting away from the fact that we who have stayed at home, no matter how much we have endured through privation and bombing, have not changed as much as he. Once a man joins up, he is at once deliberately isolated from civilian life, and locked up in the entirely different existence of the national fighting machine.

At one go he gives up his personality, his free will, his privacy, his personal belongings, his varied activities, his responsibilities as family man and citizen. He becomes a cog in the machine, taking orders without blinking, and obeying them instantly, eating, sleeping, and bathing in public, owning practically nothing except Service issue, following a whittled-down routine of " shooting and saluting " ; a mechanised man, trained to do one thing only—kill the enemy.

The thing which finally cuts the fighting man off from civilian life is the comradeship of a unique and wholly satisfying kind which his new world offers during every hour of the day.

All the usual barriers—class, occupation, wealth, dress, religion, geographical origin—are down. Everything is shared on equal terms, men invent their own private language and their own secret mythology, as in the R.A.F.'s gremlins. The feeling of " belonging," of solidarity, gets in their blood, fires their imaginations.

Then, when they reach the front line, their sense of comradeship produces some of the finest flowers in the garden of humanity. Men give up their lives for each other. They experience over and over again the ecstasy of surviving mortal danger together. They sacrifice their comfort for a wounded comrade, with all the tenderness of a mother for her child.

From these heights a man learns to scorn the petty competitions and jealousies of civilian life. His capacity for unselfish love and self-sacrifice is developed to a degree impossible in ordinary circumstances. This is what no woman must ever forget, for it marks the chief difference between her and the man who has come back to her from the front.

The shock will thus be great when he runs up against the cut-throat principle of civilian life—" each man for himself."

He will feel hurt, angry, profoundly homesick for what he has lost, and he will be in for a cynical period which may make him difficult to get along with and very unhappy in himself, if his family does not realise what he is experiencing, and give him constructive help. We can do this only by the warmest and most demonstrative possible response to his homecoming. I think your best guide might be to regard your husband or son as a boy home from school : for a while, you spoil him a bit, and it's good for him.

Then, when you have lapped him round with the comfort of your love and understanding, drawn out his whole story—if he wishes to tell it—and proved to him that he still " fits " into family life, you can safely begin to assert yourself a bit, to allow him to see that you, too, have been through it in your own way, but that you have developed, and are ready to build a new life with him.

Think of the task as an emergency engineering job. The black, swift river of wartime absence flows between you, and only you can bridge it. So you start your tough (Continued on page 190)

When They Come Back

By Louise Morgan

" THE first morning he got here the Hunt turned up, and he was too upset to contain himself. That there were people at home who were content to spend money and time keeping horses and hounds, and using petrol in some cases, in the world of to-day, was beyond his comprehension. The thought of a fox being hunted was unbearable to him. He said 'It's like a prisoner of war facing a firing squad.' "

That was a repatriated prisoner, whose words typify to some extent the changed outlook of all those returning to ordinary civilian life. What can we do to make things easier for them ?

Plant your garden for full-scale vegetable production.

There may be paper in YOUR home not helping the War Effort.

Cross with care. Road casualties are still great.

FROM A
doctor's diary

This is based on a doctor's experience of cases of V.D. It has been carefully edited so that the people concerned shall not be recognised.

" '...How can I keep it quiet, doctor ?'

He was a young lad, only about eighteen, though he looked more, a nice boy, but a bit excitable and uncontrolled. He was earning big money in a munitions factory and he'd been spending it in pubs. One night he'd met a woman much older than himself. She had suggested he should go home with her to her lodgings .... The result was a sharp attack of a venereal disease—gonorrhœa.

I'm afraid it's a common story these days. The strain of hard work. Big wages. Uncertainty. No social club in the district where the boy could have met decent companions. And then temptation comes along. But that's not really the point I want to make.

This young fellow was in a terrible state of mind. He was afraid his parents and work-mates would find out that he had venereal disease. I assured him that treatment at the V.D. clinics is entirely confidential. He thought he had to get his parents' consent to go to a clinic. That isn't so. And I emphasised that patients at clinics are known only by numbers. Then he was afraid of being seen going in, or coming out. Clinics are usually in very inconspicuous places, often inside hospitals. Would he have to lie up and take time off ? Almost certainly not. Would it mean an operation ? No. Would anyone outside the clinic have to be told about it ? No. Would treatment cost a lot ? No, it was free.

Finally, he asked a very natural question. Why did the Government take all this trouble to treat people like him, who had got themselves ill by their own doing ? My answer was this : partly it was for his own sake and to prevent his becoming a burden on the community later on; but mainly to safeguard other people from the disease. If those with venereal disease get it treated promptly they cease to be a danger to other people."

Further information IN CONFIDENCE can be obtained from your local Council's Health Department or by writing to the Medical Adviser, Central Council for Health Education, Tavistock House, Tavistock Square, London, W.C.1, enclosing stamped addressed envelope.
Issued by the Ministry of Health and the Central Council for Health Education
(VD28-18)

When They Come Back

(Continued from page 189)

and complicated job from your side, and by the time you get part-way over, he will be eagerly preparing to make a head for it on his side.

You can begin now to prepare for this woman's job of bridge-building. A little thing, but of the deepest significance, is keeping in touch with the places where your man has been, following him right through his war-time journey by maps and books.

Another extremely useful thing to do would be to read any of the well-known novels on the last war, such as Robert Graves's *Goodbye to All That*, Remarque's *The Road Back*, Ernest Raymond's *Tell England*, or Sir Philip Gibbs' *Now It Can be Told* : the mentality of the de-mobbed soldier in the last war was fundamentally the same as now.

You had better add to those books a considerable amount of other information, for every man, most particularly those who have had long pauses between campaigns, is coming back with a wider outlook, a keener brain, and a thirst for knowing the world about him. To meet him on this new level, you might " rub up " your general reading.

I have emphasised love and understanding, because these are the fundamental things in all human relationships, and if we get these straight, other things follow. The demobbed soldier who is loved and understood will settle down in a fraction of the time it takes a man in less happy circumstances, while the unhappy man may not settle down at all, or may even become an invalid.

Understanding and patience will be particularly needed in connection with the thorny question of jobs. The fighting man will have forgotten what a " job," in the civilian sense, is like. He has not had to worry about keeping or looking for a job, or competing with other men for one, since he was called up, and the thought of " competing " with other men on the financial level is revolting to one who has competed on the idealistic level of the common good and the common happiness.

Moreover, his life has consisted of alternating periods of exhausting fighting or marching, and periods of loafing about, doing nothing. He needs time to readjust to the idea of the neat little jog of a civilian job, and he may also feel he would like a completely different job from his pre-war one.

You will have to help him, course, but help must be given in practical, impersonal way. Seek t right moment to open the questic of the future, and make it plain th you feel the important thing is h happiness. With your constant su port and understanding, it will far easier for him to find the rig job and to put his heart into it. may even try a succession of jo before settling down, but you w not resent this mental adjustment.

The vital point is to keep his fai in human companionship alive. comes back with two simple reactio —the first of resentment and ha for the brutal life he has been leadin and the second of love and adoratio for the one manifestation of goodne in that life, which was the companio ship of his comrades.

If you keep his power of lovir alive, he will be able to face the bitt facts that civilian society is entire different, that men who stayed home have been making money an getting promotion while he w fighting the enemy, that his meda are useless as recommendations for job, and his superb skill in throwir a hand-grenade or leading his me in attack does not prevent his beir classified as unskilled labour unle he has some " civilian " skill knowledge.

This adjustment of the demobbe to civilian life is the most difficu demand that society makes on ar human being. To me it represen the final and most ironic injustice war. Why should one generation men be asked not only to risk the lives, and suffer untold horrors, b also to watch themselves dwind from heroes to beggars, and struggle for their existence ?

If society demands these sacrific from them, then society—and th means us—owes them in return mo than it owes any other group.

The demobilisation of Servi women and directed factory worke will not present such a great proble partly because women have be spared the experience of fighting a killing, and partly because they a born adjusters. Their minds, lil their bodies, are more plastic tha those of men, and they can cu themselves comfortably round almc any new situation.

It is the parents (especially t fathers) and the husbands of the

---

Every day in every way your Paper Salvage pile should grow Bigger and Bigger.

How much paper have YOU saved this month ? Can't you do better ?

Methodical Making-do and Mending, Mean Money saved for National Lending.

irls who will have to do most of the
djusting.

Young women by the million have
arned the joys of independence of
ind and of pocket, freedom of time,
ocial give-and-take on a large scale,
nd a jolly, bright atmosphere.

One might as well try to stop the
un rising as to put them back where
hey were at the beginning of the
ar. The thing to do is to make
heir acquaintance all over again,
nd go on from there. This can be
reat fun, and very stimulating, for
here is much that can be learned
om young women, married or unmarried, who have worked in the
ervices or factories. Some have
ad a bad time, but on the whole
hey have been very well handled,
nd have been able to lead a busy,
onstructive, satisfying life.

Girls like these should not be
sked to go back to petty social
estrictions, domestic slavery and
nancial dependence on father or
usband. Not only their families,
ut their country must realise what
 owing to them. The Government
hould see to it that by good social
onditions they will have enough
eisure to continue the wider life
hey have been living.

What about prisoners of war?
hey are heroes of a unique kind,
ith that particular brand of courage
hich goes to keeping a banner
ying, not for a glorious moment,
ut for years on end.

We should prepare for their home-
oming in much the same way as
r other Service men, but with
xtra tenderness and a great deal
ore protectiveness. Their " skins "
ave become so sensitive that a
reath will upset them. Things
hich we take for granted as part
f the normal pattern of life may
errorise them. See the letter I
cently had from a reader at Oke-
ampton whose " dear prisoner "
as just returned after four and a
alf years of captivity—you will
nd it quoted on page 44.

This is the ingrown, finely sensi-
ve, exquisitely discriminating type
f mind you will have to deal with,
nd introduce gently to the rough-
nd-tumble, crude and often brutal
fe of the ordinary world. It will
e like transplanting a rare flower.

Privacy will be one of the most
recious things you can give these
en, so don't be offended if your
risoner just wants to sit and think
r potter about at home by himself.
e probably won't want more than a
mited amount of parties and festi-
ities.

THEN

NOW

WHEN?

Reflection of the past—projection into the future. Will you be a very different woman when the lights go up again and the peace you've worked for and deserved come back again to earth? Different in some respects perhaps, changed opinions, a deeper understanding of more serious things, but outwardly unchanged! Today Elizabeth Arden is a synonym for the rare and precious, yet your observance of the simple beauty regime devised by Miss Arden will have enabled you to retain the youthful freshness and distinction that has always been yours . . . you will have bridged the years triumphantly.

Elizabeth Arden

25 OLD BOND STREET, LONDON, W.I   MAYFAIR 8211

THE lights are up again, and the shops flashing their welcome. Maybe the displays still look somewhat sparse and "war-time," and certainly the puddings and cakes lack the richness of pre-war years, but, with the gaiety of twinkling lights to glorify our long-dark streets, it seems like a new world.

And though the nightmare of War is not completely past, nor may be, perhaps, for yet another Christmas, while our men are striving in the Pacific, one era has indeed come to an end, and we are on the threshold of a new world.

Peace will bring problems as difficult and exhausting, if less horrible, than the war-time ones, but for the sake of those who have made the great sacrifice, and even more for our children's, we'll face them with the courage and determination of the last five years.

So let us get busy in the kitchen, in planning the Christmas gaiety, and in taking the children to see the brightly lit shops. We'll do it all with great thankfulness in our hearts, and with a firm determination that the years of darkness shall not have been in vain. For peace on earth we'll work and pray.

You wouldn't throw away a precious jewel – it is just as foolish to throw away the smallest scrap of paper.

Prevention is better than cure – teach your child to avoid the dangers of the road.

Good Housekeeping

May 1943

1/6

"In Georgia Now," by Randolph Lawton

CHRONICLER'S "FINGER ON THE PULSE"

The Institute's Unrivalled Services

Good Housekeeping

June 1943

1/6

"Bristol-Port of Hope," by Gail Richmond

FAITH BALDWIN : NORAH LOFTS : HELENE MANARD

The Institute and other Special Service Features

Good Housekeeping

September 1943

1/6

Canada-A Nation Grows Up by Gail Richmond

A. HENRY SAVREN : CHRONICLER : MARGARET ROGERS

Good Housekeeping

March 1944

MAURA LAVERTY : HELENA NORMANTON : KATHLEEN WALLACE

1/6 "A People with a Voice – Wales": Gail Richmond

10 Pages of Institute Recipes and Hints

Good Housekeeping

April 1944

1/6 *Princess Elizabeth, by* Hector Bolitho

W. SOMERSET MAUGHAM : MARJORIE HESSELL TILTMAN

The Institute Surveys the Domestic Help Problem

Good Housekeeping

May 1944

Long Novelette *by* Martha Cheavens

1/6 OSBERT SITWELL : GAIL RICHMOND : EDITA MORRIS

New Cake Recipes Tested by the Institute

Good Housekeeping

October 1944

S.P.B. MAIS : OLGA MOORE : KATHLEEN WALLACE

1/6 "Pacific Front" by Geoffrey Hutton

Dishes of the Month by the Institute

Good Housekeeping

December 1944

1/6 *Letters of Alexander Woollcott*

CLARE SHERIDAN : SYLVIA THOMPSON : ELIZABETH GOUDGE

GOOD HOUSEKEEPING

ONE SHILLING & SIXPENCE

JANUARY 1945

Irene Ward : Mary Roberts Rinehart : Gordon Holmes

"Bride's Guide to the U.S.A."

Scottish Cookery : Children's Party : Budgeting